D1555032

FEEDING MEXICO

The Political Uses of Food since 1910

WITHDRAWN

Enrique C. Ochoa

A Scholarly Resources Inc. Imprint
Wilmington, Delaware

FEEDING MEXICO

Scholarly Resources Inc.
104 Greenhill Avenue
Wilmington, DE 19805-1897
www.scholarly.com

Library of Congress Cataloging-in-Publication Data

Ochoa, Enrique.
  Feeding Mexico : the political uses of food since 1910 /
    Enrique C. Ochoa.
      p. cm. — (Latin American silhouettes)
    Includes bibliographical references and index.
    ISBN 0-8420-2812-9 (cloth : alk. paper)
    1. Food supply—Government policy—Mexico—20th century.
  2. Nutrition policy—Mexico—History—20th century. 3. Agriculture and state—Mexico—History—20th century. I. Title: Political
  uses of food since 1910. II. Title. III. Series.

HD9014.M62 O24 2000
363.8'0972—dc21   99-087310

ISBN 0-8420-2813-7 (pbk.)

Para mi familia

Henry José Ochoa (1935-1989),

Francesca Palazzolo Ochoa,

Gilda L. Ochoa,

Julianna Kaup,

Elisa and Ricky Ochoa-Kaup

About the Author

Enrique C. Ochoa is associate professor of history and associate coordinator of Latin American Studies at California State University, Los Angeles. A specialist in modern Mexican and Latin American history, he has edited and authored several works including *Estado y agricultura en México: Antecedentes de las reformas salinistas* (Mexico, 1994). He is a coordinating editor of the journal *Latin American Perspectives*.

Acknowledgments

This book would not have been written without the help and support of a number of people. As it evolved from a dissertation to a monograph, I met many people and became exposed to a variety of ideas that have directly and indirectly influenced this study. Because it is impossible to list all of those who have contributed, I will limit my acknowledgments to those who have had a direct impact on this study.

Several people provided encouragement and support at several key junctures of this project. Professor James W. Wilkie stimulated my interest in Latin American history and in government policy and has been an unwavering supporter. In Professor Mary Yeager's seminar, I first became interested in the subject of government regulation of food products. Among the many others who offered advice and encouragement along the way include Adolfo Bermeo, Jeffrey Bortz, E. Bradford Burns, Robert Burr, Arturo Grunstein, Sergio de la Peña, Iván Gutiérrez, James Lockhart, David LaFrance, David López, Aída Mostkoff, and Martín Valadez. I am grateful to Stephen Niblo for sending me a copy of his article on the Gaxiola affair. David Lorey provided valuable comments on a number of drafts and has been an important critic and friend throughout. Joseph Cotter first introduced me to the personal archive of Ingeniero Ramón Fernández y Fernández and together we have spent many discussing and debating the intricacies of Mexican agricultural policy. My colleagues and students at California State University at Dominguez Hills and at California State University at Los Angeles have provided a stimulating atmosphere to teach and write. Bill Beezley and Judy Ewell provided numerous thoughtful suggestions and have been a source of constant encouragement. I am thankful to Rick Hopper, Michelle Slavin, Carolyn Travers, and many others at Scholarly Resources for their role in making this study come to fruition.

The research and writing of this study were facilitated by generous support from several sources. The UCLA Program on Mexico provided me with two travel and research grants and provided support in a number of ways. I am also indebted to the Program on Mexico for including me in its research projects and allowing me to present some of my findings at conferences in Mexico. In addition, two UCLA university fellowships enabled me to carry out the bulk of the research and supported the early writing phases. At CSULA, I was fortunate to receive an Affirmative Action Grant for Faculty Research before a hostile political environment hastened the demise of such grants. I also acknowledge the able research assistance of Carlos Espinosa in collecting materials on Mexican agriculture in the 1980s and 1990s.

This work would never have been initiated, let alone completed, without the support of my family. My parents, Henry and Francesca Ochoa, first introduced me to Latin America and encouraged my study of the region and its history. They unyieldingly supported (emotionally, intellectually, and financially) all my endeavors. Tragically, my father did not live to see me complete my degree and publish this study, but his long hours of reading and discussing Latin American history with me left an indelible imprint. I have been fortunate to have been able to share my interests with my mother, who has traveled with me to Mexico and Central America on several occasions. My sister Gilda Ochoa, a sociologist, has encouraged me throughout this study and made many numerous thoughtful suggestions.

Julianna Kaup has lived through every stage of this study. There is no way to adequately thank her for all that she has contributed. I am grateful to her for having traveled to and lived in Mexico with me. By setting up a household in Mexico we were able to gain a bit more insight into the politics of food in Mexico. Julie spurred me on during the darker days of research, writing and rewriting and helping celebrate the research victories. She read and commented on portions of this study at its various stages. Our children, Elisa and Ricky, have served as a further source of inspiration and constantly force me to put my research and writing into context.

Contents

Abbreviations

AGDCA	Almacenes Generales de Depósito de Crédito Agrícola
ANC	Asociación Nacional de Cosecheros de Cereales y Productos Alimenticios
ANDSA	Almacenes Nacionales de Depósito, S.A.
ARCONSA	Almacenes de Ropa CONASUPO, S.A.
BANAMEX	Banco Nacional de México
BANCOMEXT	Banco Nacional de Comercio Exterior
BANRURAL	Banco Nacional de Crédito Rural
BAT	Biblioteca y Archivo Técnico
BNCA	Banco Nacional de Crédito Agrícola
BNCE	Banco Nacional de Crédito Ejidal
BORUCONSA	Bodegas Rurales CONASUPO, S.A.
CECONCA	Centros CONASUPO de Captación
CEIMSA	Compañía Exportadora e Importadora Mexicana, S.A.
CNC	Confederación Nacional de Campesinos
CONASUPO	Compañía Nacional de Subsistencias Populares
CONCAMIN	Confederación de Cámaras Industriales
CONCANACO	Confederación de Cámaras Nacionales de Comercio
CONDISUPO	Compañía Distribuidora CONASUPO
COPLAMAR	Coordinación General del Plan Nacional de Zonas Deprimidas y Grupos Marginadas
CRMS	Comité Regulador del Mercado de las Subsistencias
CRMT	Comité Regulador del Mercado de Trigo
CT	Congreso de Trabajo
CTM	Confederación de Trabajadores Mexicanos
DGP	Dirección General de Precios
DICONSA	Distribuidora CONASUPO, S.A.
EAP	economically active population

EPR	Ejército Popular Revolucionario
FAO	Food and Agriculture Organization
FFNN	Ferrocarriles Nacionales
FROC	Federación Regional de Obreros y Campesinos
GDP	gross domestic product
ICONSA	Industrias CONASUPO, S.A.
IMF	International Monetary Fund
IMPECSA	Impulsadora del Pequeño Comercio, S.A.
IMSS	Instituto Mexicana de Seguro Social
INEGI	Instituto Nacional de Estadística, Geografía, e Informática
INN	Instituto Nacional de Nutrición
ISSSTE	Instituto de Seguridad y Servicios Sociales para los Trabajadores del Estado
LICONSA	Leche Industrializado CONASUPO, S.A.
MACONSA	Materiales CONASUPO, S.A.
MASECA	Molinos Aztecas, S.A.
MFN	most favored nation
MICONSA	Maíz Industrializado CONASUPO, S.A.
MINSA	Maíz Industrializado, S.A.
MLN	Movimiento de Liberación Nacional
NADYRSA	Nacional Distribuidora y Reguladora, S.A.
NAFINSA	Nacional Financiera, S.A.
NAFTA	North American Free Trade Agreement
PACE	Programa de Apoyo a la Comercialización Ejidal
PAN	Partido de Acción Nacional
PEMEX	Pétroleos Mexicanos
PNR	Partido Nacional Revolucionario
PPS	Partido Popular Socialista
PRI	Partido Revolucionario Institucional
PRM	Partido Revolucionario Mexicana
PROCAMPO	Programa de Apoyo al Campo
PRONASOL	Programa Nacional de Solidaridad
SAF	Secretaría de Agricultura y Fomento
SAG	Secretaría de Agricultura y Ganadería
SAM	Sistema Alimentaria Mexicana
SEN	Secretaría de la Economía Nacional
SEN-DGE	Secretaría de la Economía Nacional, Dirección General de Estadísticas
SFA	State Food Agency

SRH	Secretaría de Recursos Hidráulicos
TRICONSA	Trigo Industrializado CONASUPO, S.A.
UGOCM	Union General de Obreros y Campesinos Mexicanos
UNAM	Universidad Nacional Autónoma de México
UNICEF	United Nations Children's Fund
USDA	U.S. Department of Agriculture

1

Introduction

Food and Society in Postrevolutionary Mexico

Following the popular uprising of 1910–1920, successive Mexican governments were pressured to create a host of institutions to address the demands of the people. This study examines the rise and fall of government intervention in the economy of basic foods in Mexico. Intervention in the food sector from the 1930s to the 1980s led to the creation of a series of subsidies for farmers, a chain of over 20,000 retail stores to provide working-class Mexicans with basic necessities at accessible prices, and numerous food-processing plants to stock the stores with low-cost nutritious foods. By exploring the social, political, and economic factors that led government policymakers to intervene in the marketing and distribution of basic foods, we can see how these policies became a pillar of social welfare policy for well over a half century. Contrary to most analyses, this study demonstrates that the growth and development of economic intervention and social policy are not ad hoc but instead are closely intertwined with political, social, and economic goals. However, these various and often contradictory goals shape policy in ways that make it look unwieldy.

An analysis of the formation of state intervention and social policy at this time in history is critical because many of the government programs created to provide a minimum social safety net for Mexico's poor have been sharply reduced or completely eliminated. Symbolic of such cuts was the ending in January 1999 of the long-standing policy of subsidizing the tortilla and controlling the price of this most basic staple of the Mexican diet. The price of tortillas quickly doubled in most regions, sparking outcries in the daily press and several spontaneous protests. Stories abounded of the hardship that the policy change caused Mexico's poor because the subsidy had helped Mexicans put tortillas on the table during nearly two decades of real wage decline.[1] The ending of the tortilla subsidy came just months after the milk subsidy ended and the price of milk was liberalized. Culminating the recent cuts was the announcement that the main food agency that has symbolized government commitment to social welfare policy since the 1930s was slated for liquidation.

The ending of basic food subsidies and the lifting of price controls are part of a series of reforms that have led to severe reductions in social spending. These economic reforms, carried out during the presidencies of Miguel de la Madrid (1982–1988), Carlos Salinas de Gortari (1988–1994), and Ernesto Zedillo (1994–2000), have been aimed at implementing market-based solutions to Mexico's economic problems, including privatizing state companies, liberalizing markets, attracting foreign investment, and negotiating the North American Free Trade Agreement (NAFTA). Since the early 1980s, most sectors of the economy have experienced privatization and reduction of expenditures, and many of the historic pieces of social legislation, including land reform and social security, have been significantly restructured to end the state's support of these policies.

The liberalization of the economy and the reduction of social expenditure cut deeply into traditional services that, however inadequate, provided a minimum social safety net and a hope that the state, with some pressure, might expand into new areas and provide even greater services to the population. Much of this hope ended with the economic reforms of the 1980s and 1990s, which were sealed with the signing of NAFTA. The loss of hope that the present system would provide for the people of Mexico was expressed in numerous ways. Social peace was broken with the uprising of the Ejército Zapatista de Liberación Nacional in Chiapas on January 1, 1994, the day that NAFTA went into effect. The subsequent appearance of guerrilla movements in Guerrero and Oaxaca, as well as the various rumors of other movements, further demonstrated the growing frustrations. This increase in armed movements and the resulting militarization of many regions of the country indicate that social programs are being replaced with private-sector and military solutions, radically transforming the nature of state-civil society relations.[2]

The replacement of state redistributive policies with market solutions is a significant departure from previous government policies that traced their roots to the revolution of 1910. That violent upheaval, which claimed the lives of hundreds of thousands, brought Mexicans from different classes, sectors, and regions together under the banner of fighting for fairness and social justice. Since the revolution, Mexican governments pledged themselves to improving the welfare and living standards of the majority of Mexicans. As a result, a number of laws were passed and a variety of programs aimed at improving the standard of living were created, addressing issues such as land reform, the expansion of education, legal guarantees for the right of workers to organize, and protective labor legislation.

As this study demonstrates, food policy has been one of the primary ways that policymakers and politicians have sought to balance the social goals of the revolution with the often contradictory goals of industrialization and urbanization. Through study of food policy, we can see how policy is formed in a way that addresses the demands of consumers, producers, and merchants while still allowing policymakers to direct food and agriculture policy in a way that is consistent with overall development policy.

Mexican Revolutionary Ideology, Social Reform, and State Intervention

The revolution of 1910–1920 was fought by large numbers of Mexicans throughout the republic. Whether Emiliano Zapata in the South, Pancho Villa in the North, or the numerous other regional leaders of the revolution, each demanded access to land, liberty, and social and political equality. Although these concepts were interpreted differently based on class, social background, and regional context, most revolutionaries argued that some form of transformation should occur.

After 1915 northern elite revolutionaries such as Venustiano Carranza, Alvaro Obregón, and Plutarco Elías Calles gradually consolidated their power and attempted to centralize authority. This centralization was achieved in a number of ways. The Constitution of 1917 served as an umbrella, addressing a wide range of concerns that appealed to the various revolutionary factions. Although the loosely constructed document was not fully implemented, it was a constant reference point for groups struggling for justice and for a piece of the revolution. Politicians played on that hope, while at

the same time moving to consolidate their power, using land reform and education to break local power blocks.[3]

The new elite that emerged from the revolution used central
government power to consolidate its rule and attempted to use
social policy to win over marginalized groups. Attempts were made
to extend the hand of the central government into the countryside
through the creation of a network of rural schools, land reform,
and a host of lesser federal programs. Contemporary scholars have
demonstrated that the complexity and durability of local customs
and values made central authority's efforts to expand its influence
and create hegemony a hotly contested process. The result was a
social peace that was often tenuous. The terms of peace were locally negotiated and constructed to bring various regions and sectors of the population into the nation-state fold while not fully
altering the goals of the nation-state as envisioned by the ruling
classes.[4] The creation of this social peace was crucial for new ruling classes to impose their authority and establish a mechanism
for dealing with issues of social justice that emerged from the revolution. The social pact, or pact of domination, as the sociologist
Viviane Brachet-Márquez has termed it, served to solidify class
domination while still providing an "escape valve" for social
mobility and an appearance of government commitment to social
justice.[5]

This complex process led to a social peace that made Mexico
one of the most politically stable countries in Latin America. Every
six years since 1934 elections have taken place with relatively little
disruption: people go to the polls and vote and those elected take
office and generally carry out their terms. The electoral process
served to maintain the Partido Revolucionario Institucional (PRI),
the self-proclaimed heir to the revolution, in office with a veneer of
legitimacy. Challenges to the ruling party often took nonelectoral
forms, such as strikes and social movements, which the ruling party
was able to disarm through a variety of tactics, including infiltra-
tion, co-optation, repression, and the granting of some concessions
once the political threat was removed.[6] In addition, government
officials extended other concessions to workers and peasants, which
created a complex welfare state that was selectively responsive.
Social peace provided stability for economic growth that occurred
from the 1940s to the 1970s.

Connected to the efforts to create social peace was the concomi-
tant goal of forging a unified modern nation-state. The goal of most

rationalist modern states, as James Scott has deftly shown, is to reduce the complex diversity of the human experience to a more manageable form conducive to census takers' and planners' attempts to quantify material goods to increase efficiency so as to more effectively govern, control, and tax the population.[7] The historical problem for policymakers and nation-state builders has been how to weave the diverse regions of Mexico, each with its own centuries of history, tradition, and language, into one system, understandable to Mexico City elites. Numerous market systems, price structures, weights and measurements, languages, and cultures that exist in Mexico are the result of its complex history. The Mexican state in the postrevolutionary era used food policy as one tool to try to extend its rule over the countryside and create one system. This strategy is intimately connected to the political, economic, and social policy of the state throughout the postrevolutionary period.

For the past half century scholars have debated the nature of the Mexican revolution and the extent to which it fundamentally altered society. A significant thread in this debate surrounds the crucial role of government intervention in this process. Early analysis centered around the structural and social aspects of revolutionary policy and tended to focus on land, labor, and education as the three major arenas for assessing the extent of revolutionary transformation. Pioneering students of the Mexican political system tended to see state participation in the economy as crucial to its success and stability. Howard Cline, for example, attributed state intervention in the economy and redistributive programs as essential elements in creating a "balanced boom."[8] Similarly, Frank Brandenburg saw different forms of ownership (including state ownership) as a major factor in explaining the success of Mexican economic growth and an essential factor in the formation of "modern Mexico."[9] The emphasis on stability and the success of the Mexican model came under fire during the late 1960s and 1970s. In the wake of the government repression in 1968, scholars increasingly depicted state intervention in the economy as a tool in the government's arsenal to be used to manipulate the population to perpetuate the authoritarian regime.[10] These works tend to focus on state intervention as a whole but with a much more critical eye than early works. By the 1980s, with the widely perceived failure of import substitution industrialization and state intervention being lambasted by the international financial community, a number of scholars began to systematically study state intervention in specific industries. Many studies explored how state intervention contributed to economic stagnation.[11] Others tied political stability in Mexico to state intervention to a greater extent than had been done in the past. Although a number of case studies have emerged, much recent analysis has centered on events of the 1980s and 1990s, and only a few works have explored the historical origins and context of such policies.[12]

Studies of social policies, such as land reform, labor, and education, have been central to our understanding of the social and political aspects of postrevolutionary governments. Numerous works have demonstrated how the state that emerged from the revolution during the 1920s and 1930s responded to pressure from campesinos and workers to initiate a land reform program and to enact labor reforms that would help improve the material well-being of the majority of Mexicans.[13] These studies have made great strides in demonstrating the complex forces working in specific industries and locales and in explaining how the revolution was created at the local level.

Despite such progress, most studies have not fully demonstrated how complex forces (both internal and external) have coalesced to initiate, shape, and alter policies over time. Although specific circumstances and patterns might exist that lead to the creation of a particular policy, these conditions often change over time, and unforeseen factors arise that policymakers then respond to. Hence, the outcome of policy is often very different from its original conception. The literature has not fully examined how factors and policies vary with different goods and industries. Moreover, given the recent boom in regional studies, it is fairly clear that the result of intervention and public policies also vary depending on the specific regional context.[14]

The majority of studies of government intervention and social reform has tracked the evolution of policy from its inception until the major thrust of the policy slowed and was bureaucratized. For example, studies of land reform and education often end by the 1940s and 1950s, when the more radical, transformative aspects of these policies had diminished. In addition, most analyses of social policy tend to focus almost exclusively on one sector and rarely demonstrate how it interrelates with other sectors' policies. This approach is problematic since social policy develops within the larger political-economic context, and policy priorities are often shaped to more effectively serve these larger goals.

The Uses of Food Policy in the Era of Economic Modernization

This study approaches postrevolutionary government policy differently than do previous works. It uses food sector policy to explore the multifaceted nature of government policy that often gets lost when one looks exclusively at land or labor policy or, more strictly, at social, political, or economic policy. Although land reform and labor issues are an important component of social policy, they became less important after 1940 as new strategies for responding to working-class and campesino militancy, including social security, public health, housing programs, and food policy, were adopted.[15] As land reform and labor reform become institutionalized and severely truncated, these initiatives become the staple of social policy. Throughout much of the twentieth century, food policy has been among the longest lasting and furthest reaching of such policies.

Food policy touches on a wide range of aspects crucial for understanding the dynamics of state policy in the postrevolutionary era. Since issues of land and agricultural production have been central to postrevolutionary policy, food has generally been discussed by scholars in relation to production and the social and political impact of production policies.[16] Food as a unit of analysis can be examined in relation to the formation of national culture, and in discussions of malnutrition and poverty.[17] Since food is crucial to human survival, how a society seeks to organize production and distribution tells much about that society. Food, then, is an important window onto dynamics of class politics, development strategy, the connection between the countryside and the city, social policy, and the formation of national culture.

Food policy in Mexico and the state's role in provisioning Mexican society provides a unique opportunity to compare the rhetoric and the reality of state social policy and its connection to the economic, social, and labor policies of Mexico's ruling party. It also provides a glimpse of the nature of state policy in postrevolutionary Mexico by illustrating how

1. The Mexican government sought to use food policy to speed up the process of market formation by attempting to create an efficient distribution system with a uniform market system of national prices and uniform units of measurements

2. The government attempted to balance the needs of producers for remunerative prices, while at the same time working to keep prices relatively low for consumers
3. The government responds to pressures to bolster sagging wages through food policy and, by keeping wage pressures down, how food policy serves as an indirect subsidy to the private sector as well as an object of social welfare
4. Policy serves a crucial social welfare function that is used to shore up political support
5. Policy that seems on the surface well planned and structured is often developed in an ad hoc manner in response to short-term social and political demands

The formation of food policy in its complex manifestations developed in piecemeal fashion throughout the twentieth century. Prior to the 1930s the federal government did not consistently intervene in the markets of staple foods, but by the mid-1980s it was one of the most active forces in nearly all aspects of the Mexican food system. The Constitution of 1917 assigned a prominent role to the Mexican state to regulate the public good and to intervene in the economy to foster social justice and protect national sovereignty. Article 28 of the Constitution empowered the state to regulate the economy to prevent monopolies and the hoarding of and speculating in basic goods. However, despite the constitutional provisions, Mexican governments were slow to intervene in the economy, and when such intervention occurred, it tended to be carried out on a case-by-case basis, depending on the conditions specific to a particular industry and in response to specific social pressures.

During the presidency of Lázaro Cárdenas (1934–1940) government policy most explicitly claimed to use state power to develop infrastructure and distribute social benefits. Beginning in 1937 the Mexican government created a host of agencies whose aims were loosely defined as ensuring that producers received a fair price for their harvest and that staple foods were available to consumers in adequate amounts for a just price. To carry out these rather vague goals, the various government agencies, collectively referred to here as the State Food Agency, began by participating in the wheat market, purchasing grains at home and abroad and absorbing transportation and storage costs. The Agency would then sell the grain to merchants and millers at a subsidized rate, resulting in lower consumer prices.

Although the initial goal of the policy was to support producers, after 1938 Mexico began to pursue a strategy of economic development based on rapid industrial growth. Modernization of Mexico, policymakers argued, would lead to significant economic growth that would ultimately benefit the majority of Mexicans. The rhetoric of the revolutionary era, which had included discussion of redistribution of land and direct social improvements, became increasingly rare and was gradually replaced by a discourse of economic growth and employment. By mending fences with private capital, pro-worker rhetoric declined, and official language became more class-conciliatory. Originally envisioned as a way of correcting market failure and breaking the control of local creditors, food policies explicitly came to be used for granting concessions to militant workers and campesinos.

The industrial boom in Mexico City and its environs increased the number of factories from 5,000 in 1930 to nearly 45,000 in 1950. This industrial expansion attracted waves of migrants from the countryside, many of whom came after 1940 when the pace of land distribution slowed. The number of employees in these factories increased from 100,000 to nearly 450,000, increasing the capital's share of the nation's economically active population from 20 percent to 30 percent.[18] The city's share of the gross domestic product (GDP) grew from 30.6 percent in 1940 to 36.0 percent in 1960.[19] As a result, urban-based industrialization led to significant rural-to-urban migration. Between 1940 and 1960, the population of the greater Mexico City region grew from 1.8 million people to 5.3 million by 1960 and two decades later, in 1980, reached 13.4 million, accounting for 20 percent of Mexico's total population. The rates of urbanization were paralleled throughout the republic; in 1940, only five cities had populations over 100,000; by 1960 there were eleven; and by 1980, twenty-one.[20]

In line with efforts to industrialize Mexico, policymakers sought to reorganize the countryside to meet urban-industrial demands. An immediate increase in the supply of inexpensive foodstuffs to provision the urban areas was needed. Large-scale production was encouraged as small-scale production, support of *ejidos*, and land reform took a back seat. This shift in policy facilitated the transition to an urban-industrialization model since sharp fluctuations in supply could raise prices, which would cut deeply into workers' household budgets and might lead to demands for wage increases or riots that would disrupt production.

Gradually, for a multitude of reasons that this study explores, the State Food Agency expanded both the number of grains that it purchased and sold and began to find different ways to intervene in the marketing of basic foodstuffs. In the process, the Agency grew to epic proportions (Table 1-1). By 1970 it had become the fifth-largest corporation in Mexico. By 1985 it was the third-largest enterprise in Mexico, involved in diverse activities: purchasing and selling twelve different grains, operating a retail store chain with over 20,000 outlets, controlling a network of grain silos throughout the country, and running a large complex of food-processing plants.[21]

In the process of analyzing a crucial aspect of social policy, this study sheds light on the complex reasons that the Mexican state appeared to develop in an ad hoc and unsystematic way. Such tentacular and financially costly growth is not the result of poor planning and inefficient administration, but instead is the direct result of political efforts to forge social peace, ameliorate class conflict, and create hegemony throughout the republic. Given the complexity of the Mexican social fabric, policymakers see a need to exert centralized control over the republic to solidify the national market and to fully draw diverse Mexicanos into the folds of their imagined community.

The Structure of the Book

In order to reconstruct the history of government intervention in the marketing and distribution of basic foodstuffs in Mexico, I have had to piece together information found in disparate archives and libraries. My investigation has turned up important materials in the various presidential, personal, and institutional papers located in Mexico's Archivo General de la Nación (AGN). Documents in the presidential archives provided insight into various social and political factors that shape the policymaking process. At the AGN, I used the personal papers of several public officials, such as those of the prominent economist Gonzalo Robles and former Secretary of Hydraulic Resources Eduardo Chávez. A number of libraries throughout the country house materials crucial for the study of Mexican government policy. At the Banco de México library, I utilized unpublished reports of agencies dealing with the food trade as well as rare published government reports. At the Colegio de Michoacán, in Zamora, the personal papers of Ramón Fernández y Fernández, a key agronomist and policymaker for much of the period under study, provided much technical insight into the intricacies of polices. In the Biblioteca y Archivo Técnico of the Compañía Nacional de Subsistencias Populares (CONASUPO-BAT), I located technical reports and documents essential to this study, including records of board meetings and the operation of the various departments of the State Food Agency during the 1940s, 1950s, and early 1960s. In addition to the Mexican archives, the U.S. National Archives were a rich source of information on Mexican agricultural policy. Consular reports offered unique insights into the local food situation, and the records of the U.S. Department of Agriculture (USDA) provided essential data that are often lacking in Mexican archives. Recent information was culled from numerous publications (pamphlets, books, and newspaper and magazine articles) and from technical reports published by government agencies. The reconstruction of state activity in the food sector and its connections to social peace and social policy were supplemented with various secondary and newspaper accounts.

To reconstruct the inner working of postrevolutionary bureaucracy in Mexico and its connection with larger social, political, and economic questions, I assembled a number of time-series statistical tables to begin to systematically examine the operation of the State Food Agency. These tables have allowed me to track the continuity of government policy, even when the seemingly ad hoc nature of policymaking made it difficult to do so. Ample qualitative data are used to explain trends and begin to assess the origins, impact, and outcomes of policy.

Because the State Food Agency has undergone six name changes throughout its history, I have generally opted not to use the various names in the text but instead simply called it the State Food Agency (Table 1-2). Although the basic goals of the various agencies were not lost in the name changes and reorganizations, the records of each institution were not uniformly maintained.

Throughout this study I use the concepts of basic grains and staple foods to refer to those foods and grains that historically have been staples of the Mexican diet. The grains basic to the diet of most Mexicans are corn and wheat. Staple foods include tortillas, beans, bread, milk, and eggs; however, this mix is not static. As Mexico underwent a transformation from a rural to an urban society, so too the diet of the people changed. In urban areas, for example, middle- and upper-income Mexicans tend to eat more wheat bread than tortillas. Poorer segments of the population both in the city and the countryside tend to rely more on tortillas than on wheat

Table 1-1. Evolution of the Activities of Mexico's State Food Agency, 1937–1994 (by function)

1937	1940	1950	1960	1965	1970	1975	1980	1985	1991	1994
Grain purchases	Grain purchases	Grain purchases	Grain purchases	Grain purchases	Grain purchases	Grain purchases	Grain purchases	Grain purchases	Grain purchases	Rural food stores
	Retail food stores	Retail food stores	Retail food stores	Retail food stores	Retail food stores	Retail food stores	Retail food sores	Retail food stores	Retail food stores	Milk reconstitution
		Corn milling	Corn milling	Corn milling	Corn milling	Corn milling	Corn milling	Corn milling	Milk reconstitution	
		Milk reconstitution	Milk reconstitution	Milk reconstitution	Milk reconstitution	Milk reconstitution	Milk reconstitution	Milk reconstitution	Wholesale food stores	
			Wheat milling	Wheat milling	Wheat milling	Wheat milling	Wheat milling	Wheat milling	Aiding small enterprise	
				Packaging	Rural development	Rural development	Rural development	Rural development		

1937	1940	1950	1960	1965	1970	1975	1980	1985	1991	1994
					Storage	Storage	Storage	Storage		
						Rural training	Rural training	Rural training		
						Retail clothing stores	Food processing plants	Food processing plants		
						Retail fresh fruit stores	Wholesale food stores	Wholesale food stores		
						Retail construction material		Aiding small enterprise		

Sources: Adapted from *Del control en el comercio triguero a la regulación integral del mercado basicos* (CONASUPO, 1987); *Gaceta CONASUPO*, no. 8 (September 1974); CONASUPO, *Informe anual* 1963; CONASUPO, *Memoria de labores, 1965–68*; CONASUPO, *Informe al consejo de administración 1964–33*; "Sistema de CONASUPO catálogo de programas 1989" (mimeo); *El mercado de las subsistencias populares: Cincuenta años de regulación* (CONASUPO, 1988); "A quién sirve la nueva CONASUPO" (CONASUPO, 1989); and *El Financiero Internacional* (various).

bread. Thus, a sharp increase in the price of tortillas is more likely to provoke a response from the inhabitants of the poorer neighborhoods than from the middle-income sectors, as the recent elimination of the tortilla subsidy demonstrated.

Table 1-2. Evolution of Mexico's State Food Agency, 1937–1999

Name of Organization	Ministry Affiliation	Date Created
Comité Regulador del Mercado del Trigo	Secretaría de la Economía Nacional[a]	June 22, 1937
Comité Regulador del Mercado de las Subsistencias	Secretaría de la Economía Nacional	March 15, 1938
Nacional Distribuidora y Reguladora, S.A. de C.V. (NADYRSA)[b]	Secretaría de la Economía Nacional Secretaría de Hacienda y Crédito Público[c]	May 3, 1941
Compañía Exportadora e Importadora Mexicana, S.A. (CEIMSA)	Secretaría de Hacienda y Crédito Público; Banco Nacional de Comercio Exterior	July 14, 1949
Compañía Nacional de Subsistencias Populares, S.A. (CONASUPO, S.A.)	Secretaría de Hacienda y Crédito Público	March 2, 1961
CONASUPO	Autonomous Agency	April 1, 1965

Sources: México, *Directorio del gobierno federal de los Estados Unidos Mexicano, 1947*; Mexico, *Manual de organización del gobierno federal, 1969–70*; México, *Diario Oficial* (various).
[a]The board of directors also comprised the secretarías de agricultura and hacienda and leaders of three regional producer organizations.
[b]On March 2, 1943, as part of the attempt to enhance coordination between government agencies during World War II, President Manuel Avila Camacho created the Consortium, which was made up of NADRYSA, CEIMSA, the Banco Nacional de Crédito Ejidal, and the Banco Nacional de Crédito Agrícola.
[c]With the dissolution of the Consortium, NADYRSA was placed under the authority of the Secretaría de Hacienda y Crédito Público.

This study shows that food programs and policies grew and expanded as a direct result of popular action. Although many policymakers wanted to use state intervention to make the market operate more smoothly and efficiently, responding to social upheaval would interrupt such projects, and therefore feeding social peace became an overriding concern, while efficient distribution throughout the country became secondary. The paternalistic role of the government in attempting to "feed" the population stemmed from its attempt to use the rhetoric of the revolution to intervene in the economy of basic foods to ameliorate social conflict. A leading opposition politician, half jokingly suggested that this study should be more aptly titled "Starving Mexico." Although large amounts of pesos were expended under the guise of feeding Mexico, the policy did not eradicate poverty. Instead, it enlarged the state: as policies aimed at giving peasants control over lands and encouraging them to produce for local demand were abandoned, the State Food Agency's role grew accordingly. Such policy was overwhelmingly driven by an authoritarian responsiveness that heard popular complaints but did not fully take them into consideration. It responded to short-term crises, often ignoring the long-term impact of its decisions. Consumers and producers were not consulted on how state power could be used to better their interests. Such a policy was unsystematic as well as very costly, but it was successful at helping to maintain social peace, reinforce class dynamics, and facilitate capitalist expansion in Mexico.

To best explain the complex development of state intervention in the food sector, this book is organized chronologically. Chapter 2 examines the historical evolution of state intervention in the food sector in Mexico from colonial times to the 1930s. It demonstrates that most early regulation was done at the local level, consistent with the structure of Mexican society and the state of market development. As efforts were made to unify the various regions of Mexico into a nation-state, the demands for a national system of regulation become greater, and initial attempts were reluctantly made, but not until after the revolution of 1910 were many concrete steps taken to integrate the market.

Chapters 3 through 9 use the six-year presidential term (*sexenio*) to analyze state food policy under each president. I decided to focus on the presidential term because the emphasis of the various agencies generally coincides with the president's overall strategy for his six-year administration.[22] Each president sought to shape the policies of public agencies to fit his own political and economic agendas, but, as this work reveals, much of the real policymaking and implementation lies within the bureaucracy, which is often only marginally influenced by presidential policy.

Between the late 1930s and 1982 the Mexican government retreated from the social goals and the promises of the revolution and concentrated on creating a modern urban industrial nation. Food policy, as one of the bastions of social welfare, played a crucial role in this transformation. As discussed in Chapter 3, during the administration of Lázaro Cárdenas, state intervention in the food sector became a priority, and agencies were established to co-ordinate production and distribution and provide remunerative prices to producers. Despite Cárdenas's initial goals, however, a series of crises transformed the agencies dealing with foodstuffs; they became a means to provide relief to workers and urban consumers to address their eroding purchasing power. Chapters 4 through 8 demonstrate the process by which the State Food Agency grew into a large and complex agency that sought to provide relief to both urban and rural areas at a time when social unrest was developing throughout the country. The demise of land reform and the consolidation of business unionism left the State Food Agency as the main arm of social welfare, responsible for providing inexpensive foodstuffs during times of rising prices, increasing producer prices, and subsidizing small business. At the same time, the State Food Agency served to consolidate agribusiness and reduce the importance of small producers and *ejidatarios*. This complex process is discussed in Chapter 8, which explains the phenomenal growth of the State Food Agency in the midst of a period of social unrest and government repression.

In the wake of the economic crisis of the 1980s, the State Food Agency experienced the fate of most government entities as it was dismantled and its segments privatized. As detailed in Chapter 9, however, this initially occurred gradually, since the State Food Agency was part of the glue that held the social pact together. Presidents de la Madrid and Salinas understood this well and moved cautiously in removing the last component of the social safety net protecting the Mexican people. Instead, a campaign to slowly discredit the agency was carried out so as to dismantle it without popular outcry. In examining the rise and fall of the use of food to support social policy, this study seeks to reinterpret food policy to connect it to both economic and social policy and to underscore how state policy responds to hard-won fights by working people in ways that reinforce the existing social structure.

Notes

1. James F. Smith, "Mexico Clamps Down on Tortilla Prices," *Los Angeles Times*, January 7, 1999.

2. James F. Rochlin, *Redefining Mexican "Security": State, Society, and Region under NAFTA* (Boulder, Colo.: Lynne Rienner, 1997). See also Sergio Zermeño, *La sociedad derrotada: El desorden mexicano del fin de siglo* (México: Siglo Veintiuno Editores, 1996).

3. See Thomas Benjamin and Mark Wasserman, eds., *Provinces of the Revolution: Essays on Regional Mexican History, 1910–1929* (Albuquerque: University of New Mexico Press, 1990); and Gilbert M. Joseph and Daniel Nugent, eds., *Everyday Forms of State Formation: Revolution and the Negotiation of Rule in Modern Mexico* (Durham, NC: Duke University Press, 1994).

4. This is the subject of a growing body of literature. See Joseph and Nugent, eds., *Everyday Forms of State Formation*; Mary Kay Vaughn, *Cultural Politics in Revolution: Teachers, Peasants, and Schools in Mexico, 1930–1940* (Tucson: University of Arizona Press, 1997); Marjorie Becker, *Setting the Virgin on Fire: Lázaro Cárdenas, Michoacán Peasants, and the Redemption of the Mexican Revolution* (Berkeley: University of California Press, 1995); and Adrian A. Bantjes, *As If Jesus Walked on Earth: Cardenismo, Sonora, and the Mexican Revolution* (Wilmington, Del.: SR Books, 1998).

5. Viviane Brachet-Márquez, *The Dynamics of Domination: State, Class, and Social Reform in Mexico, 1910–1990* (Pittsburgh, Pa.: University of Pittsburgh Press, 1994).

6. Evelyn Stevens, *Protest and Response in Mexico* (Cambridge, Mass.: MIT Press, 1974).

7. James C. Scott, *Seeing Like a State: How Certain Schemes to Improve the Human Condition Have Failed* (New Haven, Conn.: Yale University Press, 1998), pt. 1.

8. Howard F. Cline, *Mexico: Revolution to Evolution, 1940–1960* (New York: Oxford University Press, 1963), chap. 17.

9. Frank R. Brandenburg, *The Making of Modern Mexico* (Englewood Cliffs, N.J.: Prentice-Hall, 1964).

10. Among these works see Kenneth F. Johnson, *Mexican Democracy: A Critical View* (Boston: Allyn and Bacon, 1971); and James D. Cockcroft, "Mexico," in Ronald H. Chilcote and Joel C. Edelstein, eds., *Latin America: The Struggle with Dependency and Beyond* (Cambridge, Mass.: Schenkman Publishing Co., 1974), pp. 221–303.

11. Carlos Bazdresch and Santiago Levy, "Populism and Economic Policy in Mexico, 1970–1982," in Rudiger Dornbusch and Sebastian Edwards, eds., *The Macroeconomics of Populism in Latin America* (Chicago, Ill.: University of Chicago Press, 1990), pp. 223–262; Jeffrey Brannon and Eric Baklanoff, *Agrarian Reform and Public Enterprise: The Political Economy of Yucatan's Henequen Industry* (Tuscaloosa: University of Alabama Press, 1987).

12. Exceptions include Kevin Middlebrook, *The Paradox of Revolution: Labor, the State, and Authoritarianism in Mexico* (Baltimore, Md.: Johns Hopkins University Press, 1995); Brachet-Márquez, *The Dynamics of Domination*; and José A. Alderete-Haas, "The Decline of the Mexican State? The Case of State Housing Intervention (1917–1988)" (Ph.D. diss., MIT, 1989).

13. Land distribution has been the focus of numerous studies and is a primary focus of the now numerous local studies of the revolutionary and postrevolutionary period. For a general discussion of local pressures and demands in the revolutionary period, see Alan Knight's masterful *The Mexican Revolution* (New York: Cambridge University Press, 1986). For a discussion of regional agrarianism and hacendado responses, see Benjamin and Wasserman, eds., *Provinces of the Revolution*. For recent studies of local agrarian process over the *longue durée*, see Daniel Nugent, *Spent Cartridges of Revolution: An Anthropological History of Namiquipa, Chihuahua* (Chicago, Ill.: University of Chicago Press, 1993); John Gledhill, *Casi Nada:*

A Study of Agrarian Reform in the Homeland of Cardenismo (Albany, N.Y.: Institute of Mesoamerican Studies, 1991); Middlebrook, *The Paradox of Revolution*; and Brachet-Márquez, *The Dynamics of Domination*.

14. For the value of the commodity-based approach in exploring the nuances of policy and the regional variation based on a variety of factors, see William Roseberry et al., *Coffee, Society, and Power in Latin America* (Baltimore, Md.: Johns Hopkins University Press, 1995). For suggestive approaches to how state interventions impact diverse regions and how local populations respond, see Joseph and Nugent eds., *Everyday Forms of State Formation*. For a case study of milk supply in Mexico City, see Enrique C. Ochoa, "Reappraising State Intervention and Social Policy in Mexico: The Case of Milk in the Distrito Federal during the Twentieth Century," *Mexican Studies/Estudios Mexicanos* 15:1 (winter 1999).

15. For discussion of these policies, see Carmelo Mesa-Lago, "The Case of Mexico," in Mesa-Lago, *Social Security in Latin America: Pressure Groups, Stratification, and Inequality* (Pittsburgh, Pa.: University of Pittsburgh Press, 1978); Peter Ward, *Politicas de bienestar social en México, 1970–1989* (México: Nueva Imagen, 1989); Brachet-Márquez, *The Dynamics of Domination*; and Alderete-Haas, "The Decline of the Mexican State?"

16. Cynthia Hewitt de Alcántara, *La modernización de la agricultura mexicana, 1940–1970* (México: Siglo veintiuno editores, 1978), Steven E. Sanderson, *The Transformation of Mexican Agriculture: International Structure and the Politics of Rural Change* (Princeton, N.J.: Princeton University Press, 1986); and P. Lamartine Yates, *Mexico's Agricultural Dilemma* (Tucson: University of Arizona Press, 1981).

17. Jeffrey M. Pilcher, *¡Que Vivan los Tamales! Food and the Making of Mexican Identity* (Albuquerque: University of New Mexico Press, 1998).

18. Ernesto López Malo, *Ensayo sobre localización de la industria en México* (México: Universidad Nacional Autónoma de México, 1960), pp. 84–104; James W. Wilkie, "Mexico City as a Magnet for Mexico's Economically Active Population, 1935–65," in James W. Wilkie, ed., *Statistics and National Policy* (Los Angeles: UCLA Latin American Center Publications, 1974), p. 44.

19. Peter M. Ward, *Mexico City: The Production and Reproduction of an Urban Environment* (Boston: G. K. Hall, 1990), p. 14.

20. Calculated from Instituto Nacional de Estadística, Geografía, e Informática, *Estadísticas históricas de México* (México: Secretaría de Programación y Presupuesto, 1985), vol. 1, pp. 24–33.

21. David Barkin, "Mexico's Albatross: The U.S. Economy," in Nora Hamilton and Timothy F. Harding, eds., *Modern Mexico: State, Economy, and Social Conflict* (Beverly Hills, Calif.: Sage Publications, 1986), p. 113; *South*, April 1987, p. 86.

22. For a discussion of the importance of the *sexenio* for public policy, see Merrilee Serrill Grindle, *Bureaucrats, Peasants and Politicians in Mexico: A Case Study in Public Policy* (Berkeley: University of California Press, 1977), chap. 3.

2

From Local to Federal Intervention

Food Policy Prior to the 1930s

In the 1930s the federal government became the primary government entity to intervene in the marketing and distribution of basic grains. Prior to this time, federal actions were generally limited to the importation of grains in times of shortages, and the task of market regulation was relegated to local officials and institutions. This chapter traces the shift from local intervention to federal government intervention in the marketing of basic foodstuffs in Mexico from 1519, when Europeans arrived in Mexico, to the administration of Lázaro Cárdenas in 1934. By analyzing the nature of government intervention in the economy over time, we explore the reasons for increased federalization of food policy in the post-revolutionary era. In examining the role of the various governments in the marketing of basic grains during the colonial period (1519–1810), the early independence period (1810–1876), the Porfiriato (1876–1911), the revolution (1910–1917), and the aftermath of the revolution (1917–1934), this chapter demonstrates that government regulation of foodstuffs evolved in concert with the development of a national market economy. Therefore, federal government regulatory policies toward foodstuff developed as a tool in government's effort to create a national market as well as in response to growing social pressures resulting from the numerous deleterious effects of market consolidation.

Grain Regulation under European Rule

Following the European conquest early Mexican society and economy were dominated by local authorities. In the words of one historian, "Colonial Mexico was the sum of its regional economies.

Mexico City, in spite of its privileged status as viceregal capital, its dominance of overseas trade, and its demographic primacy, probably exercised less direct influence beyond the valley of Mexico than had its Aztec predecessor."[1] Although the extent of regional provincial isolation varied, local authorities and town councils oversaw the daily operations of government with a relatively high degree of independence from Mexico City.[2] Such recent interpretation of colonial society overturns years of scholarly perceptions that have painted the picture of a strong central government imposing its will on various parts of society. One reason for the persistence of the earlier interpretation, was the emphasis on analyzing Mexican history through documents and rulers who were based in Mexico City. Although edicts were issued in capital cities, oftentimes their enforcement did not extend beyond the boundaries of the city.

The first local intervention in the food markets can be traced to the arrival of Columbus in the Western Hemisphere. As early as the 1490s, when Columbus was named governor of the Indies, he was granted authority to control production and set prices of foodstuffs. Early in his administration, Columbus decreed that pricing was to allow profit, yet goods should be sold at a "fair price." He was authorized to decide what agricultural goods were to be produced and to force merchants to sell products at fixed prices if they were unwilling.[3] Although it is not clear how effective Columbus was at enforcing production and price controls or how such controls were determined, they established the pattern of government intervention in food policy in the New World that would become increasingly codified as more Europeans settled in the Western Hemisphere.

After the conquest of Mexico in 1521, European landowners began to shift the production of goods to meet the needs and tastes of other Europeans who settled in growing numbers in urban areas. Because the Hispanic settlers in New Spain were accustomed to a European diet that was wheat-based, unlike the corn-based diets in the Americas, wheat was sown shortly after settlement and was quickly followed by the milling of wheat for the production of bread.[4] In order to provision the city, preconquest communal labor mechanisms were continued to ensure a constant and steady supply of grains at affordable prices. As postcontact cities grew, due partially to the increase in the number of Hispanized Indians who migrated to the cities to fill the service sector jobs and to continued European immigration, it became increasingly important to ensure a steady supply of affordable food.[5]

Food regulation policies were instituted in New Spain within a few years of the arrival of Hernán Córtes in 1521. Increasing urbanization and unpredictable climate conditions led to periodic grain shortages, prompting governments to intervene in the marketplace. Enrique Florescano has divided basic food legislation during the sixteenth century into three general periods. The first period, 1525–1550, was anarchic, with very little legislation. In 1524 Mexico City elected its first urban food officer, the *fiel ejecutor*, to regulate weights and measures and intervene in all aspects regarding food in the city.[6] In the second period, 1553 to 1579, there was a greater effort to regulate sales as the price of corn in central Mexico increased nearly threefold and the price of wheat rose at a somewhat faster rate between 1530 and 1573. During the third period, after 1580, the city council in Mexico City created an institution that would seek to ensure a stable price and abundant supply.[7]

By 1590 two institutional mechanisms were established to overcome fluctuations in agricultural production due to unfavorable weather, labor shortages, poor distribution, and other factors.[8] The first institution, the *alhóndiga*, was modeled on institutions in Spain and Lima and began operating in Mexico City in 1580 to stem a five-year famine.[9] The *alhóndiga* was a public granary charged with ensuring a steady supply of grains at a "just" price. Local city councils established and administered the *alhóndigas*, which served as public markets where producers would bring grain from the countryside, store it, and later sell it at the *alhóndiga* at a price set by its officials. To help pay for the operation and maintenance of the granary, officials would exact a minor tax from each load of grain brought in.

The second regulatory institution, the *pósito*, was a grain reserve controlled by the city council. The city council would authorize *alhóndiga* officials to purchase grain when the price was low, so that it could be stored in the *pósito*, which was located in the same building as the *alhóndiga*. This grain was to be released on the market during periods of scarcity or high prices to encourage lower prices and discourage speculation during periods of famine.

Although the ability of the *alhóndigas* and the *pósitos* to maintain a constant supply of grains at a "fair price" has yet to be thoroughly studied, regional studies, especially on the eighteenth century, shed some light on their actual operations. During Mexico's more severe food shortages, in most cases grain-regulating institutions were unable to prevent near-famine conditions. For example, when grain became scarce during the 1620s, the viceroy ordered the purchasing of grain, but he could not stave off rapid price increases of corn that nearly caused famine.[10] Other widespread food shortages could not be prevented and caused large numbers of deaths, as occurred during the subsistence crisis of 1785–87. Nonetheless, the relative infrequency of food riots can be attributed to the ability of governments to maintain a semblance of legitimacy. The grain-regulating institutions were seen as symbols of the government's attempts to address problems in food supply.

Although grain scarcity often acted as the immediate cause for the establishment of the *pósito* and the *alhóndiga*, these institutions also thrived during periods of grain abundance. According to historian Guy Thomson, the case of Puebla demonstrates that of all economic legislation, laws regulating food supply were the most consistently applied, and they were the last to be repealed.[11] Nonetheless, problems in operating the *alhóndiga* and *pósito* were legion. Abuses of the *alhóndiga* laws were seen as the principal cause of price increases and not the consequence of the anticipated poor harvest. A study commissioned by the Puebla City Council in 1800 found that the *alhóndiga* officials were favoring large grain sellers over small local ones. The primary complaint was that larger grain merchants were allowed to sell for a longer period of time at prices above the fixed price and that officials accepted commissions from the large producers.[12] For the next forty years, the city council in Puebla sought, with futility, to reform the *alhóndiga*. Not until agriculturalists lost their political influence to industrialists was the city council able to reduce the privileged status of the large agriculturalists. The newly emerging industrialists were more concerned with the prices of foodstuffs paid by urban consumers than they were with the profits of large estate holders; for industrialists, lower and consistent staple prices allowed them to pay lower salaries and avoid disruptions of production.

Despite problems with the operation of the *alhóndiga* and the *pósito* in Puebla, these institutions were not abandoned until the 1850s, long after most other colonial economic legislation had been repealed. A 1839 study commissioned by the Puebla City Council concluded:

> In good harvest years everyone speculates and the alhóndiga sees little activity, but in years of bad harvests, speculators are few and monopolize sales. Certainly you [the council] lack the resources to remedy such unfortunate occurrences, but perhaps the public will be persuaded that the crisis was not your responsibility and not move their lips to complain; but if you auction the

alhóndiga, the public is not composed of philosophers, and left
to follow their senses, they will attribute the cause of evil to you,
and your name will be execrated as the author of their ruin.[13]

Thus, although economically the *alhóndiga* and the *pósito* could not
solve the problem of food scarcity and may have indeed added to
it, at the very least they allowed for the appearance of government
control and willingness to feed the population.

Aside from regulating the local grain markets, local governments also began to take more active roles in setting prices and
weights of bread during the eighteenth and nineteenth centuries.
Bread became one of the major staple foods of urban dwellers during this period and was one of the primary targets of government
controls. Governments tried to impose laws regulating the weight,
type, and price of bread, which many times led to unintended problems. In Mexico City, for example, it became impossible to regulate
the various laws because bakers and millers actively sought to circumvent them.[14] Despite the myriad of problems that arose from
government attempts to regulate the marketing of foodstuffs, subsequent governments continued to regulate basic foods.

During the years following Mexico's independence from Spain
in 1822, local government continued to dominate the scene as
Mexico scrambled to consolidate national order. Early republican
Mexico experienced substantial political and economic instability
during the first half century of independence. In addition to having over sixty presidents in fifty years, Mexico lost half its territory
in 1848 after the war with the United States, was invaded and oc-
cupied by the French between 1863 and 1867, and experienced numerous secessionist movements. Such instability was part of the
severe economic downturn after the wars for independence. The
depression did not hit all regions with the same magnitude, especially because the federal government lacked funds to construct
transportation and communication systems needed to unify the
country and it markets.[15] John Coatsworth calculated that Mexico's
GDP per capita fell from $73 in 1800 to $49 in 1860.[16] Hence, decreased economic activity meant fewer pesos going to government
coffers and fewer resources to enable the central government to
impose its will on the rest of the republic. Thus after independence
Mexico continued to live under regional rule.

Throughout the colonial period and the early nineteenth century, most government intervention in foodstuffs occurred at the
local level. Although Mexico City controlled the trade of goods, it

was the local governments that established institutions to attempt to ensure a steady supply of food for the other cities. The larger grain producers often used the *alhóndiga* as their own personal market by using political power to drive out competition when necessary, as they did with indigenous peoples in Puebla. Not until the introduction of the railroad and telegraph in the second half of the nineteenth century was the federal government able to begin to consolidate its power politically and gradually to lay the basis for political and economic integration of Mexico.

Indirect Federal Intervention in the Economy, 1876–1910

The reign of Porfirio Díaz (1876–1911) laid the political foundation for a consolidated nation-state. After seizing power, Díaz immediately sought to unify the various regions of the country by forging alliances with regional leaders and buttressing a rural police force. These efforts at consolidating his power enabled the Díaz administration to court foreign investors who poured an estimated 2 billion dollars into the Mexican economy.[17] The dual policy of creating political order to achieve economic progress was mutually reinforcing. With more resources at his disposal, Díaz was able to begin to create a relatively strong administrative state, so as to provide the basis for the expansion of the capitalist economy.[18]

Díaz's intervention in the economy is best exemplified by the Departamento de Fomento, established in 1880 to modernize agriculture and expand transportation and communication works so as to entice rural investment. By 1883–84, it wielded over one-third of the federal government budget, investing, for example, in the colonization of new lands and in the expansion of irrigation projects.[19] In addition, the Díaz administration initiated an aggressive policy of surveying and privatizing vast tracts of public lands, placing some 45.7 million hectares of public land in the marketplace.[20] To further spur the modernization of agriculture, Díaz encouraged the construction of irrigation works, first through monitoring water use by private owners and then by more direct management of water use of various rivers.[21] Díaz also sponsored the writing and distributing of pamphlets on modern growing techniques, borrowing many of the latest innovations in modern agriculture from French scientists.[22] These indirect measures of government intervention led to a more active federal government than in the past.

This intervention in agriculture was fueled by elite conceptions of modernization that often equated wheat-based diets with modernity and corn-based diets with backwardness. Jeffrey Pilcher has shown how Porfirian discourses on the tortilla developed in concert with the emergence of nutritional sciences and public health research that tended to link tortilla consumption with poor nutrition and a perception of Indian "backwardness." According to Pilcher, one influential figure, Francisco Bulnes, went so far as to argue "most controversially that generations of malnutrition had 'mineralized' the indigenous people, inclined them to the immutability of 'rocks,' and prevented any hope for future progress."[23] Nutrition was very much a part of elite discourse, and many argued that it was necessary to alter the basic diet of the majority of Mexicans to create a stronger population for the nation's prosperity.

Although the federal government intervened in the economy to stimulate the modernization of agriculture, it left the regulation of food distribution to local government. For years municipal governments had administered and regulated public markets and continued to do so throughout the Porfiriato. In the municipal government of Mexico City, the Department of Public Markets governed most aspects of the operation of the seventeen large markets, the numerous smaller and ephemeral markets, and the activities of the street vendors. The municipal authorities were charged with renting space in the markets, collecting taxes, overseeing construction and repair, and enforcing sanitary laws. By providing and controlling the location of public marketing, the municipal government ensured a steady income from these activities. Throughout the Porfiriato, municipal budgets demonstrated that income from markets equaled between 5 and 11 percent of the total municipal income, whereas markets accounted for an average of approximately 1 percent of the city's investments.[24] Under normal conditions, the government intervened only to regulate the conditions of distribution, and merchants purchased their goods from the countryside and the surrounding areas with little government involvement.

The federal government was slow to respond to food shortages and reluctant to intervene to alleviate such situations. During the first decade of the twentieth century, this reluctance and its consequences became clear when climatic conditions sparked severe shortages and price increases and, coupled with an economic recession, made basic foodstuffs less accessible to workers. Drought conditions during the years 1905–1907 led to alarming reports in

Mexican newspapers of grain scarcity. Basic food prices increased substantially between 1907 and 1910, with corn and wheat, respectively, increasing by 38 and 20 percent on average. In the northern states, corn shortages forced prices up by nearly 100 percent in 1909. These increases in the price of staple goods cut further into the already declining purchasing power of workers.[25] One study of the Mexican working classes during the period found that "real wages rose slowly and erratically from the mid-1890s to the turn of the century and then declined throughout the next decade as rising prices cut into workers' purchasing power."[26] In Chihuahua, the German consul estimated that in 1909 the price of basic goods increased 80 percent, while nominal wages fell by 20 percent.[27] The shortages and resultant price increases were complicated by the return to Mexico of miners thrown out of work by the 1907 economic downturn in the United States.[28]

Government intervention to alleviate scarcity first occurred at the local level. Local governments instituted standby policies of price controls and ordered municipal presidents to submit weekly reports on prices and grain stocks. In more severe cases, governments secured grain from other regions if possible. However, local government could provide only short-term relief that was often too little, too late. Such was the case, for example in Michoacán, about which Gerardo Sánchez concluded: "Local and state authorities always intervened in an untimely manner, dictating policies, such as importing grains and using public funds to sell the grain cheaply, but never being able to control the voraciousness of speculators who doubled their fortunes while the urban and rural masses suffered hunger and misery." [29]

Without a plan to respond to food shortages, the federal government did not act until 1906. In that year, government officials met with large landowners to discuss the scarcity of basic foodstuffs throughout the country and decided to intervene to alleviate the situation. Due to the gravity of the shortage, Díaz appointed Vice President Ramón Corral to form the Junta Provisional de Granos (Commission for Grain Provisions), which was charged with monitoring the supply and demand of basic grains. Corral's commission, which included prominent members of the cabinet, such as Minister of Finance José Limantour, imported large amounts of corn and wheat for domestic distribution and monitored prices of these basic grains. The government subsidized the cost of corn and wheat imports, resulting in a jump in the value of grains from 439,000 pesos between 1902 and 1906, to 2,198,000 in 1908, and to

over 15 million pesos in 1909. This intervention provided some relief to the cities where grains were in short supply. In 1910, when
the prospect of a better harvest was on the horizon and after much
of the grain imports had reached Mexico, Díaz disbanded the commission.[30] The centralizing policies of the Díaz administration led
to a more active use of the federal government in the economy.
Indeed, the federal government reluctantly intervened in the marketing of basic grains after food shortages spread beyond localities
and became a national problem.

Revolution and the Breakdown of Federal Control, 1910–1917

The outbreak of the Mexican revolution in 1910 led to a collapse in
the central government authority and control that Díaz had helped
to forge, and regional leaders again came to dominate the country.
The revolution disrupted the growing national economy that had
taken off during the Porfiriato, causing a number of problems such
as severe food shortages and near-famine conditions in a number
of places. Cut off from the national government, local governments
were forced to intervene in the economy to supply food to their
populations.

Although the tumultuous nature of the Mexican revolution did
not disrupt all economic activity, it did hinder agricultural production. Available data on corn and wheat production show various
fluctuations. With the exception of a few good years, production
generally fell below that for the prerevolutionary years. For corn
production, the average output during the violent decade was two-
thirds the amount it was during the previous decade. Wheat production faired better than corn, generally declining by 25 percent
from the amount produced during the last decade of the Díaz era.
However, the largest decline in grain production came in 1914.
According to official data, production declined by 69 percent for
corn and 144 percent for wheat in relation to the previous year.[31]
Due to the chaos in Mexico during the revolution, grain imports
could not compensate for the production declines during the
decade.[32]

Detailed price data do not exist for this period, but qualitative
evidence indicates that the 1910–1917 period was marked by intense inflation. The soaring prices were primarily the result of the
issuance of fiat currency and two poor harvests. The issuance of
paper money by the diverse revolutionary factions led to a flood of

currency circulating throughout the country. Alan Knight noted that, between 1914 and 1916, "the country was swamped by a polychrome of paper money: national and local bills, cardboard *cartones*, notes of the Henequen Regulating Commission, company *vales*, revolutionary IOU's, and the bizarre, improvised *bilimbiques* which ranged from toilet paper to shin plasters."[33] Inflation was coupled with the poor agricultural harvests of 1914 and 1915. Much of the crop that was not lost to the weather was either destroyed in battle or seized by military chieftains. Railroads and railcars had also been appropriated by military chieftains, which hindered the distribution of grain. As a result of these shortages and bottlenecks speculators and middlemen profited from price increases. In 1916, it was reported that prices of basic foodstuffs in Mexico City had increased fifteenfold since the beginning of the revolution.[34]

Scarcity of basic foodstuffs plagued Mexico during the revolutionary decade and was felt throughout the republic. Various regions of the republic reported possible crop losses. Shortages throughout the country led to public outcries that sometimes turned violent. In many cities people would rise early to stand in line for bread and tortillas several hours prior to the opening of the stores. In other areas, food riots erupted, often leading to looting. Although conditions in Mexico City began to improve in 1917, the north suffered its most severe shortage in that year: the states of Durango and Coahuila, plagued by drought, reported the loss of 75 percent of their crop.[35]

To provide relief and to prevent more civil disturbances, local governments sought to intervene in the distribution of basic foodstuffs. Because the most consistent form of government action was to publicly berate speculation and speculators, frequently "populist rhetoric was a substitute for positive action."[36] Along with the rhetoric came a number of ad hoc and largely unsuccessful attempts at price fixing and other measures. In many cases local authorities "found themselves fixing prices for food which was unobtainable anyway."[37]

Two high-profile attempts to control the price and supply of basic foodstuffs met with some success. In the state of Yucatán, during the administration of the reform government of Salvador Alvarado, basic food scarcity led to large-scale price gouging. To combat abuses by merchants, Governor Alvarado established a regulatory commission, as a subsidiary of the profitable state-operated Henequen Regulating Committee, to deal with food distribution. Although the commission was able to secure and stockpile foodstuffs and rein in prices, corrupt management caused it to become a large speculator itself. In many cases, inadequately policed merchants raised the price of goods without authorization.[38]

In Mexico City, President Venustiano Carranza initiated a second major government attempt to mitigate the effects of food shortages. To distribute foodstuffs, Carranza set up a committee to oversee the operations of a number of retail outlets where the urban poor could buy basic grains, milk, fish, meats, and clothing at substantially reduced prices. The committee contracted with other government agencies and unions to obtain approximately 250,000 bread rolls (*bolillos*) a day and then sold them at ten centavos apiece, instead of the market price of 70 centavos.[39] As in Yucatán, allegations of official corruption plagued most attempts at regulating grain trade, and many prominent local authorities were implicated in profiting from grain operations. Despite such abuses, however, government intervention served to stave off revolts.[40]

By 1917 Carranza and the Constitutionalist forces had begun to consolidate their power throughout the country. Although sporadic fighting still occurred, the assassinations of Zapata, Villa, and other agrarian leaders in the early 1920s paved the way for general political stability. As successive governments moved to rebuild the country, prices showed a general deflationary tendency. After the years of great food scarcity and rampant inflation, production began to recover, although not to the pre-1910 levels, and Carranza authorized the unrestricted importation of staple items. Prices slowly began to decline and stabilize. In comparing the retail prices in Mexico City before and after the violent phase of the revolution (Table 2-1), we can see that prices had, in most cases, doubled and tripled by 1918. Although prices would decline and stabilize during the 1920s, the scarcity of foodstuffs and hyper-inflation of the war years left an indelible impression on subsequent governments.

The Legal and Institutional Basis of Federal Government Intervention, 1917–1934

After 1917, Mexican presidents began to gradually rein in the regional strongmen of Mexico and centralize their authority. The general goals of the triumphant factions of the revolution were set down on paper during the Constitutional Convention in Querétaro. Widely hailed as one of the most socially advanced constitutions, the Constitution of 1917 gave the state increased power to intervene in the economy and granted provisions for government intervention to protect consumers from "excessive" increases in the price of basic foodstuffs.

Table 2-1. Average Retail Price of Basic Goods in Mexico City, 1910 and 1918 (pesos per kilogram)

	1910	*1918*	*Percent Change*
Corn	0.09	0.17	88
White bread	0.32	0.95	197
Beans	0.12	0.34	183
Rice	0.15	0.52	247
Lard	0.60	2.04	240
Coffee (milled)	0.80	0.49	-39
Milk (liter)	0.15	0.25	67
Salt	0.04	0.09	125
Sugar	0.17	0.63	271
Charcoal	0.04	0.05	25
Firewood	0.02	0.03	50
Rent (pesos per month)	5.00	7.50	50
Wax candles	0.33	0.90	173
Soap	0.25	0.79	216
Cloth (pesos per meter)	0.14	0.80	471

Sources: AGN-DT, caja 116, file 6; caja 144, file 2; caja 368, file 3.

The justifications for government intervention in the pricing of basic articles are contained in Article 28 of the Constitution of 1917. Article 28 declares that monopolies are contrary to the goals of the new government.[41] Under the broad definition of monopolies, Article 28 also gave its support to government intervention in the economy to protect consumers: "the law will severely punish and authorities will persecute with efficacy all concentration or hoarding of basic foodstuffs in the hands of one or a few who have as their objectives the increase of prices."[42] However, the federal government did not explicitly outline the procedures, aside from imposing fines, that the government could pursue. As the problem of scarcity of foods and inflation subsided there was less pressure for the government to articulate a detailed plan to combat grain speculation.

Widespread hunger and the resultant price increases of the period from 1914 to 1917 were fresh on the minds of those who gathered in Querétaro to draft the Constitution of 1917. In many parts of the Mexican north, severe food shortages had led to riots during the months preceding the Constitutional Convention. Small communities throughout the country, such as in San José de Gracía,

Michoacán, remembered 1917 as the year of the famine.[43] That the federal government had the right and the obligation to protect consumers against price gouging seemed to be universally agreed upon by those at the convention because the provision for it in the article was accepted without any debate.[44]

For nearly fourteen years after the promulgation of the Constitution of 1917, there was little popular pressure on the federal government to act on the antihoarding clause of Article 28. Beginning in 1918, price levels declined from their peak during the revolution. Retail corn prices in Mexico City declined steadily after the violent phase of the revolution, and with the exception of the drought year of 1921, prices stabilized at slightly above their 1910 levels (Table 2-2). Throughout the 1920s, the price of corn fluctuated relatively little in comparison to the previous decade.

Table 2-2. Retail Corn Prices in Mexico City, 1910-1936

Year	Pesos/Kilograms
1910	0.09
1918	0.17
1919	0.14
1920	0.10
1921	0.25
1922	0.11
1923	0.11
1924	0.11
1925	0.12
1927	0.12
1928	0.08
1930	0.15
1931	0.12
1932	0.09
1933	0.09
1934	0.08
1935	0.09
1936	0.10

Sources: For 1910–1929, data compiled from surveys by the Secretaría de Comercio e Industria, various years, located in AGN-DT. Data for 1930–1936 are from Secretaría de la Economía Nacional, *Anuario estadístico, 1938* (México, 1938).

By 1929 and 1930 prices began to climb, due largely to the drought and poor harvests: corn and bean production fell by 37 and 53 percent, respectively, between 1928 and 1930.[45] As production began to recover, beginning with the harvest of 1931, the decline in economic activity that resulted from the Great Depression led to depressed prices. As a result, there was great fear that merchants would buy grains in large quantities and hold them off the market to drive prices upward. During this volatile period, the federal government made its initial move to apply Article 28 of the Constitution of 1917 to prevent grain hoarding.

Explicit instructions detailing the manner in which Article 28 of the Constitution should be implemented were not put in writing until December 1931, when President Pascual Ortíz Rubio signed into law the Organic Law of Article 28. The Organic Law dealt with government intervention in the marketing of staple goods by creating local price-regulating committees, comprising representatives of various ministries, to assess the food needs of each municipality, set the maximum price levels during times of shortages, and impose fines on violators of price controls. These committees were temporary, to be created only during times of shortages or depressed prices to stave off grain speculation.[46]

In addition to granting local government price-regulating authority, the Organic Law also gave greater powers to the federal government. The early 1930s saw the federal government taking greater steps to assess the situation of consumers by tracking prices and estimating grain supply. Although the Mexican Labor Department began collecting data on the worker's cost of living on a regular basis beginning in 1918, only in 1930 did it begin to publish these data in a statistical yearbook.[47] Once consumer prices were systematically organized and published for Mexico City, the secretary of the economy commissioned the construction of the first cost of living index, and by 1934 there were two cost of living indexes: one that tracked general retail price movements and another that monitored the worker's cost of living in the Federal District.[48] Equipped with these tools, government officials could systematically track price movements and assess their impact on the population.

In the early 1930s, agricultural ministries also stepped up their attempts to monitor the supply of basic grains in order to enhance the coordination of production and consumption. During the 1920s and early 1930s, agricultural economists had cited the lack of an efficient information system as one of the major causes of the disorganization of grain markets.[49] To overcome this problem, information on prices, costs, and harvests was compiled by the Dirección General de Economía Rural of the Secretaría de Agricultura y Fomento (SAF), which began publishing a monthly bulletin in 1933 and commissioned several monographs on the marketing of various crops.[50] The commercial department of the Banco Nacional de Crédito Agrícola (BNCA) published, from 1931 to 1933, a bulletin that contained studies on the marketing of basic grains in Mexico and also analyzed government marketing organizations in countries such as the United States. Statistical methods for gathering production data began to be studied and debated in order to improve upon the existing methods.[51] Such indirect methods of assessing Mexico's food needs enabled the government to improve planning, but little direct action occurred in times of food emergencies. Because government did not control the grain supply, it could only attempt to regulate the market from the outside.

To do so, the federal government took concrete measures aimed at influencing the marketing of basic grains during the early 1930s. Beginning with the improved harvest of 1931 and the decline in economic activity as a result of the Depression, the price of basic grains fell to its lowest point in decades. In response to producer demands, the government intervened in June 1932 to prevent merchants and other middlemen from grain speculation, and BNCA created a storage subsidiary, Almacenes Generales de Depósito de Crédito Agrícola (AGDCA). According to the BNCA, the state had to build storage facilities to enable producers to store their own grain and sell it at their convenience, thus protecting them from "ruthless large middlemen and millers." At the same time, state-run warehouses were also seen as "a panacea to evils that afflict consumers."[52]

Despite government rhetoric, however, the newly founded AGDCA did not fully serve the interests of producers, as was planned at the outset. Its thirty-six warehouses, constructed in 1932 and 1933, were generally located near large cities or near large-scale production areas. By its own admission, the majority of AGDCA dealings until 1935 were not with producers, but rather with merchants and industrialists.[53] Although these initial efforts to operate in grain markets met with only limited success, the basis for more direct government intervention in production and commercialization had been established.

The federal government's goal of expanding the internal market and of exerting greater control over the production and consumption of foodstuffs was reflected in government plans and documents. The first six-year plan of the official party, the Partido Nacional Revolucionario (PNR), called for an interventionist government that would be active in promoting the economic growth and well-being of the country.[54] Vague plans were developed for coordinating basic grain production and consumption, but these plans were not fully elaborated or enacted until pressure was exerted on the government. As in the prerevolutionary period, only during times of inflation and food shortages has the Mexican government attempted to control the marketing and distribution process of food.

Conclusion

Western Hemisphere governments have been intervening in the marketing of basic foodstuffs since the arrival of Columbus. As New Spain was settled, the relative scarcity of basic foodstuffs that the Europeans were accustomed to eating, such as wheat, led to the emergence of government intervention in the market for basic grains. Because Mexico was hardly an economically integrated entity, this early intervention was expressed at the local level. Available evidence suggests that intervention on the local level tended to benefit the large producers who, for a large part of the colonial period, used their political power to gain economic benefits at the alhóndiga.

By the late nineteenth century the federal government had become better equipped to penetrate local society and to centralize power. Focused as it was on modernizing agriculture, upgrading infrastructure, and wooing foreign investors, the Díaz government even began to intervene in the distribution of foodstuffs (albeit reluctantly) during a period of acute crisis. The short-lived Junta Provisional de Granos imported large quantities of grain to stave off shortages. Once harvests recovered, the junta was disbanded so as not to disrupt the market process. The revolutionary upheaval of 1910 to 1917 led to a temporary breakdown of the federal government and its tentative forays into interventionist food policy. As the prices of basic grains rose dramatically due to the overissuance of fiat currency and the decline of agricultural production, regional leaders enacted their own food policies.

Only with the pacification of the country by the 1920s and the consolidation of a new governing group did the federal government begin to expand its authority into various sectors of the economy. It is true that Article 28 of the Constitution of 1917 established the basis for government intervention, but as dramatic price increases subsided along with the violence, government attention shifted toward the consolidation of power. With the failed harvests of 1929 and 1930, however, the federal government moved to define the parameters of Article 28 and establish provisions for monitoring food supply in the cities. When simple monitoring and regulatory devices failed to alleviate food scarcity and inflation, the federal government moved to take greater and more direct action by intervening directly in the marketing process.

Notes

1. Guy P. C. Thomson, *Puebla de los Angeles: Industry and Society in a Mexican City, 1700–1850* (Boulder, Colo.: Westview Press, 1989), p. 1.

2. Ida Altman and James Lockhart, eds., *Provinces of Early Mexico: Variants of Spanish American Regional Evolution* (Los Angeles: UCLA Latin American Center Press, 1976).

3. John C. Super, *Food, Conquest, and Colonization in Sixteenth-Century Spanish America* (Albuquerque: University of New Mexico Press, 1988), pp. 41–42.

4. Jeffrey M. Pilcher, *¡Qué vivan los tamales! Food and the Making of Mexican Identity* (Albuquerque: University of New Mexico Press, 1998), see esp. chap. 2, "The Conquests of Wheat: Culinary Encounters in the Colonial Period."

5. Super, *Food, Conquest, and Colonization*, pp. 32–33.

6. Ibid., pp. 44–45.

7. Enrique Florescano, "El abasto y la legislación de granos en el siglo XVI," *Historia Mexicana 56* 14:4 (April–June 1965), p. 604.

8. Raymond L. Lee, "Grain Legislation in Colonial Mexico, 1575–1585," *Hispanic American Historical Review* (November 1947), pp. 647–660.

9. Super, *Food Conquest, and Colonization*, p. 48; Irene Vásquez de Warman, "El pósito y la alhóndiga en la Nueva España," *Historia Mexicana 67* 17:3 (January–March 1968), pp. 395–426; Lee, "Grain Legislation."

10. Chester Lyle Guthrie, "Riots in Seventeenth Century Mexico City: A Study of Social and Economic Conditions," in Adele Ogden and Engel Sluiter, eds., *Greater America: Essays in Honor of Herbert Eugene Bolton* (Berkeley: University of California Press, 1945), pp. 245–246; Rosa Feijoo, "El tumulto de 1624," *Historia Mexicana 53* 14:1 (July–September 1964), p. 44.

11. Thomson, *Puebla de los Angeles*.

12. Ibid., p. 116.

13. Ibid., p. 127.

14. See John C. Super, "Bread and the Provisioning of Mexico City in the Late Eighteenth Century," *Jahrbuch Für Geschichte: Von Staat, Wirrschaft und Gesellschaft Lateinamerikas* 19 (1982), pp. 159–182.

15. Barbara Tenenbaum, *The Politics of Penury: Debt and Taxes in Mexico 1821–1856* (Albuquerque: University of New Mexico Press, 1986); and Romeo Flores Caballero, "Comercio interior," in Luís González et al., *La economía mexicana en la época de Juárez* (México: Secretaría de Industria y Comercio, 1972), pp. 159–186.

16. John Coatsworth, "Obstacles to Economic Growth in Nineteenth Century Mexico," *American Historical Review* 83:1 (1978). See also Stephen H. Haber, "Assessing the Obstacles to Industrialisation: The Mexican Economy, 1830–1940," *Journal of Latin American Studies* 24, pp. 1–32.

17. Stephen H. Haber, *Industry and Underdevelopment: The Industrialization of Mexico, 1890–1940* (Stanford, Calif.: Stanford University Press, 1989), p. 12.

18. Coatsworth, "Obstacles to Economic Growth"; and Haber, "Assessing the Obstacles." For a detailed dicussion of the centralization of the budgetary process during this period, see Marcello Carmagnani, *Estado y mercado: La economía pública del liberalismo mexicano, 1850–1911* (México: Fondo de Cultura Económica, 1994).

19. Don M. Coerver, "The Perils of Progress: The Mexican Department of Fomento during the Boom Years 1880–1884," *Inter-American Economic Affairs* 31:2 (autumn 1977), p. 60.

20. Robert H. Holden, *Mexico and the Survey of Public Lands: The Management of Modernization, 1876–1911* (De Kalb: Northern Illinois University Press, 1994), p. 9; Coerver, "The Perils of Progress," pp. 52–54.

21. Clifton B. Kroeber, *Man, Land, and Water: Mexico's Farmland Irrigation Policies, 1885–1911* (Berkeley: University of California Press, 1983), p. 225.

22. Joseph Cotter and Michael A. Osborne, "Agronomía Afranceada: The French Contribution to Mexican Agronomy, 1880–1940," *Science, Technology and Society* 1:1 (1996), pp. 25–49.

23. Pilcher, *¡Qué vivan los tamales!*, pp. 82–83.

24. Judith Ettinger Marti, "Subsistence and the State: Municipal Government Policies and Urban Markets in Developing Nations: The Case of Mexico City and Guadalajara, 1877–1910," Ph.D. diss., UCLA, 1990, pp. 122–124, 129, 196.

25. John Mason Hart, *Revolutionary Mexico: The Coming and Process of the Mexican Revolution* (Berkeley: University of California Press, 1987), pp. 183–184.

26. Rodney Anderson, *Outcasts in Their Own Land: Mexican Industrial Workers, 1906–1911* (De Kalb: Northern Illinois University Press, 1978), p. 62.

27. Cited in Friedrich Katz, "The Liberal Republic and the Porfiriato, 1867–1910," in Leslie Bethell, ed., *Mexico since Independence* (New York: Cambridge University Press, 1991), p. 111.

28. Friedrich Katz, *The Secret War in Mexico: Europe, the United States, and the Mexican Revolution* (Chicago, Ill.: University of Chicago Press, 1983), p. 10; Katz, "The Liberal Republic and the Porfiriato, 1867–1910," p. 110; Anderson, *Outcasts in Their Own Land* , p. 24.

29. Gerardo Sánchez, "Crisis agrícola y abastecimiento de granos en Michoacán, 1880–1910," in Gail Mummert, ed., *Almacenamiento de productos agropecuarios en México* (Zamora: El Colegio de Michoacán, 1987), p. 149.

30. Ramón E. Ruiz, *The Great Rebellion: Mexico, 1905–1924* (New York: W. W. Norton, 1980), pp. 80–83.

31. For data on corn production, see Mexico Secretaría de Agricultura y Fomento, Dirección de Economia Rural, *Estudio agro-económico de maíz*, pt. 3 (México, 1940), table 29. Wheat production data is presented in Secretaría de la Economia Nacional, *La industria harinera: Materia prima, molienda y transportes* (México: Talleres Gráficos de la Nación, 1934), p. 18. See also John Womak, "The Mexican Revolution, 1910–1920," in Leslie Bethell, ed., *Mexico since Independence* (New York: Cambridge University Press, 1991), p. 133.

32. Aída Lerman Alperstein, *Comercio exterior e industria de transformación en México, 1910–1920* (México: Plaza y Valdés Editores, 1989), pp. 45–46, 162.

33. Alan Knight, *The Mexican Revolution* (New York: Cambridge University Press, 1986), vol. 2, p. 408.

34. Edwin Walter Kemmerer, *Inflation and Revolution: Mexico's Experience of 1912–1917* (Princeton, N.J.: Princeton University Press, 1940), pp. 46–55; Knight, *The Mexican Revolution*, vol. 2, p. 413.

35. Knight, *The Mexican Revolution*, vol. 2, pp. 413–416.

36. Ibid., p. 416.

37. Ibid., p. 417.

38. Gilbert Joseph, *Revolution from Without: Yucatán, Mexico, and the United States, 1880–1924* (New York: Cambridge University Press, 1983), pp. 145–146.

39. Douglas W. Richmond, *Venustiano Carranza's Nationalist Struggle, 1893–1920* (Lincoln: University of Nebraska Press, 1983), p. 67; Gloria Hernández Fujigaki, "1915–1938, Antecedents: El Comité Regulador del Mercado del Trigo," in Compañia Nacional de Subsistencias Populares, *El Mercado de las subsistencias populares: Cincuenta años de regulación*, vol. 1 (México: CONASUPO, 1988), pp. 51–58.

40. For the case of Puebla, see David G. LaFrance, "Basic Goods Policy and the Revolutionary State: Puebla, 1913–1920," presented at the Ninth Conference of Mexican and North American Historians, Mexico City, October 1994.

41. Unions and producers's organizations were exempted from the definition of a monopoly. The federal government was granted the monopolistic right of currency emission.

42. From Article 28 of the Constitution of 1917, in Manuel Andrade, ed., *Constitución política mexicana: Con reformas y adiciones* (México: Editorial Información Aduanera de México, ca. 1936), p. 25.

43. Luís González y González, *San José de Gracia: Mexican Village in Transition*, trans. by John Upton (Austin: University of Texas Press, 1972), p. 130; Knight, *The Mexican Revolution*, vol. 2, p. 415.

44. See Félix F. Palavicini, *Historia de la Constitución de 1917* (México, 1938), vol. 2, pp. 3–52; E. V. Niemeyer Jr., *Revolution at Querétaro: The Mexican Constitutional Convention of 1916–1917* (Austin: University of Texas Press, 1974), pp. 121–122.

45. Lorenzo Meyer, *El conflicto social y los gobiernos del maximato* (México: El Colegio de México, 1978), p. 35; Enrique Cárdenas, *La industrialización mexicana durante la Gran Depresión* (México: El Colegio de México, 1987), p. 35.

46. Andrade, *Constitución política mexicana*.

47. Secretaría de la Economía Nacional, *Anuario estadístico 1930* (México, 1931).

48. Jeffrey Lawrence Bortz, *Los salarios industriales en la ciudad de Mexico, 1939–75* (México: Fondo de Cultura Económica, 1988), pp. 74–86.

49. Banco Nacional de Crédito Agrícola, *Boletín de Departamento Comercial*, no. 3, June 1931, pp. 24–27.

50. SAF, *Monografías Comerciales*, various vols. (1920s–1930s), vol. 6 is on corn.

51. See Ramón Fernández y Fernández, *Historia de la estadístca agrícola en Méxcio* (México: Talleres Gráficos de la Nación, 1933), pp. 11–16; E. Alanís

Patiño and E. Vargas Torres, "Observaciones sobre algunas estadísticas agrícolas," *Trimestre Económico* (1946), pp. 594–595.

52. Banco Nacional de Crédito Agrícola, "El Trigo," *Boletín de Departamento Comercial*, no. 3, June 1931; Banco Nacional de Crédito Agrícola, "Almacenes de Depósito," *Boletín de Departamento Comercial*, no. 6, September 1931, pp. 8–10; Eyler Simpson, *The Ejido: Mexico's Way Out* (Chapel Hill: University of North Carolina Press, 1937), pp. 399–400.

53. Ramón Fernández y Fernández, "Los almacenes generales de depósito," unpublished manuscript, ca. 1937, ARFF, caja 14.

54. See, for example, Partido Nacional de la Revolución, *Plan sexenal del PNR* (México: Partido Nacional de la Revolución, 1934); Partido Revolucionario Nacional, Secretaria de Acción Agraria, *Los problemas agrícolas de México*, vol. 2 (México, 1934), esp. Ernesto Martínez de Alva, "El crédito agrícola como fundamento de la reorganización de la economía agricola," pp. 563–583; Secretaría de la Economía Nacional, *Informe de la actividades desarrolladas por la Secretaría de la Economia Nacional durante el periodo del 1° de agostso de 1934 al 31 de julio de 1935* (México, 1935), pp. 5, 9.

3

Lázaro Cárdenas and the Politics of State Intervention, 1934–1940

Lázaro Cárdenas took Mexico by storm. During the Cárdenas presidency (1934 to 1940), Mexico witnessed the fulfillment of many revolutionary promises that previous leaders had avoided. In an effort to address social pressures and improve the material well-being of the Mexican people, Cárdenas expanded the role of the Mexican government in the economy by carrying out a large-scale land reform, increasing state spending, creating a number of public agencies aimed at aiding workers and peasants, and incorporating peasants and workers into the folds of the official party. The Cárdenas presidency set the stage for a lasting social peace and served as a transition to a period of relative political stability.[1]

It was during the presidency of Lázaro Cárdenas that the federal government took a far more active role in the food sector than had previous administrations. In his effort to expand land reform and channel resources to the countryside to more thoroughly integrate the peasantry and the countryside in general into the national market, Cárdenas initially sought to use state power to create marketing and distribution networks to aid small producers and *ejidatarios*. However, a series of crises shifted his focus and thus altered the goals of his food policy. It was in this political context that the sometimes conflicting demands by workers and peasants propelled Cárdenas to create Mexico's first State Food Agency. When the price of staples increased sharply, the federal government responded by using the Agency to provide relief to consumers. As a result of this policy, the Agency quickly grew into a major policy tool in Mexico. It was during this period that food policy became intricately linked to broader policy issues, such as labor and economic policy.

Coalition Building and Integrating the
Countryside into the National Economy

Upon taking office, Lázaro Cárdenas forged alliances with broad sectors of society to establish his political independence from Mexico's strongman, Plutarco Elías Calles. After engineering a number of astute political and military reorganizations to move Calles's supporters out of key posts and to replace them with people loyal to him, he began working to create a large power base to offset Calles's influence.[2]

Cárdenas channeled his peasant and worker support into two organizations. He supported the newly established Confederación de Trabajadores Mexicanos (CTM) by sanctioning its right to strike; the official number of strikes increased from 202 in 1934 to 642 in 1937. Organized labor was further encouraged by the fact that the government sided with workers in several high-profile confrontations with the private sector. Former president Calles opposed the strikes and argued that they were contributing to disorder in Mexico. This stance helped to mobilize and unify labor under Cárdenas's banner, which in turn enabled Cárdenas to force Calles into exile.[3] In return, Cárdenas used state powers to address labor concerns.

Cárdenas's support for the organization of the peasantry was perhaps even more deeply rooted than was his backing of urban labor. Prior to his nomination, Cárdenas had made known his support for expanding agrarian reform and organizing campesinos. Very early in his administration, he attempted to coordinate the various local peasant leagues into a national confederation that would create a large power block.[4] Cardenista policies in the countryside sought to transform peasants into Mexicans, but local officials who attempted to carry out these efforts often encountered resistance and were forced to adapt policies to fit local ideology, so that local hegemony was negotiated. Although this complex relationship disturbed traditional social relations, it was a clear attempt to integrate the countryside into the larger nation-state.

Central to Cárdenas's creation of a more inclusive power base was the restructuring of the official party and the implementation of policies that addressed the demands of workers and peasants. In 1936, the official party that Calles had created to institutionalize the revolution was restructured to incorporate various actors of Mexican society in its ranks. Each of the four sectors created— peasants, workers, military, and the popular sectors (composed primarily of state employees)—was to be able to make their concerns known within the party structure by channeling the ideas of workers and peasants to the top.

Cárdenas envisioned an expanded role for the government. He argued that the state should be an active agent for change to benefit large sectors of the population. In his inaugural address to Congress in November 1934, he urged further state intervention, reasoning, "it is fundamental to see the economic problem in its entirety and to observe the connections that link each of its parts with the whole. Only the State has the general interest, and, because of this, only it has the unified vision. State intervention has to be greater, more frequent, and deeper."[5] Hence, state power was seen as an effective tool for winning over and maintaining the political support of the masses.

The largest public policy endeavor carried out by Cárdenas was in the countryside. The most visible symbol of his policies was land reform. In his six years in office, he distributed over 10 percent of the total land surface in Mexico, benefiting over 800,000 Mexicans. Some of the land was from fertile haciendas, although other distributed lands were more marginal.[6] Cárdenas's land distribution program was coupled with efforts to provide other support mechanisms to the rural population, namely the expansion of agricultural credit, the extension of irrigation works, and the introduction of hybrid seeds and fertilizer to a greater number of farmers. To offset the hesitance of private banks to extend credit to lands held by communities, Cárdenas bolstered the public sector's agricultural credit system to aid the new recipients of land. Since its founding in 1926, the BNCA had extended few loans, and those were generally given to large, politically connected producers. In order to support more producers, Cárdenas decided to expand the lending practices of the BNCA to target larger numbers of small producers. Cárdenas created the Banco Nacional de Crédito Ejidal (BNCE) to provide financial backing to new recipients of land. From its inception on January 1, 1936, the BNCE dominated the agricultural banking scene, receiving over 90 percent of government outlays to agricultural banking during the Cárdenas years.[7]

To further reach small producers, Cárdenas shifted the general focus of government irrigation policy. According to Adolfo Orive Alba, an official of the National Irrigation Commission under Cárdenas and later a minister of hydraulic resources, Cárdenas sought to build small-scale waterways to benefit small producers and communities who were generally ignored by the large-scale irrigation operations.[8] In building small projects, Cárdenas's government targeted lands that produced basic grains. Corn and wheat received the most irrigation of all four basic grains. During the period from 1937 to 1940, the amount of land devoted to corn grew from 19 percent of the area cultivated in irrigated zones to over 28 percent, and wheat grew from 9 percent to 15 percent.[9] By 1940 when Cárdenas left office, the lands benefited by new irrigation works reached 58,000 hectares and the lands served by improvements on existing works totaled 49,000 hectares.[10]

The Cárdenas government expanded upon previous administrations' programs of modernizing farming practices. Modernization came in the form of the introduction of insecticides and new seed varieties. During Cárdenas's tenure, the SAF gave farmers a total of 15,000 kilograms of insecticide and 7.5 million kilograms of seeds to plant 15,000 hectares of beans, corn, and wheat.[11] The department established thirteen experimental farms throughout the country and lobbied the government to permit the free importation of new seed varieties from other countries. Corn and beans received only a fraction of this support: only 0.8 percent of the seeds were for beans, corn, and rice, whereas over one-third of new seed varieties imported were for cotton, and 26 percent of the seeds were for wheat. Efforts were also made to increase productivity.[12] Joseph Cotter, in his detailed study of agricultural science policy, has demonstrated the commitment made toward the countryside under Cárdenas, but Cotter also showed how lack of specific focus and numerous problems hindered the scientific program's ability to boost productivity levels.[13]

Land distribution and productivity were not the only issues affecting the countryside. Eyler Simpson, a contemporary observer of rural Mexico, argued that a major problem facing Mexican land reform was the absence of market organization: "The lack of adequate institutional structure and the disorder which have characterized the financing of agricultural operations in general in Mexico have been more exaggerated in the special field of the marketing of agricultural products than in any other dimension."[14] According to Simpson, recipients of land, both smallholders and ejidatarios, had difficulties selling their crops due to their poor bargaining position. Without adequate warehouses to store their grains, they usually sold their crop for cash as soon as possible and near to the site of production in order to avoid paying transportation and storage costs. If these producers could have stored and sold grain at their discretion, they would have gained much more.[15]

Producers echoed this argument at the first convention of wheat growers in late August 1934. At this convention, organized by the secretary of agriculture, producers of all sizes and government officials met to discuss high wheat production; to coordinate information on the types of seed varieties that mills were most likely to purchase; and to discuss sales operations, including pricing, railroad rates, and taxes. The wheat convention helped to solidify the acceptance of government intervention in the agricultural economy.[16] To increase their profits, wheat producers argued that government-controlled storage facilities would allow them the leverage to sell directly to mills instead of to middlemen. The model for this was the Sonoran Wheat Grower's Association, in which members sold over 70 percent of their grain directly to millers.[17] To further protect small farmers, growers called for the government to establish producer prices.

Demands for government intervention came from the wheat producers, not initially from corn and bean producers, due largely to the nature of the production of each crop. Wheat producers were, for the most part, market-oriented farmers with access to capital and other resources and tended to be concentrated in a few regions; therefore a substantial class cohesion existed that facilitated organization. This contrasted with producers of beans and corn, who were a diverse lot, some producing on fertile lands and others on marginal lands. Estimates of production costs during the mid-1930s show that bean and corn producers received a very low return on their crop in relation to the better equipped and more modern wheat farmer. Bean and corn producers earned an average of 60 centavos per day, 40 percent less than the 1 peso minimum wage and well below the returns received by wheat producers.[18] Since bean and corn producers were scattered throughout the country and without large amounts of resources, no strong organization initially emerged.

One of the initial responses to the marketing and storage requests by wheat producers came with the establishment in 1936 of Almacenes Nacionales de Depósito, S.A. (ANDSA), a decentralized agency that provided warehouses and market support to producers.[19] It was initially established in 1931 as AGDCA, an auxiliary of the BNCA. However, after a few years of operation, many bureaucrats involved in both the bank operations and the warehouse actions observed that since it was an agency of the BNCA, it was unable to pursue independent policies and develop the way that its functionaries saw fit. These officials felt that for the warehouses to properly store grain, their operations should be independent of the bank so that they would be able to build Mexico's agricultural infrastructure without the interference of bank politics. Officials involved with storage facilities wanted the institution to expand its operations to classify and regulate grain specifications to ensure good quality, to regulate commerce in basic goods by working with credit institutions, and to consult with the federal government on tariff policies. According to these policymakers, these goals could be achieved only if AGDCA was independent, in part because its employees were loyal to BNCA and had very little interest in the creation of storage houses.[20]

Within the first year of ANDSA's founding, it opened ten offices throughout the country controlling 177 warehouses with a capacity of over 160,000 tons. Having more than doubled the number and capacity controlled by its predecessor, ANDSA also set up the first public laboratory to grade and classify grain.[21] Depositors of grain in ANDSA warehouses could use the certificate of deposit as collateral to obtain loans to finance capital improvements or their next crop. However, producers who stored their crop with ANDSA did not immediately take advantage of these loan opportunities. In the last half of 1936, only twenty-two such loans were granted for a value of nearly 166,000 pesos.[22]

By establishing ANDSA and other institutions in the countryside, President Cárdenas had responded to some of the demands of producers in accordance with his effort at fostering a national market. Although such intervention initially helped him to build a governing coalition, eventually it led to increased tensions among various groups. When a situation arose that directly involved the interests of producers, consumers, and merchants, each group tried to exert pressure on the administration so as to maintain its share of the government largesse. How the government balanced the interests of the various groups often shaped the course of government policy. Such was the case with food policy in Mexico beginning in 1937.

Economic Crisis, Social Protest, and the Emergence of the State as Middleman

The year 1937 was a turning point for the Cárdenas administration. When its liberal spending and progressive social policies were called into question by a number of economic contradictions, the result was a bleak economic situation that caused the Cárdenas administration to slow down its reform efforts and seek ways of keeping itself afloat, as historian Friedrich Schuler has demonstrated.[23] The economic crisis was felt in the food sector and led to government intervention in this arena. Two major factors shaping government intervention in the basic grain markets were a drop in wheat production by some 22 percent in 1937 and the general inflationary trend of late 1937 and 1938. Following an abnormally good harvest in 1936, the drop in wheat production precipitated a rise in the price of wheat flour and bread. Beans and corn did not experience such a large shortfall as did wheat; production of these crops dropped off slightly in 1935 and tended to stagnate until 1938.[24] Lower production of beans and corn did not result in an immediate rise in prices, but it did increase pressure on the distribution process. The initial increase in wheat prices was followed by a higher inflationary trend that was, in part, a by-product of Cárdenas's expansionary policies.

What is of concern here is not so much the causes of inflation but the resulting political fallout.[25] Inflation meant a decline in purchasing power for consumers, who in turn sought to recoup their loss through wage increases, price controls, or pressure on government to eliminate merchants altogether. To avoid granting wage concessions, employers pressured government to intervene to mediate the conflict. It was incumbent upon the government to balance these diverse interests to maintain political stability without disrupting the economy. Avoiding a showdown was especially important given the dwindling resources of government and its need to continue its rhetoric of social justice at the same time that its initial pro-labor and peasant policies were being deemphasized.

The drop in wheat production and the subsequent price increases were felt most intensely in the burgeoning cities. Major urban areas had burgeoned during the 1930s: Mexico City grew by 30 percent, Guadalajara by 27 percent, and Monterrey by 40 percent.[26] As Mexico's population became more concentrated, especially in the largest cities, the potential for urban unrest also increased, pressuring government to preempt unrest. A reduction in basic grain production at a time of increased urbanization combined to increase the demand for food in the cities, which translated into rises in staple food prices during the later half of the 1930s, especially in late 1936 and early 1937. Between 1934 and 1938 the general cost of living rose by more than 53 percent, 58 percent for food (Table 3-1).[27]

Table 3-1. Worker Cost of Living Index in Mexico City, 1934–1940 (1934 = 100)

Year	General Index	Food	Clothing	Domestic and Services
1935	107.5	107.2	102.7	113.9
1936	114.4	113.6	118.2	116.3
1937	138.5	136.7	125.3	130.4
1938	153.3	157.9	145.5	133.0
1939	155.4	156.2	168.5	138.3
1940	157.3	153.6	185.7	152.2

Sources: México, Secretaría de Economía Nacional, Dirección General de Estadística, *Anuario estadístico de la república mexicana*, vols. 1939 and 1941.

After 1936 inflation cut deeply into the wage gains made by workers during the first years of the Cárdenas administration. During these years, the daily nominal minimum wage increased by 32 percent in urban areas and 19 percent in the countryside, while the cost of living rose 57 percent.[28] The decline in real wages hit especially hard in the last two years of the administration. Jeffrey Bortz's survey of real weekly wages in twenty-one manufacturing industries in Mexico City shows an average decline of 9.5 percent between 1939 and 1940.[29] Real minimum wages also fell by at least 3.2 percent. This drop in real wages fueled waves of protests and strikes throughout the country.[30]

At the forefront of the demonstrations against price increases was the newly consolidated union, the CTM. It called for all sectors of society to organize against price increases so that government would be forced to act.[31] However, the CTM and its leadership were careful about whom they blamed for the crisis. Their attacks were not leveled directly at the government but instead at merchants, whom they deemed "ruthless speculators." According to the CTM, these merchants were hoarding grain to force a price increase. Although it was not possible to definitively solve the problem of inflation, the CTM argued, because it was endemic to "the economic activity of the bourgeoisie regime," it called for the government to take an active role in controlling such speculation and claimed that merchants' speculation could be limited through massive importation of basic grains to flood the market, thus lowering the price.[32]

During the early years of his administration, Cárdenas had tolerated strikes and used them to his political advantage, but by April 1937 they were becoming injurious to his government by giving ammunition to his detractors, who demanded "order" to achieve economic development.[33] It was in this context, then, that upon learning of a proposed general strike, called for April 2 by the Federación Regional de Obreros y Campesinos (FROC) to protest the high cost of living,[34] Cárdenas ordered Labor Department chief Genaro Vásquez to persuade the protest leaders to halt their activities: "We have been informed that some organizations have announced new strikes protesting the high cost of living. Please tell these organizations that federal and local governments are taking action to control prices. That organizations should not continue to declare strikes to lower cost of living, as it could bring grave consequences. Government wants to avoid all new conflicts that can give rise to demands for salary increases."[35] To reduce the number of strikes and with much less political will to urge the private sector to boost wages, Cárdenas now committed his government to cushioning the impact of inflation on consumers.

As tensions mounted, the government found itself without the institutional apparatus to address the demands of rural and urban groups. The type of policies that Cárdenas undertook had to consider producers as well as consumers. On the one hand, the CTM was vociferous in its denunciation of price hikes of basic goods, and on the other hand, organized producers (who had long discussed government intervention in the marketing process to shield themselves from middlemen and from the threat of mass importation of basic grains) were also calling for government to protect them from the perils of the marketplace. Although both sectors were united against middlemen and speculation, their interests differed, with consumers calling for massive imports to bring prices down and producers demanding a "fair" price for their labors. Producers also called on the government to intervene to control the speculation of the middleman, but they did not favor massive imports because they might be injurious to their crops. Middlemen, including retail and wholesale merchants as well as millers, were also vocal in denouncing any attempts to undermine their business efforts. The differing interests led to a constant assault by all sides against government attempts to unify the diverse interests under one government agency.

As prices rose, merchants were seen as taking advantage of the situation, leading the Cárdenas government to respond. In 1937 government officials launched a media assault against speculators for "starving the population." These officials argued that the food crisis and the resultant price increases were an artificial creation of ruthless middlemen and retail merchants who tried to profit at the expense of the general population. The campaign of rhetoric set the tone and provided the justification for state action, even though there was little institutional capacity for such intervention during the first years of the Cárdenas presidency.

When price levels of basic foods began to rise in the early months of 1937, local governments, continuing in the tradition of local regulation, began to take action. In late February 1937, the governor of Durango, Enrique Calderón R., issued a decree prohibiting the private storage and concentration of corn and other basic grains, established an inspection commission to ensure that grains were not hoarded, and called for an accounting of all grains in the state.[36] Durango's early actions were lauded by the government newspaper, El Nacional, which called for more states to take such measures. Indeed, by early March other states began to follow suit. One of the primary actions taken by local government authorities, such as in Aguascalientes, Jalisco, and Oaxaca, was to establish commissions to study the high cost of living.[37]

As more and more states investigated the rising cost of prices and as labor unions began to organize campaigns against inflation, the federal government received requests to allow imports. For example, in mid-1937, merchants in the Associación Nacional de Almacenistas, Comerciantes de Víveres y Similares made frequent petitions to the secretary of the treasury to import wheat flour from the United States. Given the lack of wheat and the resultant price increases, such solicitations were approved, but not without vociferous opposition. Organizations of wheat millers and producer groups condemned the imports, arguing that they would hurt both the national milling industry and the national wheat industry. Realizing the potential threat to national industry and agriculture, the government intervened to resolve matters by establishing a federal commission to analyze the inflationary trend in the marketing of wheat.[38] The commission that met June 3, 1937, included representatives of the Departments of Agriculture, Treasury, and Economy, as well as of wheat producers and wheat millers. The commission recommended that a standing committee be established to monitor the wheat supply and that a ceiling be placed on the price of wheat.

President Cárdenas responded on June 22 by establishing the first State Food Agency, the Comité Regulador del Mercado de Trigo (CRMT). According to the presidential decree that created it, the CRMT was to purchase, store, and sell wheat under the aegis of the Secretaría de la Economía Nacional (SEN). Through importation and national purchases, CRMT was charged with maintaining a reserve of grains to be introduced into the market during times of scarcity, thus preempting the moves of speculators.[39] The CRMT comprised representatives of the same government ministries and producer groups that had recommended its establishment, and its president was the representative of the wheat producers of the northwest, Francisco C. Araiza.[40] The strength of the wheat producer organizations enabled them to control the CRMT and ensure that they would not be the victims of government policy.

During its nine months of existence, the CRMT carried out a number of functions. It collected information to facilitate the coordination of wheat consumption and production. By asking millers to report the amount of grain they milled yearly and the amount they stored, the State Food Agency was able to gather some basic information.[41] Although not all millers were forthcoming with such information, these early attempts to assess grain supply were an important step for the State Food Agency to at least gain some knowledge of the grain markets. In conjunction with ANDSA, the agency also collected samples of different wheat varieties to classify the various types in the country and ascertain the amount that each variety sold for in different regions.[42] The Agency urged producers to continue growing wheat and to use modern farming practices. To allay the fears of producers, it vowed to import wheat only when necessary to compensate for production shortfalls. The Agency imported wheat for the first time in September 1937 and by year's end had imported nearly 5,000 tons of wheat to make up for the decline in output.[43]

Throughout 1937 and 1938 the federal government continued its national campaign against the rising cost of living, focusing attention on the middleman as the major cause of the problem. In his third annual report to the nation, on September 1, 1937, Cárdenas decried the rise in price levels of basic goods as being detrimental to the working class and being the action of the intermediaries "who generally speculate with the basic needs of the poor." He vowed that the state would do all it could to stop the speculators.[44]

Although the government publicly blamed merchants for the escalation of basic food prices, privately it recognized that the problem was more complex. During the middle of 1937, the president received several memorandums from prominent economists of the day, analyzing the rise in prices of staple foods. They suggested various causes, including the increase in the money supply and the decline in per capita production.[45] With the prices of staple foods continuing to escalate in 1938, contemporary economic analysts also attributed the rise in prices to the 40 percent devaluation of the peso in March 1938 and to a decline in harvests.

The secretary of the economy appointed a technical commission of leading economists and government officials to discuss possible approaches to the changing inflationary scene. The technical commission, which included BNCA head Gonzalo Robles and the eminent economic historian Daniel Cosío Villegas, concluded that the increase in demand was not being met owing to the decline in agricultural output, poor transportation, and a resultant hoarding of goods by local merchants. To rectify the situation, the commission recommended that the government abandon all direct administrative attempts to control prices because "the legal system was not effective enough to enforce such controls."[46] Instead, the commission recommended that the best way to regulate the market was through directly participating in it, allowing the state to bring prices down by underselling private merchants.

In accord with the technical committee's recommendation, the short-lived CRMT was disbanded and replaced by the second State Food Agency, the Comité Regulador del Mercado de las Subsistencias (CRMS). The new Agency assumed the functions of its predecessor while adding new ones, including the intervention in the markets for corn, beans, and rice. The CRMS's board of directors was made up of representatives of the different government dependencies that dealt with agriculture, banking, and foreign trade.

Unlike its predecessor, the new Agency excluded producers as members of its board of directors. This change marks a shift in its priorities from rural to urban concerns. Whereas the wheat crisis of a year before had precipitated vocal responses from the very powerful and well-organized producers and millers, inflation and scarcity in general led to even louder protests by the urban labor force. As inflation became acute in mid-1938 and government found itself forced to respond to the demands of the city, the State Food Agency became refocused to favor the urban sector over the objections of wheat producers. Although the Agency relied on the official agricultural banks to speak for the diverse producer groups and did not overtly favor one group over another, wheat producers belonging to the Confederación Nacional de Productores Agrícolas, some of whose leaders had been on the board of the CRMT, argued that the Agency's pricing policy discriminated against them by not allowing for adequate remuneration.[47]

Agency financing came from various government agencies. The initial capital outlay establishing it was supplied by the liquidation of its predecessor. Subsidies came from the Comité de Aforos y Subsidios al Comercio Exterior, which was established on August 9, 1938, under the direction of the Department of the Treasury. The role of the Comité de Aforos y Subsidios al Comercio Exterior was to both appraise the merchandise for export so as to tax it at a 12 percent rate and to extend subsidies for the importation of certain goods.[48] With the subsidies from the Treasury, the total regulating fund of the State Food Agency reached over 3 million pesos.[49] The Agency was also able to obtain several loans from its principal source of credit, the Compañía Exportadora e Importadora Mexicana, S.A. (CEIMSA), which was established September 1, 1937, under the aegis of the newly founded Banco Nacional de Comercio Exterior (BANCOMEXT) with capital from other official banks (including the Banco de México, Nacional Financiera, S.A. [NAFINSA], and the BNCA). CEIMSA, which generally functioned as the commercial department of the BANCOMEXT to import goods in short supply,[50] in 1939 extended nearly 10 million pesos in credit to the State Food Agency, 30 percent of which was targeted for importation and the remainder to purchase goods from the internal market.[51] By the time of the CRMS's liquidation in 1941, it was in debt to CEIMSA for more than 12.5 million pesos.[52]

The CRMS, much like its predecessor, used the profit it obtained from its wheat operations to subsidize the operations of beans, corn, rice, and other products. In its 1938 operations the State Food Agency lost over 1.3 million pesos in the sale of beans, corn, and rice, whereas from wheat it made a profit of nearly 500,000 pesos.[53] The Agency explained this loss in the operations of beans and corn by emphasizing the increased cost of importing these crops due to the low international value of the peso, but administrative and financing costs were also involved. For these products, national purchases would have saved more money.[54] In 1939 the Agency earned 3.5 million pesos in wheat operations, compared to the 1.4-million-peso loss in the operations of the other three basic grains.

To respond to the demands of urban pressure for relief from inflation, the Agency began to expand its operations soon after its reorganization in 1938; overall operations in 1939 grew 265 percent over the previous year.[55] Furthermore, Agency expenditures were greater than those shown on the ledgers, primarily because the ledgers did not take into account subsidies for import tariffs, which added 10 million pesos to the amount given in the 1939 ledger.[56]

Coupled with the expansion in the State Food Agency's expenditures, the bureaucracy of the agency also grew substantially, to six departments by 1940. Two of these departments were general administrative departments, two were accounting departments (one to spend, one to audit), and two were commercial departments (one for all goods, one for salt). The largest department, in terms of personnel, was the commercial department for all goods, with 122 employees out of a total of 219.[57] Although the creation of the State Food Agency was a response to the political fallout extending from scarcity and inflation, its expansion met with much resistance from various sectors of the population, including those it was intended to serve. As the Agency began to assume the role of a middleman, it became more visible to the public and thus a target of increasing criticism in both the countryside and the city.

The State Food Agency and the Countryside

It was Cárdenas's view that the State Food Agency should provide marketing support to producers so that they could receive a fair price for their harvest. To this end, in conjunction with other agriculturally oriented agencies, the Agency established a number of programs aimed at incorporating producers into the national market. Cárdenas's goal of better equipping small producers to compete in the marketplace would remain largely unfulfilled. However, large producers would be better able to take advantage of the services offered by the Agency.

In its effort to reach out to peasants during the first years of his administration, the Cárdenas government buttressed a number of agencies to assist producers in the marketplace. Initially, the BNCA provided market support to small producers by establishing a storage division and by helping clients to receive a good price for their crop. Recipients of such market support, however, were restricted to bank clients. The establishment of an independent State Food Agency provided diverse groups, not tied to official banks, with an opportunity to use services offered by the state to enhance their ability to compete in the marketplace.

One of the first actions by the Agency to regulate prices in the countryside was to establish a protective producer price for the four basic crops: beans, corn, rice, and wheat. The rural protective price, established in 1938, was a minimum price at which the state would purchase crops as a last resort, ensuring the producer a guaranteed sale. The Agency purchased crops at this price in the hope that its marginal participation in the market would force the minimum price of crops up to at least the amount it paid, thus breaking the grip of local merchants. It absorbed storage and handling costs, sold them at fixed prices, and disseminated information on this protective price throughout the country, making producers aware of alternatives to selling to local merchants.[58]

Although in theory setting the rural protection price according to production costs seemed sensible, in practice it was more complex. The difficulty of setting the price rested in its dual function of ensuring a remunerative price for the producer without abandoning the purpose of ensuring a reasonable price for the consumer. To balance these two seemingly contradictory goals, various factors were taken into consideration, such as production costs, transportation costs, and quality.[59] Production costs generally fluctuated from year to year depending on a number of factors, including climatic ones, that could not be predicted.[60] Also, neither the SAF nor the State Food Agency had much experience in estimating production costs, rural protection prices did not always reflect the actual costs of the producer, and in many cases the rural protection price was set below the estimated cost of production. An example of such practices can be seen for the year 1939, when in many areas the Agency set the rural price for corn at the same amount as it had for 1938. It compounded the problem by setting prices below those recommended by the secretary of agriculture, leading to a feeling of hopelessness among small rural producers.[61]

The Agency's grain purchases seem to have benefited producers with greater access to Mexico City. In this vein, policies favored areas closer to rail lines and discouraged the production and sale of corn in more isolated areas. On the surface, large producers seemed to be at a disadvantage since the price was generally set lower than it was in areas of small-scale production. However, upon closer examination, it becomes evident that the State Food Agency often opted to purchase the less costly grains, which can be seen by comparing the price set by the Agency with the freight rate for each region. Areas with higher freight rates tended to have lower rural protective prices, thus making these areas more competitive with production center near Mexico City. The best examples of this relationship can be seen in Sinaloa, where the rural protection price was set the lowest, at 80 pesos per ton, and the rail rate was the most costly, at 28.43 pesos per ton; in comparison, in central Mexico the rural protection price was 110 pesos per ton, and fleet costs hovered between 3 and 5 pesos per ton.[62] Smaller producers in remote areas, far from rail lines or government warehouses, were less likely to transport their crop to sell at specified sites than producers whose production centers were near rail. It became easier and cheaper for the Agency to purchase grains in large quantities from large producers near railways (such as in Sinaloa). Naturally, smaller producers in more remote areas complained bitterly that they were receiving unequal treatment.

The way in which the State Food Agency set producer prices was criticized by various organizations. In a number of states there were complaints that neither the local agencies of SEN nor the state governor were informed about the factors used to determine the price of corn.[63] For example, Enrique Pawling, commercial representative of the SEN, reported protests in an *ejido* in Guadalupe Victoria, Durango, against the low prices for corn and beans. He said that the rural protection prices for these crops were set at 90 and 180 pesos per ton, respectively, which was well below the production costs in this area since a combination of drought and freezes had raised the production costs, and argued that the CRMS should adjust the price so as not to further hurt producers. The CRMS officials in Mexico City responded that prices could not be modified.[64] A similar situation occurred in the state of Colima where the governor complained that production and transportation costs of corn came to 105.50 pesos a ton, yet the State Food Agency paid only 90 pesos. Thus the producer would lose over 15 pesos per ton.[65]

Wheat producers also argued that CRMS operations were injurious to national wheat production, mostly because of the large amount of wheat being imported. They urged that these imports not be sold at prices lower than those for national wheat and suggested instead that the government pay greater prices for national wheat in order to stimulate domestic production.[66] A second complaint was that the rural protection price was set too low; producer groups argued that it should be raised. A third complaint, closely related to the first two, was that there was no longer any producer representation on the CRMS. A number of groups wrote to the president requesting that the CRMS include a representative of the Confederación Nacional de Productores Agrícolas, since this group, it was agreed, knew production costs and the capabilities of wheat producers and therefore could contribute to the discussion of these issues.[67]

Aside from the structure of the rural protection prices, the manner in which the State Food Agency acquired grains also tended to favor larger and better organized producers. In each of the two ways in which the Agency acquired grains, by full train cars or at ANDSA warehouses, the seller was responsible for the transportation of the goods to the site of purchase, and all local taxes and costs were to be paid by the seller. To deliver grains to the Agency by train, the seller had the extra task of acquiring a boxcar, which were in constant short supply.[68] Once the seller delivered the grain to the Agency it was tested to determine the exact price to be paid. Samples of the grain were taken and analyzed by laboratories operated by the ANDSA-State Food Agency. It was checked for its quality, and money was deducted from the rural protection price if the quality was not at the level demanded by the Agency.[69] Larger producers with greater capital could afford to transport their crop and not worry about the quality testing, since they had money to invest in the latest productivity-increasing techniques. Freight rates were also structured to give advantage to larger operators since full cars received reduced rates. Given the relative difficulty of selling grains to the Agency, it was more convenient for smaller producers to sell their grain locally, even at a lower price.

The inability of the State Food Agency to reach small producers is reflected in government grain purchases. During its first two years of operation, it purchased a small share of national production. Available evidence indicates that in 1939 and 1940 the Agency's purchases of national wheat equaled about 4 percent of national production and approximately 1 percent of corn production.[70] The larger amounts of wheat purchases reflect the more strategic proximity of wheat lands to both government storage facilities and rail lines. The Agency admitted that it should have been purchasing larger amounts of national production but claimed the lack of resources available to it made it unable to reach wider sectors of the producer population.[71]

The State Food Agency found it much easier to import grains than to purchase them from national producers. Given the relative ease of negotiating purchase with a foreign country and transporting the grain to Mexico, the Agency had to resist the temptation to arrange massive imports to avoid upsetting producers. Although the Agency was purchasing increasing portions of the national food supply, its efforts were mainly concentrated in importing grains. Its bean operation differed significantly from its other efforts; its purchase of nearly 38 percent of the national bean production in 1940 was largely an attempt to avoid substantial price increases owing to a 35 percent drop in production. The importation of agricultural goods to supplement production became noticeable during the last four years of the decade. Imports rose significantly for corn and wheat. The bulk of purchases of the State Food Agency during this period were imports, with wheat comprising the largest amount of imports (Table 3-2). In relation to total imports, these four basic grains were nearly insignificant. During the period before 1938, the total value of imports of the four grains was no more than 0.2 percent of total imports. By 1938, this amount had climbed to 3.5 percent, due to a substantial increase in the importation of corn and wheat.[72] Although Mexico had been importing small amounts of food to supplement production for many decades, total imports had grown significantly by the late 1930s.

Table 3-2. State Food Agency Purchases of Grains as a Percentage of National Production (P) and National Supply (S), 1937–1940

| | Beans | | Corn | | Wheat | |
Year	(P)	(S)	(P)	(S)	(P)	(S)
1937	ND	ND	ND	ND	ND	1.4
1938	ND	0	0	0.9	0	21.6
1939	5.7	10.0	1.0	4.2	4.0	15.5
1940	37.8	38.2	0	0.5	3.7	3.9

Sources: Data calculated from CONASUPO, *El mercado de las subsistencias populares*, 2 vols. (México, 1988); and Aída Mostkoff and Enrique C. Ochoa, "Complexities of Measuring the Food Situation in Mexico: Supply versus Self-Sufficiency of Basic Grains, 1925–86," in James W. Wilkie, ed., *Society and Economy in Mexico* (Los Angeles: UCLA Latin American Center Press, 1990).
Note: ND = no data.

In times of emergency and shortages the temptation to import grains was heightened by Mexico's poor transportation and storage infrastructure, which made moving goods from one region to another a slow and costly affair. Despite Cárdenas's attempt to forge alliances with regional leaders, it was difficult to penetrate the various regions of Mexico economically, many of which remained isolated. One of the major factors contributing to the lack of a fully unified country can be attributed to the state of disrepair that the transportation sector was in. At the time of the 1937 expropriation of the railroads, not only were the tracks old and poorly maintained but the national railway company, Ferrocarriles Nacionales (FFNN) was deeply in debt.[73] The structure of rates, which benefited the export sector, did not help to unify remote areas of the country.

To enhance the expansion of the internal market and the flow of basic grains from the countryside to the city, the government sought to reform the long-standing rate structure that favored the export sector and large producers. Between 1931 and 1935, it was 25 percent cheaper to transport mineral products 500 kilometers than it was to move corn the same distance.[74] Rates also favored larger producers or distributors because it was between 40 percent and 90 percent more expensive to ship by partial car than by full car.[75] Although such a rate policy may have been economically sound in encouraging advantages of scale, it indirectly undermined the purchases made by the government because when the State Food Agency purchased grains from producers, the producer was required to pay for transporting the grain to the storage facility. Thus, it was more economically sound for small producers to sell their product to merchants, who in turn could take advantage of the reduced cost of full-car transportation.

That the freight rate structure was not favorable to small producers of basic grains had been long acknowledged by Cárdenas and his advisers. However, attempts to alter rates met with intractable resistance. As Cárdenas sought to increase rates in 1937 and 1938 for the mining sector and decrease rates for basic grains, he met sharp resistance from both mine operators and miners, who argued that the downturn in the world price of minerals coupled with increase in rates would destroy the industry. Given the political clout of the miners, Cárdenas could not ignore their logic and withdrew his proposals to alter the rates.[76]

Although the rate structure did not change, during periods of crisis more space was allotted for basic grains, thereby increasing the amount of good transported on these lines. Again, however, wheat received more favorable treatment than did corn and beans. The overall space allotted for these four basic grains fell slightly from 9 percent of the total railroad cars allotted to the state in 1935 to 8 percent in 1940.[77] The transportation of grains fluctuated markedly from year to year as the State Food Agency brought grains into the cities in order to provide relief during shortages and price increases, as is evident in 1938 and 1939 (Table 3-3). Less grain was transported by railroad in 1940, partially due to increased demand placed on the railroads with the onset of World War II, the shortage of materials to repair the railroad equipment, the lack of storage facilities in the cities, and the slight increase in production of basic grains.[78]

Table 3-3. Percent Change of Staples Transported by Railroad, 1936–1940
(percent change)

Year	Total Goods	Subtotal Four Basic Staples	Beans	Corn	Wheat	Rice
1936	5.3	-6.1	-12.8	-16.6	20.9	-12.5
1937	1.3	-2.4	18.9	-2.5	-11.5	9.8
1938	1.4	5.8	-24.3	14.3	13.1	-22.3
1939	4.8	14.5	20.0	8.3	26.4	-1.1
1940	-2.2	-12.0	26.3	-13.9	-25.6	26.5

Source: Calculated from Secretaría de la Economía Nacional, *Anuario estadístico de la república*, various years.

If the transportation sector hindered the economic integration of small producers into the national market, the lack of public granaries did not do much to rectify the situation. Despite the fact that President Cárdenas had created ANDSA as a national storage facility in 1936, many analysts and producers argued that it lacked sufficient capacity and infrastructure. Officials of the BNCA complained that they had difficulties coordinating with ANDSA due to its lack of capacity. In its annual report, BNCA officials argued that if ANDSA expanded its capacity, the bank would be able to purchase more of its clients' crops, thus further shielding small producers from speculators.[79] Because ANDSA's limited operations made it seem ineffective in maintaining a constant reserve of grains and in helping small producers, it was unable to fully contribute to government efforts to stave off shortages and subsequent price increases.

The State Food Agency and the City

If the Agency proved unable to satisfy rural producers, it was more responsive to urban consumers. Beginning in late 1937 it responded to fears of social unrest due to inflationary pressure by taking a more active role in the marketing of food in urban areas. Its first action was to purchase grain and sell it at reduced prices in the city. When prices continued to increase, the State Food Agency stepped up its intervention and established its own chain of retail outlets, making it a major player in the daily grain trade in urban areas. Between September 1938 and August 1939 the State Food Agency controlled 43 percent of the corn trade, 53 percent of the bean trade, and 56 percent of the rice trade. The largest recipient of grains was Mexico City, where approximately one-half of the

Agency's total sales of rice and beans took place. Corn sales, due largely to its importance in the diet of most Mexicans, were much more evenly distributed throughout the country, with only 17 percent of corn sales in Mexico City.[80]

Since the State Food Agency's participation in the marketplace was aimed at keeping prices stable, it intervened both in wholesale markets by selling randomly at first and then more selectively in retail markets. During the early stages of its operations, it sold grain by the railroad car to those who could purchase it. The grains were sold at a fixed price to wholesale buyers, who traveled to the location of the railroad cars or to ANDSA warehouses, purchased the grain, and then transported it to market. Those who could afford to make such capital investments were the larger merchants, those whom the Agency was supposed to be combating.[81] As food prices continued their upward trend, middlemen became the target of public discontent, and the government was forced to circumvent the larger wholesalers. In many cases, the Agency received complaints that wholesalers bought low from the Agency and sold inordinately above the price that it had established.

To deal with speculation, the federal government began to set retail prices based upon recommendations by consultative committees in each state and in the Federal District. These committees were headed by the governors and comprised representatives of state government, the local chambers of commerce, worker and consumer groups, and producer organizations. Each committee provided the SEN with information on the market, which in turn set consumer prices according to the characteristics of different markets.[82] In 1938, the State Food Agency recommended that the federal government also fix the retail price of rice, meat, and beans. The Agency argued that if it was to make basic foodstuffs accessible to those pinched by inflation, it was necessary to set a maximum price for other basic foods.[83]

In 1938, to limit the influence of wholesalers and to stimulate small business, the Agency entered retail marketing. It began to sell grains to authorized retail merchants in the larger cities. These transactions occurred at a fixed price, and in return the merchant was obliged to sell the products supplied by the Agency at the official price. Authorized merchants were located in the major public markets of the major cities: Mexico City, Guadalajara, Oaxaca, Torreón, Puebla, and Monterrey.[84] As the largest market for staple goods, Mexico City had twenty-two of the Agency's authorized merchants, nine in La Merced market alone.[85] The Agency intervened to ensure that staple foods could be sold by authorized merchants at lower prices than in private markets. For example, the average price of corn was 17 centavos per kilogram in private markets in October of 1938, but it sold for 15 centavos at Agency prices. Additionally, Agency rice sold for 16 percent less than rice from private vendors (38 centavos per kilogram versus 32 centavos).[86]

The State Food Agency prices did not always prevail because some authorized merchants charged higher prices than allowed. Consequently, a corps of inspectors was created to enforce sales at the official price and weight. All merchants were ordered to post prices of the staple foods they sold in a visible place, thus making inspection easy. Likewise, merchants were required to meet minimum weight standards for their bread and tortillas.[87] Various studies by the president's advisory commission during this period discussed the folly of the authorized merchant policies because these merchants continued to ignore state directives. According to the presidential advisers, more inspectors would not rectify merchant abuses since inspectors could be corrupted by dishonest merchants. Rather than put money into a corps of inspectors, the presidential team advised that the Agency establish and control directly its own chain of stores.[88]

Initially, neither the president nor the Agency chose to heed the warnings of the presidential advisers and continued the authorized merchant policy. A year later the president's advisers submitted another report explaining that their earlier predictions about the fate of the Agency operations had come true. They argued that although the Agency had sold large amounts of grains at low prices, only a relatively few number of merchants benefited, and many of these often engaged in speculative activities that the corps of inspectors was unable to prevent.[89] Once again, the commission urged the creation of a large chain of stores controlled directly by the Agency as well as union stores and consumer cooperatives all over Mexico City.

Under the combined pressure of the CTM, which was consistently demanding benefits for inflation-harassed workers, and the presidential advisory commission, the State Food Agency finally opened its first store in late August 1939; by the end of the year it had a total of twenty-five stores in the Federal District.[90] The primary products sold in these stores were basic grains, sugar, lard, milk, and there were plans to expand the product list. They had trouble competing with the local neighborhood stores, owing to the fact that Agency stores operated only eight hours a day, whereas neighborhood stores, which were generally attached to the owner's house, operated up to fifteen hours a day. Moreover, local stores had many family members working in the store, not all of whom were paid, giving these stores a competitive edge over Agency stores with paid government employees. Consequently, the Agency stores, in nearly all cases, operated at a disadvantage and incurred financial losses.[91] Even though Agency stores had lower prices than other stores, their reduced operations hindered sales.

In its effort to provide affordable staples to the working classes, the State Food Agency also helped to create union stores and consumer cooperatives. Located in a working-class area and operated by union members, the first of such stores, "Tienda Sindical 1," was founded in Mexico City in April 1939.[92] The Agency sold the union products at its subsidized prices, thus enabling the union store to resell goods to its members at low cost. Tienda Sindical 1 had an average of 1,200 customers daily and sold goods below the prices of other nongovernment stores.[93] Stores fashioned on the union store model were established for other organizations and for consumers organized in cooperatives. These stores were seen as a way both to help workers overcome the rising cost of living and to supplement their incomes.[94]

During these years there was also a general movement to organize consumers in cooperatives so as to eliminate the middleman and lower the cost of living. Although the need for consumers to organize had long been discussed by Cárdenas and his aides, concrete measures did not come until 1937. During that year, the Labor Department established an office in charge of creating and regulating consumer cooperatives.[95] Yet, aside from the office in the Labor Department, little else was accomplished in the realm of consumer cooperatives until the inflationary crisis grew worse.

As inflation cut into wages in 1938, the government strengthened its efforts to establish consumer cooperatives. In that year the official party, Partido Revolucionario Mexicana (PRM), established a campaign to reduce the cost of subsistence foods, the task of which was to inform consumers and to stimulate the establishment of consumer cooperatives. The campaign called for eliminating intermediaries and demanded that the State Food Agency play a stronger role in setting prices as well as in the marketing process. Despite the PRM's campaign, consumer cooperatives did not catch on widely. A year after Cárdenas's term had ended, only fifty-two consumer cooperatives had been authorized in the Federal District, thirty-nine of which were operating.[96] Attempts at establishing

consumer cooperatives were only marginally successful at organizing a strong and cohesive block of consumers.[97]

Critics of the Cárdenas Food and Pricing Policy

Because the State Food Agency's actions were most noticeable in
the cities, especially in Mexico City, its harshest critics were found
there. This criticism came at a time when general feelings of inse-
curity and instability stemming from the profound Cárdenista reforms were sweeping broad sectors of Mexican society.[98] By the State
Food Agency's own admission, it was the most controversial public agency during the latter years of the Cárdenas administration.[99]
On the surface such controversy did not seem to have much effect,
but it is very likely that it prevented the state from granting additional authority to the Agency, holding in check more militant factions of organized labor who wanted to see the state take over retail
marketing altogether.

The most boisterous attacks on the State Food Agency came
from the Confederación de Cámaras Nacionales de Comercio
(CONCANACO). Comprising merchants and with branches in all
major cities, CONCANACO was able to wage an effective campaign
against the Agency by barraging the president and the secretary of
the economy with letters and telegrams, placing advertisements
and articles in the major news dailies, and publishing its own material on the Agency.[100]

During the first years of the State Food Agency, CONCANACO
dedicated numerous pages of its official organ, *Carta Semanal*, to
discrediting it. Most issues carried at least one article attacking the
Agency, and the majority of issues had more than one. The main
argument was that the state should not intervene in the economy.
According to CONCANACO, by trying to regulate prices the
Agency was only adding to the problem of inflation by creating
artificial shortages contributing to the rise of a black market. To
absolve merchants from the charges that they were hoarders and
the greatest beneficiaries of inflation and shortages, the Confederación pointed to the increase in state intervention in the agricultural
sector in the areas of credit and marketing and argued that these
measures provoked a disequilibrium in the market of basic foods
that manifested itself as inflation.[101] CONCANACO's efforts continued throughout the existence of the State Food Agency but declined noticeably during 1940. With Cárdenas's shift to a more
overtly moderate policy and with signs of price stability on the

horizon, CONCANACO accepted a belated offer by Secretary of the Economy Efraín Buenrostro to participate in the fight against inflation.[102] Although still opposed to the Agency, the Confederación began to play down its opposition and, instead, declared itself a victim of the high cost of living that was willing to cooperate with the government to put effective measures into action.

The vigorous campaign waged by CONCANACO helped keep government intervention in check because it was forced to respond to repeated attacks. Cabinet officials, such as Buenrostro, met with the Confederación's leadership to negotiate a compromise. The vociferous activities of CONCANACO and the constant pressure it placed on the State Food Agency forced government officials to pay attention to its criticisms and to harness its support.

Conclusion

The government of Lázaro Cárdenas took decisive measures in establishing institutions to deal with Mexico's food problems during the late 1930s. Along with the creation of these new institutions came an increase in government attempts to study the markets of basic grains. Government created commissions to calculate production costs of basic grains, began to track consumer prices throughout the country, carried out studies to determine the nutritional intake of the Mexican populace, and organized producer groups.

Mexican food policy attempted to respond to the demands of both producers and consumers. By establishing a rural protective price, coordinating various government agencies to purchase crops at this price, and limiting the importation of grains, the Mexican government took important steps toward protecting basic grains producers. The State Food Agency absorbed the cost of storage and handling and was able to resell grains at a subsidized price. However, several obstacles hindered all producers from benefiting: rural protection prices were not always remunerative, and poor infrastructure and inadequate storage capacity made storing and transporting grain cheaper for larger producers. As crisis beset the government, there was even less incentive to respond to the demands of smaller producers.

Government attention to urban consumers quickly became the mainstay of food policy during the Cárdenas administration. President Cárdenas's alliance with the CTM made him increasingly aware of the situation that faced the consumer. The government also began to learn more about the plight of consumers as more experience was gained in the use of consumer price indexes. The sale of grains to wholesalers and retailers increased over the State Food Agency's first three years of activity. The prices of individual items, especially tortillas, a corn-based product, and bread increased at a slower rate than the consumer price index in general. Even though real wages declined during the last three years of the Cárdenas administration, consumers benefited from stability in some prices. Consumer cooperatives, Agency stores, and union stores were not as numerous as consumer groups had wanted, but the process was institutionalized so that in latter years government could expand their numbers. To the extent that consumers benefited from this government intervention, residents of Mexico City were the most fortunate. The Agency carried out a disproportionate number of operations in Mexico City. Only corn was sold widely throughout the republic. Because the government knew the market of Mexico City better than any other, it was there that programs were first developed.

Government intervention in the marketing of basic foods under Cárdenas was, in part, created to win support from both organized labor and consumer groups, as well as from various producer groups. Despite good intentions, however, the State Food Agency was incapable from the outset of responding to all of the vested interests involved in the economy. Even as the PRM commission called for the Agency to take over all retail food operations, CONCANACO vigorously opposed such intervention in the marketplace. In the face of Agency attempts to compromise, each group complained that the government could do a more effective job of intervening in the market on its behalf.

The process of the rise and expansion of the State Food Agency under Cárdenas would characterize its modus operandi for years to come. It was established and grew in response to crisis. Inflationary pressures caused the government to attempt to correct political and economic crises with stopgap measures. The result was that state action was ad hoc and unsystematic. As we will see in Chapter 4, such unplanned expansion would increase proportionate to the depth of each crisis.

Notes

1. The literature on Cárdenas's presidency has been growing substantially, and consequently interpretations of the meaning of the Cárdenas sexenio have been changing. For overviews of the period see Alicia Hernán-

dez Chávez, *La mecánica cardenista* (México: El Colegio de México, 1979); Nora Hamilton, *The Limits of State Autonomy: Post-Revolutionary Mexico* (Princeton, N.J.: Princeton University Press, 1982); Adolfo Gilly, *El cardenismo, una utopía mexicana* (México: Cal y arena, 1994). For discussion of the various debates surrounding the meaning of Cárdenas's administration and of cardenismo, see Juan de Dios González Ibarra, *Interpretaciones del cardenismo* (México: Universidad Autónoma Metropolitana, 1988); and Alan Knight, "Cardenismo: Juggernaut or Jalopy," *Journal of Latin American Studies* 26 (1994), pp. 73–107.

2. For an excellent discussion of Cárdenas's transferring of military commanders and his shuffling of governors, see Hernández Chávez, *La mecánica cardenista*.

3. Nora Hamilton, *The Limits of State Autonomy*, p. 125.

4. This process is ably described by Lyle C. Brown, "Cárdenas: Creating a Campesino Power Base for Presidential Policy," in George Wolfskill and Douglas Richmond, eds., *Essays on the Mexican Revolution: Revisionist Views of the Leaders* (Austin: University of Texas Press, 1979), pp. 101–136.

5. "Discurso del General Cárdenas al protestar como presidente de la república ante el congreso de la unión, el 30 de noviembre de 1934," in Luis González y González, ed., *Los presidentes de México ante la nación: Informes, manifiestos, y documentos de 1821 a 1966*, vol. 4 (México: Cámara de Disputados, 1966), pp. 11–15.

6. James W. Wilkie, *The Mexican Revolution: Federal Expenditure and Social Change since 1910* (Berkeley: University of California Press, 2d ed., 1970), p. 76.

7. Wilkie, *The Mexican Revolution*, p. 141.

8. Adolfo Orive Alba, *La política de irrigación en México* (México: Fondo de Cultura Económica, 1960), chap. 9.

9. Calculated from Banco Nacional de Crédito Agrícola, *Informe anual*, 1937–1940.

10. Nacional Financiera, S.A., *50 años de revolución mexicana en cífras* (México, 1963), p. 49.

11. Secretaría de Agricultura y Fomento, *Memoria de los trabajos ejecutados por las direcciones de agricultura y ganadería e Instituto Biotecnico del año de 1935 a mayo de 1940 y dentro del periodo presidencial del C. Gral. de División Lázaro Cárdenas* (México, 1940), pp. 14–15.

12. Calculated here from ibid, pp. 24–28. The exact figure is 37 percent.

13. See Joseph Eugene Cotter, "Before the Green Revolution: Agricultural Science Policy in Mexico, 1920–1950," Ph.D. diss., University of California at Santa Barbara, 1994, chap. 3.

14. Eyler N. Simpson, *The Ejido: Mexico's Way Out* (Chapel Hill: University of North Carolina Press, 1937), p. 376.

15. Ibid., p. 381.

16. Gloria Hernández Fujigaki, "1915–1938 Antecedentes: El Comité Regulador del Mercado del Trigo," in Compañía Nacional de Subsistencias Populares, *El mercado de las subsistencias populares: Cincuenta años de regulación*, 2 vols. (México: CONASUPO, 1988), vol. 1, p. 91.

17. Secretaría de Agricultura y Fomento, *Memoria de la primera convención triguera nacional* (Mexico, 1934), pp. 111–115.

18. Moisés T. de la Peña cited these calculations in an important work entitled "El maíz, su influencia nacional," *El Trimestre Económico* 3:10 (April–June 1936), p. 196.

19. For discussion of government policy toward raising productivity through the use of improved techniques, see Cotter, "Before the Green Revolution."

20. Memorandum urging the founding of ANDSA from Ing. Ernesto Martínez de Alva and Ing. Gaspar Garza Lara to Lic. Ricardo J. Zevada, 9 Agosto 1935, AGN-GR, caja 16 bis. exp. 5.

21. Oscar Paredes Arévalo, *Los almacenes generales de depósito en México* (México: Alamacenes Nacionales de Depósito, S.A, 1955), pp. 22–23; Eyler N. Simpson, *The Ejido: Mexico's Way Out*, p. 400.

22. BNCA memorandum, October 16, 1937, ARFF, caja 198.

23. Friedrich E. Schuler, *Mexico between Hitler and Roosevelt: Mexican Foreign Relations in the Age of Lázaro Cárdenas, 1934–1940* (Albuquerque: University of New Mexico Press, 1998). For further discussion of this shift and how it connected to post-1940 developments, see Stephen Niblo's important study, *War, Diplomacy, and Development: The United States and Mexico, 1938–1954* (Wilmington, Del.: SR Books, 1995.

24. Calculated from Aída Mostkoff and Enrique C. Ochoa, "Complexities of Measuring the Food Situation in Mexico: Supply versus Self-Sufficiency of Basic Grains, 1925–86," in James W. Wilkie, ed., *Society and Economy in Mexico* (Los Angeles: UCLA Latin American Center Press, 1990).

25. For a discussion of inflation during this period, see Enrique Cárdenas, *La hacienda pública y la política económica, 1929–1958* (México: El Colegio de México, 1994), chap. 3.

26. James W. Wilkie, "Mexico City as a Magnet for Mexico's Economically Active Population, 1935–65," in James W. Wilkie, ed., *Statistics and National Policy* (Los Angeles: UCLA Latin American Center, 1974); Martín Valadez, "Guadalajara: Population Growth and Distribution of the Working Population by Economic Sectors, 1900–1980," paper presented at "Ciclos y Tendencias: Una Reinterpretación Cuantitativa," Puerto Escondido, June 1990.

27. Cited in Pedro Merla, *El costo de la vida obrera en México* (México: Secretaría de Trabajo y Previsión Social, 1942), p. 7. For discussion of the construction of this index and its limitations see Jeffrey Bortz, *Los salarios industriales en la ciudad de México, 1939–1975* (México: Fondo de Cultura Económica, 1988), esp. chap. 2.

28. *Revista de Estadística* 3:2 (December 1940), p. 149. Ramón Fernández y Fernández, "Fijación de salarios mínimos," *México Agrario* (October–December 1941), cited in Merla, *El costo de la vida obrera en México*, p. 11; see also Merla, *Estadística de salarios* (México: Secretaría de Trabajo y Previsión Social, 1942).

29. Calculated from Bortz, *Los salarios industriales*, appendix 3. For minimum wages, see Kevin Middlebrook, *The Paradox of Revolution: Labor, the State, and Authoritarianism in Mexico* (Baltimore, Md.: Johns Hopkins University Press, 1995), pp. 214–215.

30. Arturo Anguiano, *El estado y la política obrera del cardenismo* (México: ERA, 1975), p. 84; CTM (1937), "La alza de los precios," in *CTM 1936–1941* (México, 1942), pp. 251–252. Kevin Middlebrook finds a correlation between inflation and strike petitions for the early 1940s. See *The Paradox of Revolution*, p. 166.

31. CTM (1937), "La carestía de la vida y el proletariado," in *CTM 1936–1941*, pp. 237–238.

32. To President Cárdenas from Lombardo Toledano, general secretary of CTM, April 5, 1937, AGN-LC 706/73; "La CTM Frente el Alza de los Precios," *Futuro* (April 1937), pp. 20–25; CTM, *CTM 1936–1941*, pp. 235–255.

33. For discussion of the conservative opposition to Cárdenas, see John W. Sherman, "Reassessing Cárdenismo: The Mexican Right and the Failure of a Revolutionary Regime, 1934–1940," *The Americas* 54:3 (January 1998), pp. 357–378.

34. "Estudios y declaraciones sobre el alto costo de la vida," *El Economista*, no. 18, November 16, 1939, pp. 6–13.

35. Telegram from President Cárdenas to Genaro Vásquez, April 13, 1937, AGN-LC 706/73.

36. Telegram from Lic. Baltazar Dromundo, secretario particular to the governor of Durango, to President Cárdenas on February 25, 1937, AGN-LC 521.8/19; also see *El Nacional*, March 1, 1937.

37. *El Nacional*, March 16, 1937; Banco Nacional de México, *Examen de la situación económica de México, 1925–1976* (México, 1978), pp. 170–171.

38. Ramón Fernández y Fernández, "El comercio del trigo en México," unpublished draft of a report for the Comisión de Estudios Especiales of the Banco Nacional de Crédito Agrícola, BBM, 1937, pp. 310–311.

39. México, *Diario Oficial* June 29, 1937; Fernández y Fernández, "El comercio del trigo en México," p. 314.

40. *Excelsior*, June 30, 1937.

41. Letter to millers, from CRMT president Francisco C. Araiza, June 22, 1937, ARFF caja 199; Fernández y Fernández, "El comercio del trigo en México," p. 317.

42. Letter from González Calderón, secretary of CRMT, to wheat growers, July 2, 1937, ARFF, caja 199.

43. Hernández Fujigaki, "1915–1938 Antecedentes," pp. 93–96.

44. "Informe de General de División Lázaro Cárdenas, Presidente de la República Mexicana, ante el H. Congreso de la Unión, correspondiente al ejercicio comprendido entre el 1 de Septiembre de 1936 y el 31 de Agosto de 1937," *Palabras y documentos públicos de Lázaro Cárdenas*, vol. 2: *Informes de gobierno y mensajes presidenciales de año nuevo, 1928–40* (México: Siglo Veintiuno Editores, 1978), p. 111. According to the Weyls, in their laudatory biography of Cárdenas, this was not the first time that Cárdenas had encountered "ruthless speculators." During the revolution, when he returned to his hometown of Jiquilpan, circa 1915, he learned that speculators had forced the price of corn out of the reach of the poor. He then lectured the speculators, acquired large sacks of corn, and turned them over to the people. See Nathaniel Weyl and Silvia Weyl, *The Reconquest of Mexico: The Years of Lázaro Cárdenas* (London: Oxford University Press, 1939), pp. 45–46.

45. "Memoradum que presenta el profesor Federico Bach al Señor Licenciado Ignacio García Tellez sobre las problemas causas del alza de precios," August 14, 1937; and Profesor Ezequiel R. Pérez, "El alza de las subsistencias, su solución y el stock monetario nacional," September 1937, both in AGN-LC 706/73.

46. Ricardo J. Zevada, "Política de precios," *Investigación Económica* 5:4 (1945), p. 477.

47. Letter to President Avila Camacho from Fernando González and Alfonso Herrera Salcedo, president and secretary of the Confederción

Nacional de Productores Agrícolas, December 19, 1940, AGN-MAC 545.21/9.

48. *Diario Oficial*, August 10, 1938. See also El Comité de Aforos y Subsidios al Comercio Exterior, "El subsidio a la importación del trigo," mimeo, 1944, p. 54, BBM.

49. Comité Regulador del Mercado de Subsistencias, *Informes anuales*, mimeo, 1940, pp. 45, 85.

50. No history of the operations and evolution of CEIMSA exists. For this period the best description of CEIMSA functions, although uncritical, is Gonzalo Mora Ortiz, *El Banco Nacional de Comercio Exterior* (Mexico: Editorial Ruta, 1950); Blanca Torres, "1938–1949 El Comité Regulador del Mercado de Subsistencias y la Nacional Reguladora y Distribuidora, S.A.," in Compañía Nacional de Subsistencias Populares, *El Mercado de la Subsistencias Populares*, vol. 1.

51. Banco Nacional de Comercio Exterior, *Informe anual 1939*, p. 50.

52. Banco Nacional de Comercio Exterior, *Informe anual 1940*, pp. 33–34.

53. Comité Regulador del Mercado de Subsistencias, "Resumen de perdidas y ganancias al 31 de Diciembre de 1938," in *Informes anuales*.

54. Comité Regulador del Mercado de Subsistencias, *Informes anuales*, p. 30.

55. Secretaría de la Economía Nacional, *Memoria* (September 1939–August 1940), pp. 314, 319.

56. For a discussion of the way the State Food Agency expenditures were calculated, see Ulises Irigoyen, "Nueva orientación al Comité Regulador de los Precios de Subsistencias," August 10, 1939, AGN-LC 706/73; Moises T. de la Peña, "El Comité Regulador," *Revista de Economía* 2:4 (February 1942).

57. Calculated from Comité Regulador del Mercador de Subsistencias, "Proyecto de presupuesto mensual para el periodo compredido de 1° de enero al 31 de diciembre de 1941," AGN-MAC 568.3/205.

58. Ramón Fernández y Fernández, *El comercio del trigo en México*, 2 vols. (México: BNCA, 1939), chap. 15; Weyl and Weyl, *The Reconquest of Mexico*, p. 188; Comité Regulador del Mercado de Subsistencias, *Informes anuales* , pp. 22–26; Torres, "1938–1949 El Comité Regulador del Mercado de Subsistencias y la Nacional Reguladora y Distribuidora, S.A."

59. Comité Regulador del Mercado de Subsistencias, *Informes anuales*, pp. 24–25.

60. Fernández y Fernández, *El comercio del trigo en México*, vol. 1, chap. 3; vol. 2, chap. 15.

61. "'Maíz,' estmaciones de SAF respecto a cosechas, costos medios de producción por héctare y tonelada, 1939," ARFF, caja 127.

62. Ibid.

63. AGN-LC 521.6/12, 506.12/12.

64. Letter to CRMS from Enrique Pawling, December 2, 1938, and the reply on December 8, 1938. AGN-LC 521.8/19.

65. Telegram to President Cárdenas from Miguel G. Santa Ana, governor of Colima, February 5, 1939, AGN-LC 521.6/12.

66. AGN-LC 506.12/12; Fernández y Fernández, *El comercio del trigo en México*, p. 255.

67. These letters are located in AGN-LC 506.12/12.

68. Comité Regulador del Mercado de Subsistencias, *Informes anuales*, pp. 50–63.

69. *Boletín de Mercados de la Secretaría de Agricultura y Fomento*, June 24, 1939, cited in Fernández y Fernández, *El comercio del trigo en México* (México: BNCA, 1939), esp. chap. 15.

70. Compañía Nacional de Subsistencias Populares, *El mercado de las subsistencias populares*, vol. 1.

71. Comité Regulador del Mercado de Subsistencias, *Informes anuales*, p. 29–30.

72. Calculated from Secretaría de la Economía Nacional, *Anuario estadístico de comercio exterior*, 1934–1940.

73. Sergio Hernán Ortiz, *Los ferrocarriles de México: Una visión social y económica*, 2 vols. (México: Ferrocarriles Nacionaled de México, 1988), vol. 2, p. 208.

74. Moisés T. de la Peña, "Crítica de las tarifas ferrocarrileras," *Trimestre Económico*, no. 4 (1937), p. 16.

75. Federico Bach, "La nacionalización de los ferrocarriles," *Revista de Hacienda* 4:19 (September 1939), pp. 139–140.

76. Ruth Adler, "La administración obrera en los FFNN," *Revista Mexicana de Sociología* 50:3 (July–September 1988), pp. 106–108. For a discussion of the militancy and the priviledged status of the mine workers' union, see Marvin D. Bernstein, *The Mexican Mining Industry, 1890–1950: A Study of the Interaction of Politics, Economics, and Technology* (Albany: SUNY Press, 1965), chap. 19.

77. Calculated from Secretaría de la Economía Nacional, *Anuario estadístico*, 1935–1940.

78. Carlos Villafuerte, *Ferrocarriles* (México: Fondo de Cultura Económica, 1959), p. 46.

79. BNCA, *Informe al Consejo*, 1939, p. 25.

80. Calculated from Secretaría de la Economía Nacional, *Memoria* (September 1938–August 1939), p. 69.

81. Jesús Díaz Barriga, Comisión de Estudios de la Presidencia, "Aspectos del financiamiento del Comité Regulador del Mercado de Subsistencias y sugestiones para corregirlos," memo 45, October 20, 1938, AGN-LC 521/35.

82. *Diario Oficial*, October 7, 1938.

83. Comité Regulador del Mercado de Subsistencias, *Informes anuales*, pp. 28–29.

84. Comité Regulador del Mercado de Subsistencias, *Informes anuales*, pp. 69–71.

85. Departamento del Distrito Federal, *Gaceta Oficial* 3:52 (June 1938), pp. 6–7.

86. *El Nacional*, October 1, 1938.

87. Departamento del Distrito Federal, *Gaceta Oficial* , June 15, 1936, July 15, 1937.

88. Jesús Díaz Barriga, Comisión de Estudios de la Presidencia, "Aspectos del financiamiento del Comité Regulador del Mercado de Subsistencias y sugestiones para corregirlos," memo 45, October 20, 1938, AGN–LC 521/35.

89. Jesús Díaz Barriga, president of the Comisión de Estudios de la Presidencia, to President Cárdenas, memo 92, August 1, 1939, AGN-LC 706/73.

90. Comité Regulador del Mercado de Subsistencias, *Informe anual 1939*.

91. Letter from Sindicato de Trabajadores del Mercado de Subsistencias to President-Elect Avila Camacho, December 6, 1940, AGN-MAC 521.8/1.

92. Gloria Hernández Fujigaki, *La CTM en la lucha por la alimentación* (México: Sistema de Distribuidores CONASUPO, 1987), p. 68.

93. CTM, *CTM 1936–1941*, p. 1049.

94. Secretaría de Economía Nacional, "Proyecto para la organización de sociedades cooperativas militares de consumo," August 15, 1935, AGN-LC 545.3/229.

95. Departmento del Trabajo, *Memoria del Departamento del Trabajo, septiembre de 1937–agosto de 1938* (México: DAAP, 1938), pp. 329–332.

96. Secretaría de Trabajo y Previsión Social, Oficina de Cooperativos de Consumo, "Informe condensadamente sobre las labores desarrollada por esta oficina," October 20, 1941, AGN-STPS, caja 1156, exp. 13/106-13-/1.

97. Ricardo J. Zevada, "México," in Erik T. H. Kjellström et al., *El control de precios*, trans. by Javier Márquez (México: Fondo de Cultura Económica, 1943), p. 212.

98. For a discussion of the general aspects of the latter portion of Cárdenas's presidency, see Albert L. Michaels, "The Crisis of Cardenismo," *Journal of Latin American Studies* 2:1 (May 1970), pp. 51–79.

99. Comité Regulador del Mercado de Subsistencias, *Informes anuales, 1938–39*, p. 97.

100. Robert Jones Shafer, *Mexican Business Organizations: History and Analysis* (Syracuse, N.Y.: Syracuse University Press, 1973).

101. *Excelsior*, August 2, 1939.

102. "Un deber primordial nuestro: Abaratar la vida," *Carta Semanal* 4:170 (May 18, 1940).

4

World War II, Economic Modernization, Food Crisis, and Urban Relief, 1940–1946

The outbreak of World War II accelerated the trend toward greater urbanization and industrialization, which exacerbated many of the weaknesses in the country's food distribution system. On the surface, increased exports to the United States resulted in a booming economy, but Mexico found it increasingly difficult to import goods.[1] During the war years, the country became more vulnerable to shortages, panic purchasing, and price increases than anytime since the revolution. Basic foodstuffs were especially vulnerable. Lands that produced grains were shifted to cultivate highly sought-after oil seeds and export crops, resulting in a decline in the amount of land planted in corn and beans.[2] Poor weather in 1943 further reduced the corn harvest and, coupled with transportation bottlenecks, led to widespread food shortages and spiraling prices. This crisis of the production and distribution systems increased the potential for social unrest, and such conditions forced the government to respond to consumer demands. In the process, the State Food Agency became the largest and most visible relief agency in the country; however, this crisis-driven policymaking moved the Agency farther away from its initial aim of benefiting small producers and more toward ameliorating social conflict and establishing social peace.

The Mexican Economy during World War II

Manuel Avila Camacho's presidency (1940–1946) was marked by a call for political unity and a movement away from the nationalism and redistributive programs of the early Cárdenas administration. Although Avila Camacho's national reconciliation program was driven in part by the opposition of some sectors of the population to Cárdenas's policies, it also reflected changing world contexts. This new foreign and domestic climate led Avila Camacho to continue Lázaro Cárdenas's shift to focus more on economic growth and away from redistributive policies.

Closer cooperation between the United States and Mexico resulted in the signing of a major economic treaty in 1942 and with the United States granting Mexico most favored nation (MFN) status. In accord with the agreement, each country lowered tariff barriers, and Mexico agreed to supply the U.S. market with primary goods needed during the war, such as rubber, cotton, and vegetables, as well as labor. Thus, the war helped to spur the Mexican economy by providing a secure market for Mexican goods.

As the government extended incentives to stimulate the manufacturing sector, the number of urban jobs expanded, and there was an increased movement of population to urban centers. One estimate placed the number of people leaving the countryside between 1940 and 1944 at 400,000.[3] Increased demand in urban areas placed pressure on government to ensure a steady supply of inexpensive goods. The resulting unplanned growth of the cities, especially Mexico City, also sparked the need for infrastructural developments to accommodate the burgeoning urban population.

In the countryside, land redistribution and peasant-oriented policies began to give way to efforts aimed at increasing productivity through large-scale agriculture. Land distribution, which had begun to wane during the latter part of the Cárdenas administration, declined to approximately one-third of its level during the period 1934–1940.[4] President Avila Camacho granted certificates of inaffectability, exempting land from the land reform process, for over 400,000 hectares of agricultural land, 661 percent more than under Cárdenas.[5] Government commitment to collective agriculture began to decline during this period. *Ejido* farming accounted for 44.1 percent of total cropland in 1950, down from 47.4 percent in 1940.[6] Also noticeable during the 1940s was the decline in agricultural credit granted. The real amount of credit allocated by the federal government during the Avila Camacho administration fell from 3.2 pesos per capita in 1940 to 1.4 pesos per capita in 1946.[7] In addition, although the agricultural banks still gave priority to basic grains, the trend of funding cotton, begun under Cárdenas, was expanded under Avila Camacho.[8] Private sources increasingly became the primary financiers of agriculture during this period and made up for the decline in federal agricultural credit, but they tended to target larger and more market-oriented producers.

The 1940s also witnessed the expansion of export crops. Although these shifts did not lead to immediate declines in the per capita production of basic grains during the first two years of the decade, as the decade wore on the situation deteriorated. The amount of cultivated land used to plant basic grains dropped from nearly 80 percent in 1940 to 72 percent in 1943.[9] This decline in emphasis on basic grain production was coupled with other shifts in Mexican agriculture, including government investment in the expansion of irrigation works and in the implementation of other modern farming techniques. Many of the irrigation works were targeted for commercial and export crops. The federal government allotted greater amounts of money for the expansion of irrigation works, as much as 15.7 percent of the total federal expenditure.[10]

Along with irrigated lands came a greater emphasis on improving yield. To improve seeds and develop hybrids suitable to Mexico's soils and varied climatic regions, in 1943 the Rockefeller Foundation sent a team of experts to work with the secretary of agriculture. Over the next several years studies were carried out to determine which were the highest-yielding seed varieties for Mexico, beginning with corn and wheat. Although these programs started during the Avila Camacho administration, results in greater yield were not made for at least ten years.[11]

Problems created by the war hindered effective distribution of grains. With economic activity spurred by the war, the distribution of food throughout the country fell victim to Mexico's decrepit transport system, which could not absorb the demands placed on it. On a steady decline for a number of years, in 1940 the transportation system was so deficient that experts argued that it did not have the capacity to adequately service the needs of Mexico City.[12] With war pressure placed on railroads to ship goods to the U.S. market, the railroads transported decreasing quantities of basic grains as they shifted to beer and cement for export.[13] As agricultural production began to shift to the production of exports, Mexico became more reliant on imports, yet transportation bottlenecks slowed the distribution process. These factors often contributed to shortages and price increases, prompting the government to take action.

The Organization of the State Food Agency and the Response to Inflation

Because of a brief hiatus in inflation during the first two years of the Avila Camacho administration, the Agency was less active than it had been under Cárdenas. By the end of 1942, however, war-generated inflation hit urban areas hard, causing food shortages and cutting deeply into consumer cost of living. The urban population responded in various ways to the increase in the cost of living, including organized strikes and demonstrations and spontaneous food riots. Popular protests shaped the growth and emphasis of the Agency.

Price Stability and Marginal Intervention, 1940–1942

President-elect Manuel Avila Camacho was pressured by various sectors of society to alter the role of the government in the marketing of basic goods. The State Food Agency's own workers complained that the stores were not open long enough and could not compete with family-operated stores that stayed open fifteen hours a day.[14] A variety of groups, including merchants, criticized the Agency for being too interventionist, arguing that its actions led to more bottlenecks. Many workers, including CTM officials, felt that the Agency should be more even more active in controlling the basic food markets.

To respond to these diverse critiques of the State Food Agency, President Avila Camacho appointed Secretary of the National Economy Francisco Javier Gaxiola Jr. to study the reorganization of the Agency at the end of January 1941. The Gaxiola commission concluded that it was essential to continue to have a government agency charged with the regulation of the market of staple goods. The problems, they claimed, lay within the old State Food Agency. The commission advocated the creation of a new agency that would correct past mistakes and include producers and consumers on the board of directors.[15]

Avila Camacho liquidated the CRMS in May 1941 and established the new agency as the Nacional Distribuidora y Reguladora, S.A. (NADYRSA). The objectives of the new agency, despite the Gaxiola commission's recommendation, were very similar to those of its predecessor: to intervene marginally in the marketing of basic grains by purchasing grains at home and abroad and then selling them, after absorbing storage and transport costs, in order to regulate and monitor prices. NADYRSA also aimed to create better storage and transportation facilities to maintain a reserve of basic grains. It was seen as essential that the new agency have more capital to work with than did the CRMS, but to begin with it operated with the same amount as did its predecessor. Following the recommendations of the Gaxiola commission, the peasant (Confederación Nacional de Campesinos [CNC]) and worker (CTM) sectors were included on the board of directors of the new agency.[16] Gaxiola also recommended that representatives of the Mexican Chamber of Commerce be placed on the board of directors, but because the government's antimerchant rhetoric was still strong, merchant groups were excluded from NADYRSA's board.

Despite the structural reorganization of the State Food Agency, many observers of the day argued that NADYRSA was basically the same institution as its predecessor. Immediately after the establishment of the new Agency, its predecessor's longtime foe, CONCANACO, launched a public attack on the institution. In a letter to Avila Camacho, the president of the commercial organization, Leopoldo H. Palazuelos, criticized the establishment of NADYRSA and said that there was not a real difference between the two agencies.[17] Palazuelos further charged that the new Agency did more to increase prices of basic grains than to halt the price escalation. Another contemporary stated that all that changed was the address.[18]

During its first two years, the new State Food Agency grew in size and activity compared to its predecessor. It was divided into fifteen different departments, all directly accountable to the general manager, with no intermediary steps. This organizational structure was suitable for an agency of such small size. As the Agency became more prominent, intense pressure would be placed on the general manager, who had to process information from fifteen different departments.[19] To manage the new Agency, Avila Camacho appointed Ignacio Lapuente, an old friend from his hometown of Teziutlan, Puebla. According to Secretary of the Economy Gaxiola, however, Lapuente was incompetent, and Avila Camacho, at the urging of his brother Máximo, quickly replaced him with Amado Trejo, who was said to have had more experience in such matters.[20]

The State Food Agency concentrated its resources in its wheat and corn operations between 1941 and 1943. The value of the sale of these two crops jumped markedly during this period, from 2.5 million pesos to 13.9 million pesos for corn and from 17.5 million pesos to 75.3 million pesos for wheat. Operations for rice and beans, which together accounted for approximately 20 percent of total sales in 1941, dropped to roughly 13 percent in 1943 (Table 4-1).

Table 4-1. Value of State Food Agency Sales, 1941–1943 (current pesos)

	1941	1942	1943
Total	25,849,061	47,344,402	111,856,719
Corn	2,540,215	7,622,464	13,907,512
Wheat (National)	0	10,918	0
Wheat (Imported)	17,519,007	27,584,081	75,342,700
Beans	4,550,696	1,015,115	1,200,224
Rice	404,180	5,046,420	13,070,844

Source: El Comité de Afóros y Subsidios al Comercio Exterior, "El subsidio a la importación del trigo" (México: Oficina de Subsidios y Estudios Especiales, 1944), mimeo.

Because the state-run retail stores had lost money under Cárdenas, they were closed during the first year of the Avila Camacho administration, and the administration was reluctant to reopen them.[21] The retreat from the retail market was possible because of the relatively moderate inflation levels during the first year and a half of the Avila Camacho administration.[22] Although the thirty stores that the State Food Agency had operated under Cárdenas had sold goods cheaply, they had never reached all areas of the city and served merely as a palliative.

By the middle of 1942, however, the Mexican economy began to feel some of the side effects of the changes wrought by shifts in the Mexican economy during the war. One of these by-products was the renewal of a general inflationary trend that began to cut into the workers' wages and sparked growing concern among the general population. The secretary of labor held several meetings to study the rising cost of living. Of the five recommendations that emerged from those meetings, three dealt with expanding the role of the State Food Agency. Most important, the secretary of labor called for the Agency to be granted more funds to buy directly from producers and to sell directly to consumers, thus circumventing the middleman.[23] This suggestion was a definite break with how the Agency had operated in the past. Instead of limiting itself to the thirty stores operated under Cárdenas, the secretary of labor called for the state to be an active large-scale merchant.

The Rapid Growth of the State Food Agency, 1943–1946

The secretary of labor's recommendation to expand the merchandising functions of the State Food Agency was not carried forward until early 1943, when the rate of inflation nearly doubled in four months.[24] Surging prices were caused in part by the anticipation of a poor corn harvest and led to near-panic conditions in the larger cities. According to Jeffrey Bortz's calculations, worker cost of living in Mexico City climbed from an index level of 134 in 1942 to 171 in 1943 to 238 in 1944 and 349 in 1946. The rising cost of living cut deeply into the pockets of urban workers; the average real industrial wage in Mexico City declined from 25.73 pesos a week in 1940 to 20.20 pesos in 1942, and to 14.15 pesos in 1946.[25] Data on real minimum wages also indicated a decline by slightly less than one-third during this same period. This sharp decline in real wages for a growing portion of the population caused alarm among CTM leaders, who had won important concessions for their adherents during the Cárdenas years, only to see them stripped away by inflation.

Under pressure from the rank and file, CTM leaders constantly called for greater government intervention. Organized labor stepped up the number of strikes throughout the country, putting pressure on the government to take more active steps to alleviate the plight of workers from inflation as well as to demand higher wages from private employers. The CTM launched a vigorous campaign to increase the salaries of its members by 50 percent. Worker militance grew during this period and took the form of a substantial increase in strike petitions and strikes. According to official government statistics, strike petitions increased from twenty-one in 1942 to 654 in 1943 and to 759 in 1944.[26] Kevin Middlebrook has demonstrated that there was a statistically significant correlation (albeit weak) between strike petition activity and inflation, indicating that it was an important issue in the minds of workers.[27]

A poor corn harvest for 1943 exacerbated the decline in real wages. The precise amount of the decline is not clear. Official figures show that the crop was three-fourths the amount of the 1942 harvest, but according to the director of the State Food Agency, it is more likely that the corn harvest was only 58 percent of the 1942 harvest.[28] This sharp decline led corn prices to increase by over three times the average rural price. Official studies claimed that corn was purchased by speculators at the time of harvest at low prices, and in turn, they slowly released the grain on the market to drive up prices. Although the Agency sought to counteract such speculative tactics, it did not have the storage capacity to purchase large amounts of grain, and it was also unable to import large amounts of corn due to wartime hostilities.[29] Thus the decline in the corn harvest and the rising prices of staple goods forced the state to further intervene in the basic grain market.

Given the gravity of the food situation, the federal government and decentralized agencies began to concentrate resources in the State Food Agency. In March 1943 the federal government increased its investment in the Agency by 900,000 pesos.[30] Aside from capital holdings, the amount of federal government subsidies for Agency operations also increased sharply, from 536,380 constant pesos in 1942 to nearly 3,226,175 pesos in 1943, a fivefold increase in one year (Table 4-2). Subsidies were also granted for the importation of grains. Although the total amount of the subsidies is unknown, by using data for selective years and crops, we can see that these subsidies amounted to substantial sums. For example, subsidies for the importation of wheat grew significantly: between 1943 and 1945, federal government subsidies increased ninefold to 28 million pesos.[31] Decentralized agencies also played a large role in financing the State Food Agency. Of all the loans extended by Mexico's foreign trade bank, BANCOMEXT, growing shares went for the regulation of prices of goods in short supply; in 1943 this amount was 33.5 percent of bank loans; in 1944, 64 percent; and in 1945, more than 55 percent. Most of this money was funneled through the Agency for the purchase of basic grains at home and abroad to subsidize their sale for the urban market.[32]

As the internal effects of Mexico's wartime participation became more acute, the federal government moved to gain greater control over the economy. On March 2, 1943, President Avila Camacho created a Consortium aimed at increasing the efficiency of food distribution and reducing prices to consumers. It was composed of the State Food Agency; the agricultural banks; CEIMSA; the Secretariats of Agriculture, Economy, Transportation, and Treasury; and later (beginning April 7) the Comité de Aforos y Subsidios al Comercio Exterior. These agencies were to modify their operations to meet the same goal as the State Food Agency: coordinate production and consumption of basic grains by purchasing from producers at fair prices, maintain a reserve, and sell the grains in the city at fixed prices.[33] It was hoped that this integrated approach would help keep agencies from working at cross-purposes.

Table 4-2. Federal Government Subsidies to the State Food Agency, 1942–1945 (pesos)

Year	A^a Total Subsidy	B^b Wholesale Price Index (1940 = 100)	C (A/B) Real Subsidy
1942	630,009	117	536,380
1943	4,533,826	140	3,226,175
1944	40,548,117	180	22,504,538
1945	55,321,807	198	27,908,613

[a]Secretaría de Gobernación, *Seis años de actividad nacional* (México: Secretaría de Gobernación, 1946).
[b]Index from James W. Wilkie, "From Economic Growth to Economic Stagnation in Mexico: Statistical Series for Understanding Pre- and Post-1982 Change," in James W. Wilkie, David E. Lorey, and Enrique Ochoa, eds., *Statistical Abstract of Latin America*, vol. 26 (Los Angeles: UCLA Latin American Center Publications, 1988), p. 924.

The importance of the Consortium was indicated by the fact that Secretary of the Treasury Eduardo Suárez was named the chairman of the board, signaling the centrality of basic grain imports. Because the treasury granted subsidies for goods to be imported, Suárez tried to use his influence in the United States to lobby for grain imports, but owing to the difficulty in acquiring transportation from the United States to Mexico, he was not completely successful. This failure made the Consortium and the State Food Agency targets of more public criticism. The Consortium never operated as anticipated because of numerous political power struggles between the various agencies.

In part due to its expanded operations, the State Food Agency became the target of criticism for the rising cost of living. Traditional supporters of this institution, especially the CTM, launched campaigns against it. At the CTM's twenty-first congress in April 1943, the labor confederation called for the state to take over the sale of all staple items.[34] CTM officials demanded the liquidation of the Agency and the creation of a more powerful organization headed by the president himself, so that the government would be better able to maintain price stability, and food distribution would not be subject to the whims of the numerous bureaucratic agencies involved in its operation.[35] Such calls for increased intervention grew louder as wages were further eroded by price increases and the Agency seemed unable to flood the markets with imported grains.

By the middle of 1943, the effects of the poor corn harvest were reverberating throughout a number of cities. Maize mills were unable to open due to a lack of corn. One large mill cooperative had closed the doors of 150 of its 400 mills. As housewives had difficulty finding corn, *masa*, and tortillas to purchase, spontaneous protests occurred. A number of women's groups organized to protest the lack of maize and to urge direct and decisive action on the part of the federal government. In May, there were riots in Mexico City because of the lack of corn.[36] Such actions were not isolated and occurred more frequently as basic foods became more scarce and more expensive. According to one contemporary observer, "The pinch was felt as early as May, 1943, when bread riots were of daily occurrence in the industrial city of Monterrey. . . . By June of that year greenstuff had all but disappeared from the markets of Mexico City. By September, 1943, in Nuevo Laredo on the banks of the Rio Grande, there was no maize in the public market. . . . In Guanajuato people stood in line all night in the hopes of getting a handful of maize for the day's tortillas. In Tulancingo, Hidalgo, and in Celaya, Guanajuato, panic and bread riots became routine."[37]

To alleviate the shortages, Secretary of the Treasury Eduardo Suárez, after making a number of failed attempts to import corn from the United States, contracted with the governor of Nayarit, Gilberto Flores Muñoz, to have large quantities of corn transported to Mexico City. In July 1943, after weeks of scrambling to get railcars to transport the grain, corn from Nayarit began to arrive in Mexico City.[38] This use of Nayarit to supply Mexico City with corn became common throughout the 1940s.

Despite the government's efforts to abate the grain shortages, the public's anger and frustration was not assuaged, since local government officials were popularly known to be among the largest speculators. The State Food Agency was seen as unable to halt such abuses.[39] Although charges had been made against local officials, none caused a greater uproar than the public accusations launched against Secretary of National Economy Francisco Gaxiola Jr. Charges were made that the secretary himself was profiting from price controls through black market operations. The accusations gained national attention in July and August when three articles in the weekly magazine *Hoy* accused Gaxiola of colluding with unscrupulous merchants. Gaxiola was nearly forced to resign over such accusations but was able to strike a deal with the president so that the State Food Agency's general manager, Amado Trejo, would be the scapegoat. According to Gaxiola, the president allowed him to dismiss Trejo personally.[40] Trejo's ouster was attributed to his inability to import grains and to a failed plan to import Argentine corn.[41]

Although Gaxiola was initially publicly absolved of the charges, the affair brought out in the open what many had suspected and what the British chargé d'affaires called " 'an open secret' that the very agency established to control shortages was led by men who were 'cornering and selling to the black market at profits which vary in direct proportion to the artificially produced scarcity.'"[42] With the appointment of Nazario Ortíz Garza, a former governor and senator from Coahuila,[43] to replace Trejo, the various ministries developed a closer working relationship, enabling the State Food Agency to take more decisive action in importing and distributing foodstuffs.[44] Gaxiola would continue to be plagued by allegations of speculation and corruption until he was forced to resign in June 1944.[45]

Beginning in late 1943, then, Ortíz Garza led the expansion of the State Food Agency, which would emerge as one of the largest and most visible public agencies in Mexico. Federal subsidies targeted for the Agency grew by phenomenal rates: from 1943 to 1944, real subsidies to the Agency went from 3.2 million pesos to 22.5 million, and during the following year the amount grew to 29.9 million pesos (Table 4-2). During the same year, the Agency became the predominant client of BANCOMEXT receiving well over 50 percent of all bank loans.

The sharp increase in the operations of the State Food Agency was most notably reflected in its grain acquisitions. Total operations, including purchases of goods and their sale, amounted to 296,655 tons of basic foodstuffs in 1942 and over 1 million tons in 1944.[46] In 1941 the State Food Agency sold slightly over 1 percent of the total corn supply, which increased to 3.1 percent in 1943 and 15.5 percent in 1944. The expansion of the operations for wheat was even more dramatic. In 1939, 11 percent of wheat supply was sold by the Agency; by 1944 this amount reached nearly 70 percent. Data for 1943 indicate that wheat sales accounted for approximately 67 percent of the total grain sales, whereas corn sales comprised a mere 12 percent.[47] The wheat sold by the agency was entirely imported.

The heightened visibility of the State Food Agency made it ripe for further charges of corruption. As the state became an important player in the basic grain market, blame for the shortages and price increases was shifted away from the merchants and onto public

officials. After Gaxiola's ordeal, corruption continued to be publicly viewed as rampant in the Agency operations. The process of
distribution of the grains was ripe for graft. One prominent former
congressman, César Cervantes, who oversaw the distribution of
corn to mills in the Federal District, was fired by Ortíz Garza after
allegations that Cervantes skimmed off money from each sale of
corn. The rapidity with which Ortíz Garza dismissed Cervantes led
some to complain that Ortíz Garza was trying to avoid an in-depth
investigation of corruption in the Agency.[48]

The Urban Bias of the State Food Agency

The gravity of the crisis of general inflation, coupled with grain
scarcity and declining real wages, demanded that the State Food
Agency channel its efforts and resources into alleviating the situation in urban areas. This required that attention be given to coordinating supply and distribution of basic foods, so that a steady
supply of grains would flow from production regions to consumers in a timely manner that did not lead to further price increases.

One of the major challenges facing policymakers was coordinating the internal movement of grain. Foremost among such problems was the lack of available railcars to transport grains from
various parts of the country to the city and the lack of government-
controlled warehouses to store grains in various regions of the country. As early as June 1941, Secretary of Agriculture Marte R. Gómez
recommended to the president that he order the railroad companies to allot cars directly to the State Food Agency and to the agricultural banks.[49] By 1943, when the food situation worsened, there
was an increased demand to transport grains to the cities, yet on a
number of occasions grains sat in the port of Veracruz or near production centers waiting to be transported.

Throughout the Avila Camacho administration, railcars remained difficult to obtain. Even when Avila Camacho declared the
movement of grains by rail a national priority, the FFNN, not only
autonomous but notoriously inefficient, did not allot the number
of cars it needed. The State Food Agency did not have better luck
in obtaining railcars in the United States. The U.S. government refused to allot cars for transportation of wheat because the railway
had not returned empty U.S. cars from a previous shipment.[50] Merchants were notorious for failing to unload their wares from railcars in a timely manner, and there was no penalty for failing to do

so until mid-1945.[51] Hence demurrage of railcars made coordinating grain supply and consumption even more difficult.

Thus, as wheat and bread prices were soaring in 1943 and the Mexican milling industry was nearly idle due to a lack of wheat, the State Food Agency's wheat purchases sat in the United States, unable to supply the entire milling operation in Mexico City and other areas. Not until the U.S. government, perturbed that 2 million bushels of wheat that Mexico had purchased several months earlier were still in the grain elevators of the Commodity Credit Corporation in Laredo, Texas, demanded that this grain be moved did the railway agree to give those grains priority.[52]

To speed up the distribution of basic grains, the federal government authorized the State Food Agency to participate directly in retail marketing. The reestablishment and expansion of a chain of "popular stores" became the most recognizable sign of federal government activity in the marketing of basic goods for the average Mexican citizen. By 1944, there were 898 popular stores located throughout the republic. The biggest concentration was found in the Federal District, where there were 179; the remaining 719 were scattered throughout the various states. During the first nine months of 1944, 19 million pesos' worth of goods were sold in the Federal District, and 10 million pesos' worth in the stores in the various states. Many of the stores sold more than fifty types of products, up from the four with which they began. By the end of 1946, the Agency had established 2,500 stores.[53] To reach consumers in areas where there were no popular markets, the Agency purchased a fleet of forty trucks, each with a 5-ton capacity. These mobile truck stores traveled to humble areas of the Federal District and sold basics such as beans, corn, rice, sugar, powdered milk, and coffee.[54]

The official prices of goods sold in the State Food Agency's stores increased at a slower rate than did prices in private stores throughout the inflationary period of 1944 to 1946. For example, corn in Agency stores sold for 37 centavos a kilogram in 1946, and the average price in private stores was 46 centavos a kilogram (Table 4-3). The data, unfortunately, do not show the extent to which goods were actually sold at the official prices. Given the discrepancies in pricing and the prevalence of black market operations, this point is significant. Nevertheless, Agency prices had propagandistic value, since they were posted in front of stores and published in newspapers. These published prices showed readers and consumers that the government was interested in the welfare of the consumer and also served as a warning to merchants.

Table 4-3. Average Prices of Selected Items in State Food Agency Stores, Compared with the Average Retail Price in Mexico City, 1944–1946 (pesos/kilogram)

Year	Corn SFA	Corn Private	Beans SFA	Beans Private	Flour SFA	Flour Private
1944	0.31	0.43	0.37	0.43	0.43	0.52
1945	0.36	0.39	0.37	0.43	0.51	0.53
1946	0.37	0.46	0.53	0.95	0.63	0.90

Sources: Adapted from *Revista de Economía* (1944–1946); Secretaría de la Economía Nacional, *Compendio estadístico, 1948* (México: Secretaría de la Economía Nacional, 1948), pp. 225–229.

The State Food Agency also began to open other retail outlets that sold specific products, the two most prominent being milk and meat. Beginning its foray into the milk market in May 1944, it opened outlets that sold 15,000 liters of milk a day at 15–20 centavos less than the market price.[55] By 1946, it had stepped up its purchase and sale of milk in the cities, selling up to 20,000 liters a day.[56] Although this amount is relatively small in comparison to the total amount of pasteurized milk consumed in Mexico daily, it served for the poorer sectors of the population as a constant source of unadulterated milk. The Agency also began to establish meat outlets. According to Ortíz Garza, its intervention in the market for fresh meat would have been deemed more effective if it could have obtained one or two packing plants in the cattle region.[57]

Beyond its local store operation, the State Food Agency began to create consumer cooperatives as an important mechanism to alleviate the rising cost of living. Although Cárdenas had proposed the establishment of consumer cooperatives throughout the country, few had been organized, and even fewer continued to operate. In a survey of consumer cooperatives in 1941, commissioned by the secretary of labor and welfare, José González Padilla found that only thirty-nine of the fifty-two authorized units were in operation.[58] To invigorate the cooperative movement, the secretary of labor coordinated with unions and companies to expand the number of cooperatives throughout the republic and to enhance their operation for their members. By 1943, the number of consumer cooperatives had increased to 110, with nearly 45,000 members. Further, an Academy for Cooperation was established to teach members how to operate them, and the noted economist Federico Bach was charged with its direction. Although food shortages during 1943 and 1944 threatened to shut down a number of consumer cooperatives, the secretary of labor sought to ensure the food supply to the cooperatives. After several meetings between Ortíz Garza and the secretary of labor, the State Food Agency agreed to supply all consumer cooperatives with basic foodstuffs throughout the country. This agreement ensured that cooperative stores could continue to operate and would not be closed due to lack of merchandise.[59] By July 1944, the number of cooperative societies had increased to 163, with over 120,000 members.

It was also during these years that the public sector began to establish its own stores for government employees. In most cases these stores were established via an agreement made between the union and the public agency. One of the first of these "company stores" was established for workers of Mexico's FFNN, and was called "Tienda Ferronal." Under a presidential decree of August 30, 1944, it received its initial capital from the railroad company, which also appointed its management.[60] These stores were exempted from all federal sales and import taxes, and they were granted a 50 percent reduction in transportation and storage costs. In January 1945, the first store was opened, and several others opened within the next couple of years. Each family was issued a ration card for goods that they were authorized to purchase.[61] The prices of the basic goods sold in the stores were not only less than retail prices but also less than prices at the State Food Agency's popular stores.

To keep prices in check, the federal government also sought to impose price controls. It set up local committees in June 1943, dubbed Consejos Mixtos de Economía Regional to monitor the local economic situation. The councils comprised the local representatives of cabinet officials, including the secretaries of economy and agriculture, and were headed by the governor of each state. They were charged with assessing the food situation of each region, setting prices for basic foodstuffs, and enforcing them.[62] Although all states formed mixed regional economic councils, it is unclear how active they were. A few kept President Avila Camacho informed, detailing the amount prices were set for and how many local inspectors were hired. Others detailed the problems faced by local government in supplying the state with adequate amounts of food. One of the most active local committees charged with price control was found in the Federal District. Created in October 1944, the Comisión de Control de Precios worked closely with the State Food Agency to sell grains to small merchants and help small businesses deal with large wholesalers.

To enforce the price controls, a corps of inspectors was enlisted to work with various agencies, such as SEN and local governments, to verify that merchants posted official prices and sold at those prices. At the height of price increases, a large numbers of merchants were fined or jailed for selling above the fixed price. During a three-day period in May 1942, some seventy-five merchants were fined for charging above the official prices for basic foodstuffs in Mexico City.[63] In March 1945 it was widely publicized that thirty-two merchants were jailed for selling above fixed prices.[64]

Despite efforts to control prices, not all merchants complied with government directives. They showed creativity in their attempts to circumvent the maximum prices set by government officials. In the case of meat, for example, it was often reported that merchants would explain to customers that "the official price is such and such, but if you give me less than so much, there is no meat."[65] Similarly, enforcement of controls was not always uniform. Stories abounded of inspectors and police officers taking bribes to ignore price violations.[66] A government memorandum to President Avila Camacho pointed out that consumers who complained usually received no satisfaction because the officer receiving the complaint refused to intervene on jurisdictional grounds.[67] This inability to enforce price controls plagued government officials endlessly. Several proposals were made to forge cooperation between the police department and SEN on the matter. Other plans included giving police officers more incentives to fine merchants by giving them a percentage of the fine paid. Yet, none of these proposals was enacted, and price controls and the lack of adherence to them continued to raise the ire of consumers and merchants alike.

Like the general question of corruption in Mexico, the complaints and allegations that public officials were profiting from food shortages through their own speculation are difficult to document, even in the most high-profile cases, such as the Gaxiola case.[68] Although this topic demands further investigation, it may be that officials acted as middlemen and sold grains to the State Food Agency or contracted sales from friends and relatives in a manner that was not necessarily illegal, but that reflected a conflict of interest.[69]

The wheat-milling industry was one of the primary beneficiaries of both the policies of the State Food Agency and of the maize shortages during this period. Heavy government subsidies provided the incentive for the massive importation of wheat, with the aid of U.S. officials, to meet the demands of urban consumers. The

United States, fearing that Mexico's food problems could lead to an explosive situation, procured large amounts of wheat for sale to Mexico, which helped raise wheat consumption by nearly 50 percent, to its highest level in recent years.[70] The wheat imported by the Agency amounted to nearly half that consumed during the height of the war years, 1943–1946. The treasury secretariat extended subsidies for nearly 200,000 tons of wheat at some 20 percent of its cost. Most wheat went to millers by prearranged contracts. Because the subsidy policy favored Mexico City (85 pesos per ton versus 25 pesos per ton for the rest of the states), the effect was to encourage the milling of wheat in Mexico City (Table 4-4).

Table 4-4. Federal Government Subsidies for Wheat and Corn, 1944 (pesos per ton)

	Purchase Price	*Selling Price*	*Subsidy*
Corn			
National	312	252	60
Import	400	252	150
Wheat			
Import			ND
Federal District			85
The States			25

Source: Memo to Manuel Avila Camacho from Nazario Ortíz Garza, January 16, 1945, AGN-MAC 521.8/188.
Note: ND = no data.

According to a report by the treasury secretariat, the subsidy generally remained in the hands of the miller and did not always get passed down to the consumer.[71] As a result of the subsidy policy, the following years saw an explosion in the number of mills as they were established to benefit from government policy. The amount of wheat milled nearly doubled between 1939 and 1944, owing largely to the increase in imports of wheat (Table 4-5), and the increase was also reflected in the operations of individual mills. For example, one medium-sized wheat mill in Mexico City, "Molinos Hercules," increased the amount of wheat it milled from a monthly average of 21,381 kilograms in 1942 to 151,244 during the first five months of 1944 (Table 4-6). The wheat that Molinos Hercules milled was both domestic and imported. Thus, the combination of an increased subsidy and the importation of wheat provided handsome benefits to millers.

Table 4-5. Wheat Milled in Mexico, by Milling Years, 1938–1944 (tons)

Year	National	Imported	Total
1938	N.D.	N.D.	354,215
1939	N.D.	N.D.	333,951
1940–41	440,004	31,443	471,447
1941–42	393,033	152,858	545,618
1942–43	471,270	123,175	594,396
1943–44	336,292	363,708	700,000

Sources: For 1938 and 1939, Secretaría de la Economia Nacional, "Estadística de la industria de molinos de trigo, 1942"; for 1940–1944, "Punto de vista del Sr. Nazario S. Ortíz Garza, Gerente General de la Nacional Distribuidora y Reguladora, S.A. de C.V. para el H. Comité Ejecutivo," April 24, 1944, AGN-MAC 521.8/188.
Note: ND = no data.

Table 4-6. Wheat Milled by "Molinos Hercules," Mexico City, 1942–1944 (kilograms)

Year	National	Import	Total	Monthly Average
1942	256,580	0	256,580	21,381
1943	1,154,487	0	1,154,487	96,207
1944 (January–May)	451, 175	305,049	756,219	151,244

Source: "Informe de la visita practicada al molino de trigo Hercules, May 31, 1943, and March 15, 1945." AGN-DGI, Caja 97 391/302: 319(04)/30.

In its scramble to rapidly supply urban Mexico with inexpensive foodstuffs during the war years, the State Food Agency paid little attention to the needs of the countryside. Although the rural protection price system established under Cárdenas remained on the books, it was largely symbolic because the state had only weak mechanisms through which it could purchase and store grains in the countryside. Prices were kept low in order to reduce the urban consumer's cost of living. This decision to give consumer demands primacy was reflected in the actions of the Agency officers. This urban bias can be seen in the setting of the guaranteed price for corn in 1945. On the one hand, various groups lobbied to raise the guaranteed price of corn, including a congressional committee charged with studying Mexico's food problem, which recommended that the guaranteed price for corn be set at 300 pesos per ton.[72] On the other hand, Ortíz Garza and other government officials, including Secretary of Agriculture Marte R. Gómez, urged lower prices. Ortíz Garza, with the support of Gómez, asked Treasury Secretary Eduardo Suárez to set the guaranteed price at 275 pesos per ton and tried to minimize warnings of the congressional committee that if the guaranteed price was set at less than 300 pesos, more than half of the *ejidatarios* would stop growing corn and there would be a grave shortage. Ortíz Garza argued that if 300 pesos per ton was paid, plus 25 pesos for the cost of storage, 50 million pesos would be needed to finance the Agency's operations, and the cost of living would rise excessively.[73] Gómez hinted that he would be willing to back an even lower guaranteed price for corn, since he felt that the coming corn harvest would be so abundant that producers could sell at market price and no longer need price incentives.[74]

Producer groups lobbied to maintain high guaranteed prices for corn. The CNC, through its representative on the board of directors of the State Food Agency, Leopoldo Flores Zavala, lobbied intensely for increases in the guaranteed price of corn. Given its relatively close relationship with the government, the CNC had to dilute its criticism of certain policies. Its main concern throughout the 1940s was the low guaranteed price of grains, especially corn, set by the Agency.[75] Flores Zavala argued that low guaranteed prices did not provide an incentive for campesinos to produce corn for the national market. As rational economic actors, campesinos would produce only goods that provided them enough food and income to survive. Although the State Food Agency paid lip service to increasing the guaranteed price, Flores Zavala knew that this was unlikely to occur. He urged peasants throughout the country to calculate their production costs and send them to him so that he could better lobby for them.[76]

The case of wheat was different from that of corn. The sharp downturn in wheat production, beginning in 1943, forced Mexico to import approximately 60 percent of its wheat supply in 1943.[77] This dependence on foreign wheat coupled with rising wheat prices in the United States made agency officials such as Ortíz Garza amenable to the idea of increasing the guaranteed price of wheat to stimulate production, which was seen as more cost effective than investing in higher subsidies for corn, since their long-term goal was to increase wheat production.[78] Hence, the State Food Agency and various related ministries and agencies raised the guaranteed price. With the exception of a dramatic dip in 1942, wheat subsidies increased notably (Table 4-7).

Table 4-7. Wheat Prices and Subsidies, 1941–1944 (pesos/ton)

Year	Guaranteed Price	Average Rural Price	Selling Price of Imports	Subsidy
1941	185	190.00	190	13.11
1942	190	188.79	200	1.63
1943	230	246.19	230	10.96
1944	300	284.12	250	62.26

Source: Secretaría de Agricultura y Fomento, *Plan de movilización agrícola de la república mexicana* (México: SAF, 1945), pp. 8–9.

The overarching problem of the State Food Agency was its inability to purchase corn from producers throughout the country. In his study of the economy of Zacatecas, conducted between late 1943 and 1945, the economist Moisés T. De la Peña reported that peasants were still obligated to sell their crops immediately after harvest at low price. De la Peña argued that better rural prices would be obtained with a more efficient and all-encompassing transportation system.[79] The lack of warehouses continued to be a major obstacle in the Agency's ability to influence the marketing of grains in the countryside. Without such facilities, the Agency could not buy grain from peasants on a large scale. In 1943, it was estimated that merely to handle the grain harvests, not to mention reaching out to peasant producers, the state needed at least 10 percent more warehouses.[80] Increased storage capacity would have better prepared the Agency to meet demand for basic foodstuffs.[81]

The state storage facility, ANDSA, did not expand its operations during the Avila Camacho period. After Cárdenas created ANDSA and then expanded it three years later, its operations declined over the following fifteen years. Real income and expenditures of the state storage facilities were noticeably lower after 1940,[82] and the average annual amount of stock in ANDSA warehouses declined by approximately 15 percent.[83] The majority of the ANDSA warehouses were located in large cities, with very few in the countryside to store crops after harvest. Although this system enabled cities to store some grain, it hurt small producers, most of whom did not have state-of-the-art warehouses and were forced to sell their grain as soon as it was harvested.[84]

The scarcity of storage facilities was most noticeable at harvest. The lack of abundant space in warehouses for new harvests sometimes caused bureaucratic struggles. As the maize harvest was nearing completion at the beginning of 1945, Secretary of Agriculture Gómez called for the removal of the imported wheat stored, most of which had arrived excessively damp and not fit for human consumption.[85] A conflict ensued between Gómez and Ortíz Garza over this issue, in which Gómez, in conjunction with producers, accused the State Food Agency of purchasing poor grains that took up valuable storage space. The CNC argued that ANDSA's lack of warehouses and their overwhelming concentration in major consumption sites did not benefit producers or consumers, but instead aided merchants and "monopolizers."[86] Indeed, the lack of storage facilities limited the government's ability to purchase crops at the guaranteed price, thus leaving producers to the terms set by private merchants, resulting in "highly variable prices."[87]

The Persistence of the Food Crisis

Despite numerous attempts to lower rising prices in the city, scarcity persisted and prices continued their upward spiral throughout late 1945 and 1946. This occurred after a temporary reprieve during the first half of 1945, when the food situation was improved due to a strong corn harvest in 1944 and increased imports from the United States. Despite the boost in production, inadequate transportation and storage facilities led to continued scarcity and consequent price increases in many locales. The 1945 harvest was not as favorable as that of 1944, compounding an already dire situation.[88]

Throughout late 1945 and 1946, a skyrocketing cost of living was reported throughout the country. In many regions, including Veracruz, Monterrey, and Chihuahua, there seemed to be no end to the spiraling cost of foodstuffs. In these regions as in others, organized labor, housewives, and others took to the streets to demand relief. In Jalapa, Veracruz, the entire city was shut down for a day in May 1945 to protest a 100 percent increase in the price of bread.[89] In Chihuahua, the U.S. consulate reported: "It is certain that further strikes will occur, unless government intervention succeeds in controlling prices, as most local industries are now paying wage scales which they are not economically able to increase, and still labor is not receiving sufficient money to afford a decent living."[90]

The U.S. embassy monitored these conditions very closely and became increasingly alarmed. In August 1945, the embassy was reporting that the pending shortfall in grain production for 1945 and the ongoing transportation bottlenecks would necessitate increased importation of grains.[91] However, there were a number of signs that the U.S. government contemplated not providing Mexico with the amount of grain it had during the war. As the United States concentrated its efforts in rebuilding Europe in the postwar era, its attention shifted away from the Americas. Throughout 1946, U.S. ambassador George Messersmith made repeated requests to the USDA and to the State Department that grains be sold to Mexico to stave off the pending crisis. His April 5 request to the State Department exemplifies the urgency of his request: "I need not tell you that if we don't get enough wheat, corn and fats to Mexico we as well say good-bye to the Mexico which has collaborated with us in the last few years in the way it has."[92] After traveling to the United States, Messersmith received the assurances of the secretary of state and the secretary of agriculture that Mexico would receive 1,200,000 bushels of corn for April, May, and June. However, by the end of April, Mexico still had not received any shipment of grains. Ambassador Messersmith, in a memorandum dated April 27, 1945, again urged that Mexico receive grain shipments and repeated the argument he had made to government officials in Washington: "unless Mexico was assured the minimum needs of wheat and corn for which she was completely dependent on us for her deficit, there would be economic distress of the gravest character in this country, which would lead to revolution and the red flag in three months time."[93] Although Messersmith may have been exaggerating his case, the urgency of the food situation even at the conclusion of World War II is clear.

Conclusion

The economic situation created by World War II led the federal government to expand its operations in procuring and distributing basic foodstuffs. Mexico sought to shift its economy to meet wartime demands for products in the United States, which created a booming Mexican economy. However, as agricultural land was being shifted away from production for the internal market, Mexico became more vulnerable to food shortages. This was especially true given the difficulty in importing grain from abroad during the international crisis. Grain from the United States was also difficult to import due to a limited supply of railcars in both the United States and in Mexico. Grain shortages reached crisis proportions in 1943, when climatic conditions contributed to a poor corn harvest in Mexico. As the price of corn rose in the cities, protests from consumers grew louder and led to riots in some areas.

To respond to such urban pressure and in order to stave off further protests, the government reorganized and expanded the functions of the State Food Agency, greatly increasing its funding to enable it to purchase more goods abroad and establish more retail stores throughout the country. Although the Agency was able to set prices lower than market prices, it had difficulty enforcing such controls, and a black market emerged, often in the Agency's own grains. As prices continued to increase, the federal government extended more power and more funds to the Agency, and, consequently, it grew and expanded its functions.

Despite the important roles the State Food Agency played in the Mexican economy, it brought only temporary respite to urban workers. By 1946, issues of food scarcity and rising prices were still a significant part of Mexican life. The Agency effectively brought prices down and made basic foods accessible to a wider segment of the population, but it did little to boost agricultural production. Despite repeated calls by peasants and CNC leaders, the bulk of the Agency resources went to urban areas.

Notes

1. World War II's effect on Mexico is only recently receiving scholarly attention. Stephen R. Niblo, *War, Diplomacy, and Development: The United States and Mexico, 1938–1954* (Wilmington, Del: Scholarly Resources, 1995); and Blanca Torres, *México en la segunda guerra mundial* (Mexico: El Colegio de México, 1979) provide important overviews of Mexico in this period. For an in-depth narration of events, see Gustavo Abel Hernández Enriquez and Armando Rojas Trujillo, *Manuel Avila Camacho: Biografía de un revolucionario con historia*, tomo 2 (México: Ediciones del Gobierno de Puebla, 1986). Howard F. Cline, *The United States and Mexico* (Cambridge, Mass.: Harvard University Press, 1953, revised and enlarged edition published in 1963 by Atheneum Press) chap. 14, is still a useful treatment of this period.

2. For discussion of the impact of the war on agriculture, see Stephen R. Niblo, "The Impact of War: Mexico and World War II," La Trobe University Institute of Latin American Studies, Occasional Paper No. 10 (1988); and John Heath, "El abasto alimentario en la economía de guerra," in Rafael Loyola, ed., *Entre la guerra y la estabilidad política: El México de los 40* (México: Grijalbo, 1990), pp. 223–256.

3. Ramón Fernández y Fernández, *Los salarios agrícolas en 1944*, cited in Cynthia Hewitt de Alcántara, "The 'Green Revolution' As History: The Mexican Experience," in *Development and Change* 5:2 (1973–1974), p. 28.

4. For a general discussion of the shift in land reform during the Cárdenas presidency, see Dana Markiewicz, *The Mexican Revolution and the Limits of Agrarian Reform, 1915–1946* (Boulder, Colo.: Lynne Rienner, 1993), chap. 14.

5. James W. Wilkie, "The Six Ideological Phases of Mexico's 'Permanent Revolution' since 1910," in James W. Wilkie, ed., *Society and Economy in Mexico* (Los Angeles: UCLA Latin American Center Press, 1990), pp. 7–9.

6. Dana Markiewicz, *Ejido Organization in Mexico, 1934–1976* (Los Angeles: UCLA Latin American Center Publications, 1980), p. 14. For case studies of this shift, see Daniel Nugent, *Spent Cartridges of Revolution: An Anthropological History of Namiquipa, Chihuahua* (Chicago: University of Chicago Press, 1993); and John Gledhill, *Casi Nada: A Study of Agrarian Reform in the Homeland of Cardenismo* (Albany: Institute for MesoAmerican Studies, SUNY, 1991).

7. James W. Wilkie, *The Mexican Revolution: Federal Expenditure and Social Change since 1910* (Berkeley: University of California Press, 2d ed., 1970), p. 139.

8. John W. Mogab, "Public Credit Institutions as Development Agencies: The Case of Mexico's Ejido Credit System," Ph.D. diss., University of Tennessee at Knoxville, 1981, p. 145.

9. Calculated from INEGI, *Estadísticas históricas de México*, vol. 2 (México, 1985).

10. Adolfo Orive Alba, *La política de irrigación en Mexico* (Mexico: Fondo de Cultura Econónmica, 1960), p. 82. For these figures expressed in per capita terms, see Wilkie, *The Mexican Revolution*, pp. 134–135.

11. For discussion on the origins of the Rockefeller mission in Mexico, see E. C. Stakman, Richard Bradfield, and Paul C. Mangelsdorf, *Campaigns against Hunger* (Cambridge, Mass.: Belknap Press of Harvard University Press, 1967); Joseph Eugene Cotter, "Before the Green Revolution: Agricultural Science Policy in Mexico, 1920–1950," Ph.D. diss., University of California at Santa Barbara, 1994.

12. Geo D. Camp, consulting engineer to the Oficina del Plan Regulador del Departamento del Distrito Federal, "Apuntes relativos del problema urbana ferrocarrilero de la ciudad de México," June 25, 1940, AGN-GR, caja 55, exp. 2.

13. Secretaría de la Economía Nacional, *El desarrollo de la economía nacional bajo la inflación de la guerra, 1939–45* (Mexico: Oficina de Barometros Económicos, 1945), p. 47; memo of Mexico-U.S. Committee for Economic Cooperation, Sub-comisión de Mantenimiento y Mejoramiento de Medios de Transportación, June 24, 1943, AGN-GR, caja 34, exp. 19.

14. To President-elect Avila Camacho from El Sindicato de Trabajadores del Mercado de Subsistencias, December 6, 1940, AGN-MAC 521.8/1.

15. "Memoradum que se refiere a la creación del nuevo organismo de mercado que substituirá al Comité Regulador del Mercado de la Subsistencias," F. Javier Gaxiola Jr., February 25, 1941, AGN-MAC 545.21/9; Lic. Antonio Luna Arroyo, "La Nacional Distribuidora y Reguladora, S.A. comentarios para El Universal," AGN-MAC 545.2/78; Francisco J. Gaxiola, *Memorias* (México: Porrúa, 1975), p. 299.

16. "Iniciativa presidencial para resolver el problema de las subsistencias," March 27, 1941, AGN-MAC 545.21/9.

17. Palazuelos to Avila Camacho, April 1, 1941, AGN-MAC 545.2/73.

18. Raúl Salinas Lózano, *La intervención del estado y la cuestión de los precios* (México: Editorial America, 1944), p. 42.

19. Blanca Torres, "1938–1949: El Comité Regulador del Mercado de las Subsistencias y la Nacional Distribuidora y Reguladora, S.A.," in Compañía Nacional de Subsistencias Populares, *El Mercado de las Subsistencias Populares: Cincenta años de regulación*, vol. 1 (México: CONASUPO, 1988), p. 146.

20. See Gaxiola, *Memorias*, pp. 299–300.

21. Ricardo J. Zevada, "Política de precios," *Investigación Económica* 5:4 (1945), p. 495.

22. See James W. Wilkie, "From Economic Growth to Economic Stagnation in Mexico: Statistical Series for Understanding Pre- and Post-1982 Change," in James W. Wilkie, David E. Lorey, and Enrique Ochoa, eds., *Statistical Abstract of Latin America*, vol. 26 (Los Angeles: UCLA Latin American Center Press, 1988), pp. 924–925.

23. *El Nacional*, May 16, 1942.

24. For contemporary debate on the causes of inflation during the war years, see John S. DeBeers, "El peso mexicano, 1941–1949," in *Problemas Agrícolas e Industriales de México* 5:1 (January–March, 1953), pp. 7–134, and the various comments by Mexican economists in the same volume.

25. Jeffrey L. Bortz, *Los salarios industriales en Mexico, 1939–1975* (Mexico: Fondo de Cultura Económica, 1988), p. 266. For minimum wage data, see Kevin Middlebrook, *The Paradox of Revolution: Labor, the State, and Authoritarianism in Mexico* (Baltimore, Md.: Johns Hopkins University Press, 1995). The Bortz data has elicited some debate. However, what concerns us here is the wage trend and the popular reactions that it created. See Peter Gregory, "'The Effect of Mexico's Postwar Industrialization on the U.S.-Mexico Price and Wage Comparison' by Jeffrey Bortz: A Comment," in Jorge A. Bustmante, Clark W. Reynolds, and Rául A. Hinojosa Ojeda, eds., *U.S.-Mexico Relations: Labor Market Interdependence* (Stanford, Calif.: Stanford University Press, 1992); and Peter Gregory, *The Myth of Market Failure: Employment and the Labor Market in Mexico* (Baltimore, Md.: Johns Hopkins University Press, 1986).

26. *Excelsior*, November 3, 1942; Secretaría de la Economía Nacional, Dirección General de Estadisticas, *Anuario Estadístico 1943–1945*; also see Jorge Basurto, *La clase obrera en la historia de México: Del avilacamachismo al alemanismo, 1940–1952* (Mexico: Siglo Veintiuno Editores, 1984), p. 94. Kevin Middlebrook provides slightly different figures, although the trend is the same, in *The Paradox of Revolution*, pp. 164–164.

27. Middlebrook, *The Paradox of Revolution*, pp. 162–172.

28. "Punto de vista del Sr. Nazario S. Ortíz Garza, Gerente de la Nacional Distribuidora y Reguladora, S.A. de C.V. para el H. Comité Ejecutivo," April 24, 1944, AGN-MAC 521.8/188.

29. Cámara de Diputados, *La cámara de diputados y el problema de las subsistencias* (México: Ediciones de la "Editorial de Izquierda" Cámara de Diputados, 1945), p. 20.

30. "Informe de Avila Camacho al H. Congreso de la Union. 1 Sept. 1944 al 31 August, 1945," in Secretaría de Hacienda y credito Público, *Memoria de la Secretaría de Hacienda y Crédito Público* (December 1, 1940–November 30, 1946), vol. 1 (Mexico, 1955), p. 31; *El Universal*, November 23, 1944. Estados Unidos Mexicanos, *Directorio del gobierno federal 1948* (Mexico: Dirección Técnica de Organización, Secretaría de Bienes Nacionales e Inspección Administrativa, 1948), p. 628, gives this date as February 1946, yet other sources do not confirm this.

31. El Comité de Afóros y Subsidios al Comercio Exterio, *El subsidio a la importación del trigo* (Mexico: Oficina de Subsidios y Estudios Especiales, 1944).

32. Calculated from Banco Nacional de Comerico Exterior, *Informe al consejo de administración*, various.

33. "Organismos de emergencia en la administración económica," AGN-MAC 545.22/160-1-33.

34. Torres, *Mexico en la segunda guerra*, p. 333.

35. Letter to President Avila Camacho from CTM, September 25, 1943, AGN-MAC 545.2/73.

36. See "Asaltos y motines por el hambre," in Alfonso Taracena, *La vida en México bajo Avila Camacho* (México: Editorial Jus, 1976), pp. 431–434.

37. Lesley Byrd Simpson, *Many Mexicos* (Berkeley: University of California Press, 1966), 4th ed., p. 345.

38. Eduardo Suárez, *Comentarios y recuerdos (1926–46)* (México: Editorial Porrúa, 1977), p. 253; Hernández Enriquez and Rojas Trujillo, *Manuel Avila Camacho*, p. 140.

39. See, for example, "Influyents y políticos son los cupables de la carestía," *Excelsior*, November 6, 1942; and "Eliminando coyotes y acaparadores puede hacerse aumentar la producción de trigo," *Excelsior*, November 6, 1942; Niblo, "The Impact of War," p. 31.

40. See Gaxiola, *Memorias*, pp. 300–307, for his defense against the accusations and his negotiation with the president; see also Niblo, "The Impact of War," p. 32.

41. Amado Trejo, "Informe a la Junta de Económia de Emergencia," July 19, 1943, AGN-MAC 550/44-2. For an analysis of the events surrounding Gaxiola's resignation, see Stephen R. Niblo, "Decoding Mexican Politics: The Resignation of Francisco Javier Gaxiola," *Anales* (University of New South Wales) 2:1, 1993.

42. Quoted in Niblo, "The Impact of War," p. 32.

43. Roderic A. Camp, *Mexican Political Biographies, 1935–1981* (Tucson: University of Arizona Press, 1982), p. 224.

44. Gaxiola, *Memorias*, p. 300.

45. Niblo, "Decoding Mexican Politics."

46. Secretaría de Gobernación, *Seis años de actividad nacional* (México: Secretaría de Gobernación, 1946).

47. El Comité de Aforos y Subsidios al Comercio Exterior, *El subsidio a la importación del trigo*, pp. 61–62.

48. Rafael Saavedra Q., secretary general of the Federación Obrera de la Industria Alimenticia del D.F., to President Avila Camacho, October 2, 1945, AGN-MAC 604.71/2-2.

49. "Memo sobre el mercado del trigo," June 18, 1941, AGN-MAC 521/4.

50. Letter to President Avila Camacho from Secretary Gaxiola, March 18, 1943, AGN-MAC 521/4.

51. William F. Busser, second secretary of embassy, "National Railroads Increase Demurrage Charges on Carload Lots," August 14, 1945, USNA RG 166-5-321.

52. National Grain Corporation to Avila Camacho, August 26, 1943; Margarito Ramírez manager of FFNN to Ortíz Garza, September 17, 1943, AGN-MAC 521/4.

53. *La cámara de diputados y el problema de las subsistencias* (México, 1945), p. 17.

54. *El Universal*, March 10, 1946.

55. Ortíz Garza to Avila Camacho, May 2, 1944, AGN-MAC 521.8/194.

56. Report on NADYRSA milk purchases, AGN-MAC 545.2/91.

57. Ortíz Garza to Avila Camacho, May 2, 1944, AGN-MAC 521.8/194.

58. "Projecto de programa minimo de labores para el año de 1941, que desarrollaron la Oficina de Cooperativos de Consumos de la Secretaría de Trabajo y Provisión Social (STPS) y que somete a la consideración de la superioridad El C. Prof. José González Padilla, Jefe de Oficina," May 19, 1941, AGN-STPS, caja 1156, exp. 13/100 (014)/1.

59. Secretaría de Trabajo y Prevision Social Oficina de Cooperativos de Consumo, "Informe de labores," August 8, 1945, AGN-STPS, caja 1156, exp. 13/106-3/1.

60. *El Universal*, October 25, 1944.

61. "Informe de Tiendas Ferronales," January 1, 1945, AGN-MAC 521.7/165; to Avila Camacho from Luis Gómez Z. and Valentín Campa, Sindicato de Trabajadores Ferrocarriles de Mexico, June 15, 1945, AGN-MAC 521.7/165.

62. Avila Camacho to governors, June 9, 1943, AGN-MAC 545.22/160-1-33.

63. *La Gaceta Oficial del DDF* 1:34 (May 31, 1942).

64. *El Universal*, March 17, 1945.

65. "Informes confidenciales al margen de los precios," May 24, 1943, AGN-MAC 545.22/160-1-8.

66. Sergio de la Peña and Marcel Morales Ibarra, *Historia de la cuestión agraria mexicana: El agrarismo y la industrialización de México, 1940–1950* (Mexico: Siglo Veintiuno Editores, 1989), p. 87.

67. "Informes confidenciales al margen de los precios," May 24, 1943, AGN-MAC 545.22/160-1-8.

68. For a systematic study of corruption in Mexico, see Stephen D. Morris, *Corruption and Politics in Contemporary Mexico* (Tuscaloosa: University of Alabama Press, 1991).

69. For an interesting discussion of some of the ways public officials become rich while in office, see the interview with Ramón Beteta, "Ramón Beteta, político y hacendista," in James W. Wilkie and Edna Monzon de Wilkie, *México visto en el siglo XX: Entrevistas de historia oral* (México: Instituto de Investigaciones Económicas, 1969), pp. 21–71.

70. The politics behind the U.S. exports of grain to Mexico are discussed in Niblo, "The Impact of War."

71. El Comité de Aforos y Subsidios al Comercio Exterior, *El subsidio*, pp. 62–63.

72. *La cámara de diputados y el problema de las subsistencias* (México, 1945).

73. Ortíz Garza to Eduardo Suárez, January 11, 1945, AGN-MAC 521.8/188.

74. Marte R. Gómez to Ortíz Garza, February 6, 1945, AGN-MAC 528.8/188.

75. For a general discussion of the CNC and its relationship with the state, see Moisés González Navarro, *La Confederación Nacional de Campesinos en la reforma agraria mexicana* (México: El Día en Libros, 1985).

76. Leopoldo Flores Zavala, "El precio rural de maíz," *Siembra* 1:8 (November 1, 1943), p. 18; Zavala, "La política económica y los precios rurales," *Siembra* 1:3 (June 1, 1943); Acta de Asamblea de Accionistas y Sesiones del Consejo de NADIRSA, No. 87, July 30, 1947.

77. Aida Mostkoff and Enrique C. Ochoa, "Complexities of Measuring the Food Situation in Mexico: Supply versus Self-Sufficiency of Basic

Grains, 1925–86," in James W. Wilkie, ed., *Society and Economy in Mexico* (Los Angeles: UCLA Latin American Studies Press, 1990).

78. Memorandum to President Avila Camacho from Ortíz Garza, November 23, 1943, AGN-AC 521/4.

79. Moisés T. de la Peña, *Zacatecas económico* (México, 1948), pp. 432–433.

80. See the comments of the subsecretary of agriculture, Alfonso González Gallardo, "La orientación de la agricultura mexicana," *El Trimestre Económico* 9:4, pp. 527–528; see also John Heath, "El abasto alimentario en la economía de guerra," in Rafael Loyola, ed., *Entre la guerra y la estabilidad política: El México de los 40* (México: Grijalbo, 1990), pp. 223–256.

81. Ricardo J. Zevada, "El control de precios en México," in Erik T. H. Kjellström et al., *El Control de Precios*, trans. by Javier Márquez (Mexico: Fondo de Cultura Económica, 1943), p. 242.

82. Calculated from Roberto Santillán López and Ancieto Rosas Figueroa, *Teoria general de las finanzas públicas y el caso de México* (Mexico: UNAM, 1962), deflated using DGE wholesale price index.

83. Almacenes Nacionales de Depósito, S.A., *Informe del consejo de administración a la asamblea general ordinaria de accionistas* (México, 1949).

84. "Balance general de ANDSA," March 1943, AGN-MAC 565.1/63.

85. Marte R. Gomez to Ortíz Garza, February 6, 1945, AGN-MAC 521.8/188.

86. "Exposición doctrina del programa del CNC," *Siembra* no. 9. December 1, 1943, pp. 22–24, 42–49.

87. Juan F. Noyola, "Economic Survey of Mexico," IMF Research Department Staff Memo No. 138, November 7, 1947, p. 16, AGN-GR, caja 44, exp. 30.

88. J. Barnard Gibbs, "October 1945 Semi Annual Grain and Feed Review, American Embassy, October 31, 1945, USNA RG 166-5-311.

89. American Consulate in Veracruz, "Monthly Economic Report," May 4, 1946, USNA RG 59-812.50.

90. "Resumé of Economic Conditions in Chihuahua, January 1946," USNA RG 59-812.50.

91. J. Barnard Gibbs, "October 1945 Semi Annual Grain and Feed Review, American Embassy, October 31, 1945, USNA RG 166-5-311.

92. Letter to Department of State from Ambassador Messersmith, April 5, 1946, USNA RG 59-812.5018/4-546.

93. Ambassador Messersmith to William Clayton, Assistant Secretary of State, April 27, 1946, USNA RG 59-812.5018/4-2746. See also Lester D. Langley, *Mexico and the United States: The Fragile Relationship* (Boston: Twayne Publishers, 1991).

5

Between Economic Efficiency and Political Expediency, 1946–1952

The State Food Agency that emerged from World War II was three times the size it had been before the war. Despite its increased size, it was unable to solve Mexico's food problems: goods were still in short supply, and prices continued to rise. Miguel Alemán entered the presidency with a new plan to solve Mexico's food crisis and to launch the country on the fast track to industrialization. In contrast to past presidents, Alemán felt that the most effective way to abate rising price levels was to concentrate resources on increasing the production of grains in Mexico.

In keeping with this supply-oriented policy, Alemán initially sought to liberalize price controls and shift the policies of the State Food Agency away from subsidizing consumption and toward improving grain storage and handling techniques to make basic food distribution more efficient. However, as prices rose with renewed vigor after 1948, Alemán was compelled to restructure and buttress Agency programs that he had sought to dismantle. Political forces caused Alemán to modify his liberalization programs and to expand the functions of the State Food Agency to further the primary aim of his administration—fostering the industrialization of Mexico. However, the way in which the Agency grew and initiated new food policies was consistent with Alemán's general economic approach to provide incentives for the private sector, encourage lower prices, and use the federal government to enforce the laws. The results of Alemán's policies proved to be an insufficient hedge against inflation and did not endear Alemán to wide sectors of the population.

An analysis of the factors behind the shifts in Mexican food policies under Alemán reveals the reasons for the failure of his liberalization plan and the political problems it fueled. After analyzing agricultural policy under Alemán and exploring the structure and operations of the State Food Agency, this chapter surveys the reorganization and strengthening of the agency in July 1949. It then examines the crisis-ridden industries of this period—milk and corn milling—to give a better understanding of Alemán's use of the state in food policy in this latter section.

Agricultural Policy under Alemán

During the presidency of Miguel Alemán, Mexico underwent an extensive industrialization process that helped fuel the "Mexican miracle" that would characterize the following two decades.[1] The federal government invested large quantities of money in the industrialization process: providing credit through a strengthened industrial development bank, granting tax exemptions, and setting relatively high tariff barriers for manufactured goods. Abundant agricultural production was seen as essential to facilitating the industrialization process, since inexpensive foodstuffs would enable employers to keep wages low and keep inflation in check.

Sensitive to the inflation that plagued his two predecessors, Alemán was committed to combating the rising cost of living. However, in contrast to the Cárdenas years, merchants were not publicly assailed for "starving the populace." Instead, Alemán argued that Mexico's major agricultural problem lay in its insufficient production, and once this was rectified distribution bottlenecks would be eliminated. Both on the campaign trail during the height of Mexico's wartime inflation in 1945 and upon taking office, Miguel Alemán vowed to fight the high cost of living with the increased production of agricultural goods.[2] In making his pledge, he distinguished between political and economic measures of combating high prices. He saw political measures, such as price controls and fines for selling above the fixed price, as merely temporary and complementary measures. The real issue, according to Alemán, was the need to concentrate on expanding internal production of basic grains.

Because the expansion of output was central to Alemán's food policy, production was explicitly given primacy over land distribution for the first time in several decades. The land reform provision in the Constitution of 1917, Article 27, was amended within days of Alemán's assumption of the presidency. Greater protection was granted to private land holdings. The amount of land exempted from land reform increased by some 57 percent over that of his predecessor. By the same token, the amount of land redistributed was 18.5 percent less than that granted by Avila Camacho and 73 percent less than that granted by Cárdenas.[3]

With the reduction in land distribution under Alemán came a decrease in the amount of credit extended to the *ejidal* sector. State agricultural credit targeted for basic grain production by BNCE declined from between 70 and 80 percent of its operations during the Avila Camacho administration to 60 percent under Alemán. As under Avila Camacho, cotton continued to be the crop most commonly financed by both agricultural banks.[4] The deemphasis on public credit was supplemented by increased private financing of agriculture during the Alemán administration. Much of these loans, both public and private, went to wheat and export crops, and very little reached corn and beans, which provided lower rates of return.

To increase production, emphasis was placed on modernization of production techniques. The Secretaría de Agricultura y Ganadería (SAG) continued to work with the Rockefeller Foundation in an effort to create high-yield seed varieties for basic grains. During Aleman's first full year in office he invested more money in agricultural research programs than his predecessor did in his last three years.[5] The two major crops targeted by the Rockefeller Foundation and the Mexican government were corn and wheat. The first task of the Rockefeller Foundation's agricultural program was the improvement of corn yields. Beginning in 1943, numerous seed varieties were tested by the corn breeding team headed by Edwin J. Wellhausen. By 1946, the first selected seed varieties were distributed to farmers. To complement the Rockefeller Foundation programs, President Alemán established the Corn Commission in January 1947. Wellhausen and his team turned the improved seeds over to the Corn Commission, which was charged with distributing them to farmers. The seeds were said to yield 15–20 percent more than unimproved varieties. The major problem with the seeds was found in their distribution because, according to the Rockefeller Foundation, only a few "progressive" farmers were willing to make use of the seeds owing to their expense.[6]

Although the corn improvement program was in full swing at the beginning of the Alemán administration, the wheat program lagged slightly behind. The wheat program began over a year after the initiation of the corn program, in October 1944. Under the direction of Norman Borlaug, new seed varieties were developed and tested at a rapid pace, so that by 1951 nearly 70 percent of the wheat acreage was planted with new vareties. That most wheat farmers benefited from the seeds can be attributed to the fact that they produced for the market and not for subsistence. Since wheat was generally planted in irrigated lands or better rainfed lands and farmers made use of fertilizers and other new farming technologies, they were in a good position to take advantage of the new seeds.

Coupled with the program aimed at creating high-yield seeds, the Alemán administration invested heavily in other agricultural modernization programs. Large-scale irrigation works were the most visible sign of the states' commitment to agricultural modernization. President Alemán upgraded the status of the irrigation commission to a cabinet-level position at the end of 1946 and gave it one of the largest budgets of any secretariat.[7] Efforts were also made to expand fertilizer and pesticide production and use.

Aimed at expanding output, these modernization programs also led to the concentration of public investment in agricultural development in northern Mexico. The BNCE agencies centered in Torreón and the North Pacific agency, with offices in Ciudad Obregón and Los Mochis, received more than 60 percent of total *ejidal* bank loans throughout the Alemán administration. Such was also the case for highway and irrigation construction. Between 1940 and 1960, the northern region of the country received over 50 percent of the new paved roads and between 70 and 80 percent of new irrigation works.[8]

Modernization accelerated the bifurcation of agricultural production, dealing a severe blow to small producers and *ejidatarios*. The modernized sector received enormous sums of government subsidies, increasing their production for the national market and for export. These policies were detrimental to small producers and campesinos in traditional agricultural areas,[9] leading to increased rural-to-urban migration and accelerating the trend of *ejidatarios* illegally renting out their parcels of land or supplementing their income from work in the city or in the United States.[10]

Linked to the expansion of agricultural production was the need to enhance the distribution system so that grains could be efficiently moved from production to consumption centers. The first three years of Alemán's administration were aimed at increasing storage capacity and modernizing handling techniques to accommodate the expansion of agricultural output. The emphasis on storage and handling signaled a major restructuring of the role that the State Food Agency had played during the World War II years.

Storage and Efficiency in the State Food Agency, 1946–1949

After investing substantial resources into the State Food Agency from 1937 to 1946, the federal government under Miguel Alemán began to reassess its operations. The Agency assumed a more active role in increasing the efficiency of grain storage and distribution than it had done in the past in order to complement Alemán's emphasis on increased production. The efforts to restructure the Agency were linked to his wider program of abating the rising cost of living that had plagued Mexico for the past decade. Alemán argued that increased production would result in an abundant supplies that would drive prices down, and he wanted the State Food Agency to complement the work of SAG to stimulate agricultural output.[11]

President Alemán began to deemphasize the importance of the State Food Agency. Its manager under Avila Camacho, the politically prominent former governor of Coahuila, Nazario Ortíz Garza, was appointed to the important post of secretary of agriculture, and lesser known bureaucrats, Carlos Cinta (1947–1949) and Eduardo Ampudía (1949–1952), were appointed to succeed him at the Agency. Ortíz Garza had coordinated the rapid expansion of the Agency during the war years and had demonstrated great skill in using the agency to stave off large-scale famines, at least temporarily. In contrast, Alemán's directors of the Agency would seek to slim the agency, downplay its social welfare functions, and increase its efficiency.

When Carlos Cinta took over the State Food Agency, he set out to correct many of the inefficiencies that had been created by its rapid expansion during the war years. He undertook an evaluation of its finances and ordered an external audit of the agency's operations. The audit demonstrated that the operations for 1946 showed the "most grave irregularities," caused by a "lack of discipline in the auditing department."[12] Upon firing the chief internal auditor and twenty accountants, Cinta urged the Agency board of directors not to approve the 1946 year-end financial statement because "it had erroneous figures that falsify the economic situation of the company."[13] Listed in the ledgers were various persons who owed money to the Agency but could not be located and others who were completely insolvent or without proper documentation, thus making it impossible to pursue legal action against them. The amounts lost due to this mismanagement added up to hundreds of thousands of pesos.[14] The audits also discovered a number of irregularities in the handling of grains. The new auditor found that sixty-four cars of wheat had been counted twice, which meant the Agency had smaller reserves than had been thought. Further, random inspections of stored merchandise revealed that goods were unaccounted for in several warehouses, including those of ANDSA and other privately owned institutions, that were rented by the Agency. These losses also amounted to several hundred thousand pesos.[15]

In line with his effort to make the State Food Agency more efficient, Cinta attempted to discontinue several operations it performed that he deemed unnecessary and too costly. One of the first measures taken by Cinta was to reduce the amount of subsidies granted to the wheat-milling industry. By raising the price at which the Agency sold wheat to millers, it was calculated that the agency would save some 2.5 million pesos monthly, and if any deficit was incurred in these operations it would amount to no more than 170,000 monthly, a substantial reduction from the deficit of the World War II era, which amounted to 29.3 million pesos in 1944.[16] This gradual retreat from heavy wheat subsidies extended to other areas as well.

The Agency sought to consolidate its control of the food trade by absorbing and eliminating various local regulatory agencies that had been created during the expansionary wartime period. Cinta met with representatives of the Department of the Federal District to eliminate the city's Committee on Corn Distribution. Cinta argued that the inspectors of this committee did not coordinate efforts with his inspectors and that the committee had continued to proportion corn to mills that had closed, so that most likely much of this corn was sold on the black market.[17] Such charges of black marketeering by government agencies were widespread. In fact, similar charges were levied against the Agency.

The director of the Federal District's General Commission of Supplies, a local food-regulating committee, alleged that his agency had carried out an extensive investigation of the corn allocation to mills in December 1947. The results of the investigation demonstrated that many of the mills that the State Food Agency was supplying with corn did not exist and that these buyers received corn at the subsidized price of 251.50 pesos a ton and then would resell it for up to 400 pesos a ton. In forty-five days they found many such cases and were able to suppress the illegal sale of 738 tons of corn monthly at a value of 36,900 pesos.[18] As a "reward" for this investigation, the federal government liquidated the Federal District's General Commission of Supplies in February 1948, ostensibly so that the Agency could gain control over its distribution operation.

In a further effort to improve the effectiveness of the State Food Agency, Cinta sought greater cooperation between state agencies. On a trip to Washington, DC, in July 1947, he discovered that various Mexican agencies had been working at cross-purposes in the acquisition of U.S. grains. Meetings with Mexico's ambassador in Washington and with representatives of the USDA revealed that the Agency had been lobbying the USDA to allot Mexico 420,000 tons of wheat for the 1947–1948 year, while at the same time another Mexican government organism had been lobbying for 600,000 tons. The USDA had sent out questionnaires regarding Mexico's grain needs, but the secretary of agriculture never returned them. Also, Cinta learned that at the same time Mexico was seeking U.S. wheat, Yucatán was exporting wheat.[19] Such lack of coordination was seen as obstructing the Agency from efficiently carrying out its prescribed duties.

The expansion of infrastructure was an essential component of Alemán's desire to integrate the various regional markets of Mexico. Central to Alemán's larger program of integrating the country was the expansion of roads and the emphasis on local farm-to-market roads. At the end of 1938 Mexico had only 6,428 kilometers of all-weather roads, of which approximately half was paved. By 1947 the road network had increased by nearly 11,000 kilometers.[20] Although most of the roads that existed prior to the 1940s paralleled the railroad or led to the U.S. border, this began to change. In the midst of this road construction was the expansion of the construction of transversal roads that linked the provincial centers to one another. In 1948 the government initiated a project of rural road construction. The funding for the construction of farm-to-market roads was initially funded by both the federal and the state government, but within a year the latter and private investors became the premier financiers of rural road development. Between 1948 and 1951, approximately 1,678 kilometers of farm-to-market roads were constructed; 6 percent of these roads were paved, and the rest were hard-surfaced.[21]

To enhance the position of small producers, Alemán felt that they had to have greater access to national markets; thus, along with road construction, the expansion and improvement of federal storage and handling facilities were central in this process. Although the problem of the lack of state-owned and -operated storage facilities had long been recognized, little concrete action had been carried out to rectify it. Upon leaving office in 1946, Marte R. Gómez, the secretary of agriculture under Avila Camacho, explained the situation to his successor Nazario Ortíz Garza:

> The Secretary of Agriculture has not had money with which to construct silos for corn, and this has contributed to speculation. If you succeed in constructing, in strategic locations, silos that store surpluses, and in acquiring financing to purchase corn directly from peasants, at remunerative prices, it would be a great step for corn production, which is to say a benefit for the most humble peasants in our country.
>
> Grain elevators with equipment to unload corn and move it from time to time, with periodic fumigations and with everything necessary for adequate conservation of the product, needs the good-natured intervention of the Mexican state, and hopefully you can obtain it.[22]

As expectations for increased yields of basic grains began to be realized, the imperative of an effective storage system became greater. To learn firsthand about the operation of grain elevators, milling operations, and grain exchanges, Cinta visited the United States and Canada in July 1947. Impressed with what he saw there, Cinta urged the construction of grain elevators in at least thirteen strategic places in Mexico, and he commissioned the construction firm of Jones-Hettelsater, with whom he had made contact in Kansas City, Missouri, during his trip to the United States, to study the possibility of constructing grain elevators.[23] The U.S. firm concluded its study in November 1947, stating that "present methods of handling grain are not at the present time adequate to properly store, condition, and distribute the various cereal grains and that modern elevators should be built in the Federal District, Ciudad Obregón, Torreón, and Irapuato."[24] Jones-Hettelsater criticized Mexico's common method of storing grains in bags, which kept wheat moist and made it vulnerable to weevil and rodent infestation. With a modern system of grain elevators, the firm believed that Mexican cities could maintain a large grain supply for up to ninety days, thus taking pressure off the overburdened railroad system, which had to transport grains on a nearly daily basis. The overall cost of implementation of the proposal was extremely high. For Mexico City alone it was estimated that it would cost 12 million pesos and take eighteen months to build.[25]

Following the recommendations of Jones-Hettelsater and faced with the ever-growing demand for storage facilities, the State Food Agency, in cooperation with ANDSA, oversaw the construction of several warehouses during this period. The first priority of the warehouse construction was to enhance storage of grain in Mexico City. In Nayarit, the state that provided the most corn to Mexico City during the war years, two warehouse alongside the railroad were built and operational in time for the harvest of 1948.[26] In the port of Veracruz, the major gateway for imported grain, Alemán ordered the construction of a port granary complete with modern equipment, soon after one was constructed in the port of Tampico.[27] The most ambitious undertaking was the construction of the storage facility on the northern outskirts of Mexico City, in Tlalnepantla. The Tlalnepantla warehouses, known as the Silos Miguel Alemán, were aimed at storing wheat and other grains for Mexico City. The 50-thousand-ton-capacity warehouses were equipped with some of the most modern equipment, including grain cleaning and drying machinery, vacuums, and elevators. The Silos Miguel Alemán was the first major warehouse built to store grains for the city and would help ensure that a constant supply of grains would be in government hands, to be released during times of shortages.[28]

In the countryside, government-controlled warehouses tended to concentrate in larger production areas and did not readily expand into small producer-dominated areas. The majority of ANDSA's warehouses were rented (147 of 193), and as with other infrastructure such as roads and irrigation, the northern area and the Pacific Northwest benefited the most, with more than 25 percent of new storage facilities being located there.[29] The warehouses were built in this region to serve the large wheat producers, who were expanding their production and had been demanding government support in storing their crops. More remote states often complained of the lack of government-controlled warehouses in their states. In the southern state of Campeche, for example, the governor reported that in 1950, there were no more than six warehouses for corn storage in the entire state, and all were operated by private merchants. The governor felt that the federal government should open some warehouses to maintain a reserve of grains as was being done in other parts of the country.[30]

Although Alemán saw state-operated storage facilities as being essential to efficient agricultural distribution, in reality there was little knowledge of how the storage process operated. The first study conducted by the State Food Agency and ANDSA on the actual workings of government storage policy found that there was a basic contradiction in government policies. On the one hand, the Agency was interested in maintaining high reserves of basic grains to counteract shortages and speculative marketing practices on the part of private merchants. On the other hand, the government wanted to limit the amount of reserves that private merchants kept in state warehouses to prevent them from hoarding. The result was that many producers were still forced to sell at a low price immediately after harvest to middlemen with their own warehouses who could afford to wait until prices rose. Thus instead of keeping prices down by discouraging hoarding in public granaries, private hoarding was occurring, and prices continued to increase.[31]

Federal government concerns about the operation of the state storage facilities led to greater oversight of ANDSA. The financial operations of ANDSA had not been audited for several years. After a scandal became public in which employees were found to be writing certificates of deposits for goods not deposited, ANDSA decided, in July 1949, that it would set up an office of an internal auditor.[32]

The emphasis that the Alemán administration placed on storage and grain handling was the largest such effort that the state had taken to store grain using modern methods. Because Alemán's agricultural goals for Mexico included increasing production of basic grains by aiding large-scale holdings, much of the storage and handling policies of both the State Food Agency and ANDSA benefited larger and more modern producers. The building of warehouses to store the grain from small *ejidos* and remote lands was not a priority of the Alemán administration. Instead, storage of grains was aimed at enhancing the distribution mechanism of larger cities by enabling the state to store grains near the capital or in ports so as to mobilize them rapidly, be prepared to meet demand, and avoid the food panics that had occurred during the war years.

Under Alemán, the State Food Agency purchased larger shares of national grain production than it had in the past. Because annual reports were not systematically kept during this period, it is difficult to ascertain the total yearly purchases and sales of the Agency. But data do exist for the period from September 1948 to August 1949. Information for this year is important because it is a pivotal year for Agency operations. The federal government granted it 65.5 million pesos for wheat and corn operations. Seventy-three percent of the total subsidies were pegged for wheat operation and the remainder for corn. In the internal market, the Agency played the most active role in purchasing corn from national producers, buying 323,000 tons, or approximately 11 percent of the corn crop for 1949.[33] Although purchases during this period were far less for beans (4.3 percent), rice (3.3 percent), and wheat (6.2 percent), they were probably up from the war years, when the bulk of Agency operations involved imports.

Despite the fact that national purchases were increasing, the State Food Agency seemed to favor a relatively small number of states. In general, those states favored in purchases were the ones with larger and more organized production, which were in better positions to take advantage of the services offered by the state, including the guaranteed price and the use of state warehouses. The majority of the wheat consumed in Mexico City came principally from three states in the north: Sonora, Sinaloa, and Baja California. Similar patterns can also be observed for corn and bean production. Despite the fact that corn and beans are grown throughout Mexico and tend to dominate land use in Mexico's central plateau, three states comprised nearly 70 percent of the corn sold in Mexico City: Mexico, Nayarit, and Veracruz (Table 5-1). Two of these states (Nayarit and Veracruz) were not among those that traditionally produce most of Mexico's corn. Mexico's traditional corn producers, such as Jalisco and Michoacán, sent relatively small amounts of corn to Mexico City. This may be explained in part by the number of subsistence farmers who sold small surpluses locally; who were not benefiting from pricing policies, low railroad rates, and warehouses; and who often had to sell substantially below the guaranteed price.

The price paid for local production of corn hovered around 300 pesos a ton for most of the period. This price paid by the State Food Agency was not widely publicized by the government, nor did the Agency attempt to make this price accessible to all producers. Frequently, the result was that small producers sold their crops to local merchants for 110 pesos a ton, and these merchants would in turn sell to the Agency at around 300 a ton, making a sizable profit.

The State Food Agency continued to import basic foodstuffs, yet in smaller quantities than during the War. Although Mexican wheat production was on the rise, it did not meet demand and continued to be Mexico's major grain import. Large portions of Mexico's imports came as a result of Mexico's signing the World Wheat Treaty, in which it agreed to purchase at least 170,000 tons a year for seven years. In contrast, the importation of beans and corn declined somewhat throughout this period.

Table 5-1. Full Cars of Corn Entering Mexico City, by State of Origin, 1946–1951

State	1946	1947	1948	1949	1950	1951
Total	5,691	6,072	5,187	3,150	4,203	4,190
Monthly average	474.3	506.0	432.3	315.0	350.3	349.2
Coahuila	13	51	3	0	81	37
Chihuahua	1	147	162	5	522	21
Durango		47	50	30	175	19
Nuevo León	9	7	1	5	8	9
San Luis Potosí	4	0	27	11	1	4
Tamaulipas	16	9	10	12	12	926
Zacatecas	0	1	7	143	146	59
Veracruz	1,143	354	372	33	104	747
Tabasco	0	0	0	0	9	29
Nayarit	784	1,444	1,418	655	1,565	1,031
Sinaloa	19	96	25	36	58	136
Sonora	1	5	1	2	2	30
Colima	321	290	198	113	179	144
Chiapas	187	116	293	411	238	419
Guerrero	11	30	28	60	9	29
Oaxaca	58	32	14	2	21	38
Aguascalientes	15	1	13	4	11	0
Guanajuato	19	76	62	113	78	35
Hidalgo	23	23	9	41	24	6
Jalisco	434	373	109	39	102	201
México	2,107	2,653	1,975	759	531	67
Michoacán	13	78	127	284	292	82
Morelos	12	0	7	97	1	53
Puebla	442	80	232	205	16	52
Querétaro	5	19	19	11	8	1
Tlaxcala	54	29	25	79	10	15

Source: Secretaría de Agricultura y Ganadería, *Boletín menusal de la Dirección General Economía Rural* (various).

Financial efficiency was the goal of the State Food Agency during the first three years of the Alemán presidency. Cost saving, however, meant the reduction of a number of services beneficial to urban labor, including reduction in wheat subsidies and a liberalization of pricing policies. Rather that take such drastic action, the Agency adopted a policy aimed at increasing storage capacity so as to maintain larger regulating stocks. Such a policy demonstrated the use of the Agency for long-range goals, something that was fairly unique to this period.

The actions of the State Food Agency under Cinta sparked CTM and CNC complaints. These groups of workers and peasants used their seats on the board of directors of the Agency to voice their growing opposition to its operations. Both representatives felt that it had ceased to act in the interests of those it was designed to protect. During 1947 and 1948, the peasant sector's representative, Leopoldo Flores Zavala, complained bitterly that the board of directors met too infrequently to even discuss their view that the Agency's intervention in the bean and corn markets was to the disadvantage of small producers.[34]

CNC allegations that the State Food Agency's operations were sacrificing producers for the benefit of consumers were confirmed and defended by the majority on the board of directors. While Flores Zavala lobbied for the Agency to establish remunerative guaranteed prices to give incentives to small producers to sell to the state as opposed to local merchants, other board members argued that the role of the State Food Agency was to merely regulate the market by maintaining reserves and not actively participate in it. Secretary of the Economy Antonio Ruiz Galindo, who presided over the board of directors, argued that prices should be competitive and that the Agency should not intervene in the pricing process. Furthermore, Ruiz Galindo felt that the guaranteed price never reached most peasants because, being far from population centers, they had to sell to intermediaries. In Ruiz Galindo's view, "the guaranteed price was an obstacle in lowering prices for the consumer, and if . . . we pay a guaranteed price, when goods get to market they will be more expensive."[35] Galindo's views went unchallenged by all the board members except Flores Zavala, who could not accept the idea that low producer prices were needed to convert Mexico into an urban industrialized country.

In dropping the long-held rhetoric of aiding small producers and the beneficiaries of land reform, President Alemán and General Manager Cinta spoke incessantly about the need for the State Food Agency to better coordinate the distribution of grains through alliances with new producer groups. In public pronouncements, references to the CNC when discussing producers were replaced with newer private sector-oriented producers whom the government privileged. One such group was the Asociación Nacional de Cosecheros de Cereales y Productos Alimenticios (ANC). Founded in 1947 with the support of Alemán, the ANC was an umbrella organization encompassing 620 producer groups representing private farmers.[36]

The ANC took the lead in overtly supporting Alemán and the State Food Agency's policies of enhancing distribution mechanisms to lower the cost to consumers. In early 1949, the ANC inaugurated a distribution center in Mexico City to sell the cereal goods of its members. The center sought to facilitate the direct sale of goods to consumers by producers by avoiding the added costs of the middleman and trying to break the monopoly of city markets.[37] The actions of the ANC were praised by officials as a model for private action in attempting to combat the rising cost of living. However, the economic and political conditions that enabled the State Food Agency to concentrate on reforming its operations by enhancing the coordination of production and consumption did not last forever. This rather unique hiatus in crisis-oriented planning was interrupted by renewed inflationary pressures.

Renewed Inflation and Reorganization of the State Food Agency, 1949–1952

The 1949 increase in prices was, in part, triggered by the devaluation of the peso. From June 1948 to June 1949 the peso was allowed to float, and its value fell by over 100 percent from 4.25 to 8.65 pesos to a dollar during the period. Alemán had been very reluctant to devalue because he knew that the resultant price increases would bring demands for increased salaries. However, he felt that gradual devaluation was the only way to stimulate the Mexican economy out of its postwar recession. The devaluation of the peso coupled with the poor agricultural harvest of 1950–1951 led to the renewed inflation, which pinched the pocketbooks of workers and the middle class.

After the devaluation, consumer prices began to rise, and worker and consumer demands for wage increases became more vocal. Real wages, which had plummeted during the war years and had been making a slow recovery during the early Alemán period, renewed their downward trend (Table 5-2). Militant unions in the railroad, petroleum, and mining sectors were active in fighting to improve wages, working conditions, and democracy in unions, overtly challenging Alemán's modernization plans. Throughout 1948 and 1949, the government cracked down on militant sectors of labor and the left in general. In January 1949, Minister of Labor Manuel Ramírez Vásquez told the U.S. embassy's labor officer that the government dominated the industrial unions, and he predicted that after the election in July the CTM would have greater congressional representation.[38] The taming of labor and the left, then, occurred through a variety of mechanisms, including breaking strikes, appointing sympathetic labor leaders to head unions, and extending token reforms to foster social peace under the new order.

Although Alemán had tamed much of the union movement by purging militant sectors, there were still some demands for substantial wage increases.[39] The Alemán administration met these demands by granting some wage concessions, substantially less than those demanded by more independent unionists, and greater job control to unions. Further anticipating the inflationary effect that the devaluation might have on the general population, many cabinet members pushed for the establishment of subsidies and price controls on basic foodstuffs.[40] Once again, in the process of rolling back the social promises of the revolution, food subsidies were offered as a substitute for wage gains, union democracy, and improved standard of living.

Table 5-2. Consumer Cost of Living and Real Wages in Mexico City, 1946–1952 (1939 = 100)

Year	Cost of Living Year Index	Average Real Wage Index
1946	385.67	49.75
1947	416.70	50.49
1948	417.59	56.72
1949	442.86	56.68
1950	459.92	60.13
1951	545.62	55.31
1952	607.00	53.90

Source: Jeffrey L. Bortz, *Los salarios industriales en la ciudad de México, 1939–75* (México: Fondo de Cultura Económica, 1988), pp. 252, 266.

The State Food Agency was the major agency to benefit from these new subsidies. Renewed inflation, coupled with Alemán's strategy for crushing labor militancy, forced him to alter his liberalization and rationalization policies and to expand the Agency as part of his labor policy. Food subsidies became an important tool that benefited the private sector by relieving business of demands for wage increases. Hence, the Agency expansion remained consistent with Alemán's overall policy of stimulating the private sector.

In response to both complaints against its operations and in accordance with Alemán's overall economic strategy, in July 1949, NADYRSA was disbanded and its functions absorbed by an existing agency, CEIMSA, a branch of national foreign trade bank.

Since 1936 CEIMSA had operated as the commercial wing of BANCOMEXT, importing and exporting agricultural goods. This change was consistent with the belief that importation should be the main strategy for compensating for drops in production.

As Cinta left the expiring State Food Agency in 1949, the directors voted him a 20,000-peso bonus. Representatives of CTM and CNC did not vote against the bonus but abstained, silently voicing their opposition to the change in the direction of the Agency's priorities over which Cinta had presided.

CEIMSA's role as the new State Food Agency was part of Alemán's plan to bring it under the control of government agencies linked to foreign trade policy. Recall that after the dismantling of the Consortium in 1944, the Agency had been transferred from the control of the internally oriented SEN to the more externally oriented Department of the Treasury. Now, in 1949, the entire operation of the Agency was linked to BANCOMEXT. Although the stated purpose of the Agency remained very similar to that of its predecessors, its structure became much more complex. It was divided into three submanagement units—commercial, administrative, and financial—each with between seven and ten departments. These three units reported to the general manager, who in turn reported to the board of directors. This organizational design allowed the director some freedom from being involved in the day-to-day operations of each of the twenty-nine different departments. Under the structure of the old Agency, there were no intermediate steps between the general manager and the different departments (accounting, public relations, silos, and legal); all reported directly to the manager. The structure of the new agency underscored Alemán's emphasis on constructing storage facilities.

To overcome Alemán's earlier reduction in funds to the State Food Agency, BANCOMEXT allotted a 30 percent real increase between 1949 and 1952 to food regulation (Table 5-3). Much of this money funded increased purchasing operations for the Agency and the expansion of urban programs.

Public debate concerning the operation and powers of CEIMSA filled the editorial pages of Mexico City dailies during January 1950. Its power was criticized by merchants who claimed that it was a new monopoly.[41] *El Universal* lambasted it as a violation of a number of constitutional articles, namely Article 28, the antimonopoly article that the government itself used to justify its intervention in the economy.[42] Specifically, it was criticized for being the sole importer of grains. It was argued that CEIMSA, because it was able to import inexpensive grains, would be able to sell at cheaper prices than would general merchants. These later critiques were buttressed by numerous legal petitions that sought to circumvent CEIMSA's power.[43]

Table 5-3. BANCOMEXT Credit Allotted for Price Regulation, 1946–1952

Year	Credit Extended for Price Regulation as a Percentage of Total Credit	Real Amount of Credit Extended (thousands of 1950 pesos)
1947	43.5	615,993.6
1948	29.4	513,277.5
1949	26.0	505,694.0
1950	54.1	514,723.7
1951	48.2	557,251.2
1952	54.9	657,735.8

Sources: Calculated from BANCOMEXT, *Informe del consejo* (various years). Deflated using the wholesale price index in James W. Wilkie, "From Economic Growth to Economic Stagnation in Mexico: Statistical Series for Understanding Pre- and Post-1982 Economic Change," in James W. Wilkie, David Lorey, and Enrique Ochoa, eds., *Statistical Abstract of Latin America*, vol. 26 (Los Angeles: UCLA Latin American Center Publications, 1988).

The government responded to each of the criticisms first by trying to allay the fears of merchants and then by amending CEIMSA's functions. The State Food Agency's new general manger, Eduardo Ampudía, repeatedly stated that it was not a profit-motivated monopoly, but rather an agency for the public good. Responding to critiques of CEIMSA's privileged position as sole importer of grains, Ampudía argued that it could import grains only with the consultation of the secretary of agriculture, hence only when national grains were scarce.[44] Apparently, critics were not satisfied with Ampudía's assurances, and by the end of January 1950, CEIMSA's trade operations were amended, enabling it only to make grain exchanges and not to enter into the free purchase and sale of grains. This concession on the part of Alemán was met favorably by critics, and many of the petitions were withdrawn.[45]

Although the State Food Agency was weakened by Alemán's concession, attention was diverted from its purchasing operations, and it was able to concentrate on becoming more active in its urban operations. In keeping with Alemán's general liberalization policies, the Agency intervened most in areas that were deemed in crisis, such as the milk industry. In other areas the state would intercede as a last resort to provide the populace with access to inexpensive foodstuffs.

As Alemán sought to tame labor unions, his reorganization of the State Food Agency served as a substitute for substantial wage increases.[46] The renewed inflation and resulting labor and urban pressure caused Alemán at first to expand the operation and the numbers of urban stores and increase enforcement of price controls. When those measures did not alleviate the problem, the Agency became an active participant in the food processing industry, as we will see occurred with milk and corn meal.

In October 1949, the new State Food Agency announced the launch of "a second front in the war against the rising cost of living." It planned to triple the total number of stores it operated by expanding the number of wholesale stores and increasing from 105 to more than 200 the retail stores it had in Mexico City. Also, Ampudía entered into negotiations with the merchants in Mexico City's public markets to purchase more of their basic foodstuffs from the Agency's wholesale markets.[47] Within a month, some eighty stores throughout Mexico City had been established to sell goods to small businesses at reduced prices.[48]

The sharp increase in the cost of living also forced Alemán to break with his past liberalization policies. After a brief suspension during the early part of his administration, price controls were reimposed on many basic items, and an agency was established, in April 1951, to set prices and to enforce the controls. During its first two months of operation, the Dirección General de Precios (DGP) of SEN fined 698 establishments 98,750 pesos for selling above the set price, for selling products under the established weight, and for not posting prices in the stores. In many instances, these operations were temporarily shut down. This move toward enforcing controls, originally conceived as a temporary measure to alleviate the impact of inflation on workers' wages, became yet another facet of the government's intervention in the marketplace.[49]

Alemán's food policies also focused on milk distribution and production. Mexico's outbreak of hoof and mouth disease (Aftosa) in late 1946 and the subsequent cow eradication program increased the demand for imported milk, which had been imported to supplement milk production since the early 1940s. Although aggregate figures on milk production do not exist on a yearly basis, other qualitative information points to a decline in production after the outbreak. For example, in May 1947, the Nestlé milk canning plant in Ocotlán, Jalisco, received approximately 7,000 liters of milk per day, a far smaller amount than the 16,000 liters the plant handled during the same period the year before.[50] This drop can be directly attributed to the hoof and mouth eradication campaign, which required the slaughter of a number of milk-producing cattle in the region and prohibited Nestlé from receiving milk from producers in Michoacán.

Initially, the Alemán administration sought to increase imports and to stimulate the private sector to build and operate recombination plants and pasteurization plants. However, when sanitary problems and scarcity persisted, the federal government began to intervene directly. Because statistical data on milk production are scarce and very unreliable for this period, data on imports can give us insight into the gravity of the shortage. In 1947, the first full year of the Aftosa crisis, the importation of milk and milk products increased markedly: 13.2 million kilograms of powdered milk were imported in comparison to 4.9 million the year before. By the same token, the amount of butter, cheese, and fresh milk imported also reflected all-time highs (Table 5-4).

Table 5-4. Milk and Milk Products Imports, 1942–1952 (kilograms)

Year	Fresh Milk	Condensed, Powdered, and Evaporated Milk	Butter	Cheese
1942	11,025	628,720	43,999	201,558
1943	4,571	567,200	13,395	101,411
1944	99,440	1,469,210	18,056	147,843
1945	17,822	3,944,478	18,930	203,117
1946	6,750	4,944,901	233,187	260,026
1947	143,745	13,280,891	1,058,898	677,557
1950	22,594	4,342,040	44,550	424,416
1951	20,000	5,725,000	39,000	456,000
1952	6,000	6,207,000	66,000	768,000

Source: Secretaría de Agricultura y Ganadería, *Resumen de Informe de labores de la Secretaría de Agricultura y Ganadería* (various years).

During World War II the importation of milk and milk products increased markedly and continued to increase in the postwar era. Milk and powdered imports nearly tripled between 1944 and 1947 and continued to remain above the pre-1945 level for several years. The importation of powdered milk was seen as a viable partial solution to decline in Mexico's milk production, since it was relatively easy to transport, store, and reconstitute. Given the lack of large numbers of refrigerated railcars and cold storage facilities,

Mexico could not handle the importation of fresh milk or its products in large quantities, let alone distribution of its domestic production of fresh milk. To overcome such obstacles, the federal government began to help stimulate the expansion of powdered milk.

The increasing importation of powdered milk (Table 5-4) can partially be attributed to the ease with which this compact nonperishable product is transported and to the increased incentives that the federal government began to extend for the establishment of milk recombination plants. At the end of 1946, Lechería Nacional was built at the urging of the federal government. In return for its tax-exempt status and other benefits, it agreed to sell milk at a price set by the government.[51] After Lechería Nacional began operations, other milk recombination plants were set up but were confined to certain regions. These plants were able to take advantage of the recent advances in milk recombination technology; by the late 1940s, the process of dehydrating milk and recombining it with water had improved so that taste was reportedly not sacrificed.[52]

Despite the fact that they were heralded as the solution to Mexico's milk problems, the recombination plants did not immediately alleviate the milk shortage. The scarcity of milk persisted in Mexico City during the late 1940s, giving rise to the selling of unpasteurized and unsanitary milk under the official prices. One survey of 14,393 samples of milk analyzed between May 1945 and November 1946 showed that 54 percent was deemed bad quality.[53] In 1949, it was reported that the clandestine stables had come to account for one-fifth of the milk sold in Mexico City, much of which sold for 15 percent under the price of milk in supermarkets. The pervasiveness of unregulated milk was seen as a contributing factor to the vast increase in gastrointestinal diseases reported by the General Hospital.[54]

To control the clandestine sale of unregulated milk, the secretary of health was authorized to wage a massive campaign to expose and fine the operators of these stables. In June 1949, ten stables were charged with the sale of unregulated and diluted milk and forced to close down their operations. The largest plant closed, at San Simeon, had thirty cows, but for the most part, the government closed small clandestine operations with a few cattle.[55] Despite government efforts, clandestine production persisted for a number of years (see Chapter 6).

The spread of Aftosa throughout the Mexico City area contaminated nearly every herd in the region, leading to a dramatic drop in the supply of fresh milk, substantially below the normal 400,000 liters delivered daily. This led to the increase in demand for milk from Lechería Nacional. The recombination plant expanded its output from 8,000 liters a day when it opened on November 4, 1946, to 25,000 liters by the end of the month, and to 40,000 by the end of December. By mid-January 1947 it was producing between 45,000 and 50,000 liters daily. The U.S. embassy reported that as publicity of the disease spread, many feared that it would be transmitted to humans, thus increasing the demand for Lechería Nacional milk. The demand was so great that Lechería Nacional rapidly depleted its supply of powdered milk, forcing it to fly in three planeloads of powdered milk from the United States by January 1947. The company claimed that as a result of the outbreak of Aftosa, they had daily orders for 150,000 liters of milk,[56] causing them to design plants to increase production to 500,000 liters a day.[57]

Milk shortages persisted and were compounded by a sharp rise in prices in the early 1950s. The price of fresh milk in Mexico City had held at around 99 centavos a liter between 1948 and 1950 but rose to 1.38 in 1952.[58] In order to better control milk prices and eliminate the need for clandestine milk sales, the Alemán administration saw that its only recourse was to construct its own milk recombination plant to target working-class neighborhoods. Since direct economic intervention had generally been avoided by Alemán, the State Food Agency went to great lengths to explain the social welfare nature of the milk recombination plants. Although the Agency's recombination plant did not open until 1953, during the administration of Adolfo Ruiz Cortines, it was the Alemán administration that foresaw its political and economic need.

Direct government intervention in corn milling followed the pattern of intervention in the milk industry. The State Food Agency intervened in the corn-milling industry partly as a result of problems the Agency itself had helped to create. In Alemán's reassessment of its overall operations, one area that came under scrutiny was the Agency's dealings with corn millers. It had come to heavily subsidize the sale of grains to millers. Millers had been an important group for the government to appease since 1937, when they had vocally opposed the importation of already milled flour, as seen in Chapter 5. By 1946 politicians and policymakers realized that the subsidies to these industries were too high and that they were helping to enrich many millers. To correct this problem, Alemán's administration scrutinized the milling industry and its unique history.

The corn-milling industry had gradually spread throughout the country during the early decades of the twentieth century. Hand grinding of corn was replaced by machine grinding, first in the major cities and then in rural communities as electricity became available during the 1920s.[59] Although the number of mills substantially decreased due to the decline in consumption that accompanied the Great Depression, the number slowly rebounded by 1940 (Table 5-5). During the war years, the number of mills did not grow much, but in an effort to stimulate milling and decrease the price to the consumer, the government sold grains to the milling industry well below the market price, thus subsidizing the millers. The subsidies extended for the milling of corn proved lucrative for millers. Unfortunately, yearly data on subsidies do not exist, but we can get periodic insights from government reports. A 1950 report noted that "the sale of subsidized corn has been a magnificent business for millers; the State Food Agency delivers it to them at 348 pesos per ton, and then purchases the finished product at 610 pesos a ton."[60] The result of such subsidies led to a doubling of the number of mills between 1945 and 1950, yet the total value of the production did not increase. The expansion in the number of mills competing for subsidized grains exerted pressure on the State Food Agency, which was felt especially in Mexico City (see Table 5-5).

Table 5-5. Corn Mills in Mexico, 1930–1955

Year	Number of Mills	Real Value of Production (thousands of 1950 pesos)
1930	3,770	156,543
1935	927	102,542
1940	5,944	341,920
1945	5,853	532,102
1950	10,990	509,176
1955	11,709	535,907

Sources: Secretaría de Industria y Comercio, *Censo Industrial 1955, Resumen General*, vol. 1 (México, 1955). Deflated using the wholesale price index in James W. Wilkie, "From Economic Growth to Economic Stagnation in Mexico: Statistical Series for Understanding Pre- and Post-1982 Change," in James W. Wilkie, David Lorey, and Enrique Ochoa, eds., *Statistical Abstract of Latin America*, vol. 26 (Los Angeles: UCLA Latin American Center Publications, 1988).

By 1950 the disparity between the growth in the number of mills and the decline in the corn subsidy led to a cry of shortages of raw materials. Many mills disrupted their normal production cycle or slowed output in order to pressure the federal government to proportion more corn at subsidized rates. While such disruptions in the milling industry continued between 1950 and 1952, the federal government sought ways to influence the milling industry.

With the financial backing of its development bank, NAFINSA, in 1949 the federal government established the first publicly owned corn flour mill, Maíz Industrializado, S.A. (MINSA).[61] MINSA worked closely with the State Food Agency, milling Agency corn and selling it to the public. MINSA produced some 5 tons of corn flour by the end of 1949. The idea was to provide a better quality, inexpensive substitute for cornmeal that could be stored virtually anywhere until it was used. To make the tortilla dough, only water had to be added to MINSA's corn flour.[62] Despite the convenience of MINSA's product, at first it did not gain wide acceptance. The strength and influence of the milling industry's association and the employees' unions blocked government attempts to pursue a more vigorous campaign to expand the output of corn flour.

President Alemán tackled the 1949–1952 inflationary spurt differently than had his predecessor. Alemán saw government intervention in the prices and market of staple foods as only a temporary measure of last resort and sought to forestall it for as long as possible. When stimulating the private sector production of these goods did not alleviate political pressure from consumers, the federal government, even if reluctantly, took direct action in the marketplace. Both the case of milk and corn flour demonstrate the last resort character of government intervention.[63]

Conclusion

Although Alemán tried to reduce state control over food policy, by the end of his presidency the State Food Agency was nearly as active as it was prior to his assumption of office. At first Alemán reformed the Agency, reducing its policy priority, auditing its finances to detect and eliminate waste, and shifting from direct intervention in urban markets to developing storage facilities and grain elevators. Because Alemán saw Mexico's food problem as one essentially of production, he used the Agency to provide the infrastructure for the increased production that was being fostered by the Rockefeller Foundation in its work with the agriculture secretariat.

Renewed inflation, coupled with his project to tame labor militancy, and the other factors such as the outbreak of hoof and mouth disease led Alemán to reorganize and expand the Agency to combat new political and economic pressures. Unlike his predecessors, Alemán augmented the Agency only reluctantly, and he made it clear that such government actions were only temporary. He used it to stimulate private businesses to enter into the food-processing industry to produce nonperishable and steady supplies of corn flour and milk at stable prices for urban consumers. When private industry did not respond as enthusiastically as Alemán had hoped, the government intervened more directly to establish its own processing plants. Alemán's attempts to control the growth of state intervention in the marketplace ultimately failed as he was overtaken by events and responding to them. His restricted use of the interventionist state and preference for "freer markets" would be abandoned for some thirty years as successive presidents likewise used the State Food Agency to respond to various crises.

Notes

1. Although the work on Alemán is sparse, there are a few general overviews of the period. George S. Wise's book, *El México de Alemán* (México: Editorial Atlanta, S.A., 1952), trans. by Octavio Novaro, provides a good, albeit unabashedly partial, introduction to Alemán's plan for Mexico. A more recent interpretation of the period can be found in Tzvi Medin, *El sexenio alemanista* (México: Ediciones ERA, 1990). For a discussion of the economy and economic policy under Alemán, see Blanca Torres, *Hacia la utopía industrial, 1940–1952* (México: El Colegio de México, 1984), and Stephen R. Niblo, *War, Diplomacy, and Development: The United States and Mexico, 1938–1954* (Wilmington, Del.: SR Books, 1995).

2. Miguel Alemán, *Programa de gobierno* (México, 1945), p. 18; Miguel Alemán, "Primer informe presidencial" (September 1, 1947), in Luis González y González, eds., *La hacienda pública a tráves de los informes presidenciales* (México: Camara de Diputados, 1963), vol. 2, pp. 279–285.

3. For an overview of Alemán's land reform policies, see María Rodríguez Batista, "El problema del reparto agrario en el régimen alemanista," *Estudios Sociales* (Guadalajara) 6:2, pp. 4; and Sergio de la Peña and Marcel Morales Ibarra, *Historia de la cuestión agraria mexicana: El agrarismo y la industrialización de México, 1940–1950* (México: Siglo Veintiuno Editores, 1989). Data on land distribution and on certificates of ineffectability are from James W. Wilkie, "The Six Ideological Phases of Mexico's 'Permanent Revolution' since 1910," in James W. Wilkie, ed., *Society and Economy in Mexico* (Los Angeles: UCLA Latin American Center Publications, 1990), pp. 7–9.

4. John W. Mogab, "Public Credit Institutions as Development Agencies: The Case of Mexico's Ejido Credit System," Ph.D. diss., University of Tennessee at Knoxville, 1981, p. 183.

5. Nicolás Ardito-Barletta, "Costs and Social Benefits of Agricultural Research in Mexico," Ph.D. diss., University of Chicago, 1971, p. 11.

6. E. C. Stakman, Richard Bradfield, and Paul C. Mangelsdorf, *Campaigns against Hunger* (Cambridge, Mass.: Belknap Press of Harvard University Press, 1967), pp. 51–68.

7. Adolfo Orive Alba, *La política de irrigación en México* (México: Fondo de Cultura Económica, 1960), pp. 90–112; Martin Harry Greenberg, *Bureaucracy and Development: A Mexican Case Study* (Lexington, Mass.: D.C. Heath, 1970), chap. 3.

8. Clark W. Reynolds, *The Mexican Economy: Twentieth-Century Structure and Growth* (New Haven, Conn.: Yale University Press, 1970), p. 158.

9. Cynthia Hewitt de Alcántara, *La modernización de la agricultura méxico, 1940–1970* (México: Siglo Veintiuno Editores, 1978); and Steven E. Sanderson, *The Transformation of Mexican Agriculture: International Structure and the Politics of Rural Change* (Princeton, N.J.: Princeton University Press, 1986).

10. For examples of this, see Daniel Nugent, *Spent Cartridges of Revolution: An Anthropological History of Namiquipa, Chihuahua* (Chicago: University of Chicago Press, 1993); and John Gledhill, *Casi Nada: A Study of Agrarian Reform in the Homeland of Cardenismo* (Albany, N.Y.: Institute for Mesoamerican Studies, SUNY, 1991).

11. "Precios," editorial in *Revista de Economía* 9:11–12 (December 31, 1946), pp. 5–6.

12. NADYRSA, "Acta de asamblea de accionistas y sesiones del consejo," no. 85 (April 14, 1947), CONASUPO-BAT.

13. NADYRSA, "Acta de asamblea de accionistas y sesiones del consejo," no. 89 (October 22, 1947), CONASUPO-BAT.

14. NADYRSA, "Acta de asamblea de accionistas y sesiones del consejo," no. 85 (April 14, 1947), CONASUPO-BAT.

15. Ibid.

16. NADYRSA, "Acta de asamblea de accionistas y sesiones del consejo," no. 84 (January 24, 1949), CONASUPO-BAT; Secretaría de Agricultura y Fomento, *Plan de modernización agrícola de la república mexicana* (México: SAF, 1945), pp. 8–9.

17. NADYRSA, "Acta de asamblea de accionistas y sesiones del consejo," no. 84 (January 24, 1949), CONASUPO-BAT.

18. For discussion of the various agencies charged with enforcing price controls and for the views of the last director of the General Comission of Food Supplies in the Federal District, see Guillermo Martinez Dominguez, *Intentos de control de precios en México* (México: Secretaría de Educación Pública, 1950), p. 166.

19. Carlos M. Cinta to President Alemán, July 31, 1947, AGN-MA 523.1/68.

20. Calculated from the Combined Mexican Working Party of the International Bank for Reconstruction and Development, *The Economic Development of Mexico* (Baltimore, Md.: Johns Hopkins University Press, 1953), pp. 276–277.

21. Ibid., pp. 298–299.

22. Marte R. Gómez to Nazario Ortíz Garza, December 6, 1946, in *Vida política contemporánea: Cartas de Marte R. Gómez*, vol. 1 (México: Fondo de Cultura Económica, 1978), p. 741.

23. To Carlos Cinta from Ortíz Garza, October 17, 1948, AGN-MA 562.4/106.

24. To Carlos Cinta from Jones-Hettelsater Construction Co., November 17, 1947, AGN-GR, caja 13, exp. 110.

25. Ibid.

26. "Informe sobre el estado que guardan los almacenes propiedad de CEIMSA ubicado en Nanchi, Ruíz, y Acaponeta del Estado de Nayarit," August 1, 1958, CEIMSA, documentos relativas de las actas (July 1958), CONASUPO-BAT.

27. Memorandum from chief of the Departamento de Transporte Martimo de CEIMSA, Enrique Pawling, to the manager of CEIMSA, Roberto Amóros, October 8, 1959, in CONASUPO, Documentos Gerencia General, tomo 1, 1-100, CONASUPO-BAT.

28. CONASUPO, *El mercado de subsistencias populares: Cincuenta años de regulación* (México: CONASUPO, 1988), vol. 1, p. 161.

29. Almacenes Nacionales de Depósito, S.A., *Informe del consejo de administración a la 13th asamblea general ordinaria de accionistas, 1949*.

30. Lic. Carlos Sansores Pérez to President Miguel Alemán, November 2, 1950, AGN-MA 512/4436.

31. Memo to President Miguel Alemán, July 12, 1949, AGN-MA 705.1/218.

32. "Condiciones económicas de Almacenes Nacionales de Depósito," June 1949, AGN-MA 705.1/218.

33. "Actividades de la Nacional Distribuidora y Reguladora S.A. de C.V. durante el periodo Comprendido 1° septiembre 1948 al 31 de agosto 1949," AGN-MA 565.1/85.

34. NADYRSA, "Acta de asamblea de accionistas y sesiones del consejo," no. 90 (June 24, 1948), CONASUPO-BAT.

35. NADYRSA, "Acta de asamblea de accionistas y sesiones del consejo," no. 89 (October 22, 1947), CONASUPO-BAT.

36. Hubert C. de Grammont, "Los empresarios también se organizan: La unión nacional de cosecheros," in Julio Moguel, ed., *Historia de la cuestión agraria mexicana: Política estatal y conflictos agrarios 1950–1970* (México: Siglo Veintiuno Editores, 1989), pp. 46–61.

37. *Excelsior*, January 2, 1949; Hubert C. de Grammont, "Los empresarios también se organizan," p. 53.

38. Barry Carr, *Marxism and Communism in Twentieth-Century Mexico* (Lincoln: University of Nebraska Press, 1992), pp. 171–173.

39. Jeffrey Bortz, in *Los salarios industriales el la ciudad de México, 1939–1975* (México: Fondo de Cultura Económica, 1988), shows average real wages increasing slightly during this period; however, for a number of individual industries real wages decline or stagnate. Richard Ulric Miller shows real wages declining in the petroleum and steel industries during the period 1946–1951; see "The Role of Labor Organizations in a Developing Country: The Case of Mexico," Ph.D. diss., Cornell University, 1966, pp. 122, 158.

40. Torres, *Hacia la utopía industrial, 1940–1952*, pp. 119–126.

41. See, for example, *Excelsior*, January 9, 1950; and Hugo Azpeitia Gómez, *Compañía Exportadora e Importadora Mexicana, S.A. (1949–1958): Conflicto y abasto alimentaria* (México: Centro de Investigaciones y Estudios Superiores en Antropología Social, 1994), pp. 49–58.

42. "Nuevo monopolio," *El Universal*, January 11, 1950.

43. *Excelsior*, January 25, 1950.

44. *Novedades,* January 3, 1950; and Azpeitia Gómez, *Compañía Exportadora e Importadora Mexicana, S.A,* pp. 54–58.

45. *Excelsior,* January 25, 1950.

46. Alemán's labor policy is discussed in Jorge Basurto, *La clase obrera en la historia de México: Del avilacamachismo al alemanismo (1940–1952)* (México : Siglo Veintiuno Editores, 1984), p. 2; and in Norman Caulfield, "Mexican Labor and the State in the Twentieth Century: Conflict and Accommodation," Ph.D. diss., University of Houston, 1990, chaps. 5 and 6.

47. *Últimas Noticias,* October 25, 1949.

48. *El Nacional,* November 17, 1949.

49. See Secretaria de la Economía Nacional, *Memoria,* September 1950–August 1951 (México, 1951), pp. 165–171; Leopoldo Ortega Cruz, "El control de precios y su importancia en la economía del país," tesis de licenciatura (México: Escuela Nacional de Economía, UNAM, 1965), pp. 50–56.

50. Edward N. McCully, U.S. vice consul in Guadalajara, "Foot-and-Mouth Disease Curtails Production of Nestlé Milk Production in México," November 17, 1947; USNA RG 166-5-826.

51. *Gaceta Oficial del Departamento del Distrito Federal* 6:195, November 20, 1946, pp. 1–2.

52. On the history and process of milk powder and recombination, see Otto Frederick Hunzicker, *Condensed Milk and Powdered Milk: Prepared for Factory, School, and Laboratory,* 7th ed. (La Grange, Ill., 1949); and D. R. Strobel and C. J. Babcock, *Recombined Milk: A Dependable Supply of Fluid Milk Far from the Cow* (Washington, D.C.: U.S. Department of Agriculture, Foreign Agriculture Report No. 84, 1955).

53. See Guillermo Martínez Domínguez's article in *Excelsior* on December 20, 1948, "Un litro de 'leche' para cada 4 personas," reprinted in Guillermo Martínez Domínguez, *Quince años de periodismo al servicio de México* (México: Ediciones Asociación Mexicana de Periodistas, 1958), pp. 166–170.

54. *Excelsior,* June 11, 1949.

55. *Excelsior,* June 14, 1949, pp. 16, 18.

56. Thurston to Secretary of State, January 14, 1947, USNA RG 166-5-826.

57. "La producción de leche aumentara," *El Universal,* December 29, 1946.

58. Secretaría de la Economía Nacional, Dirección General de Estadisticas, *Compendio estadístico,* 1950, 1953.

59. For discussion of the transformation from hand grinding to milling of corn, see Arnold J. Bauer, "Millers and Grinders: Technology and Household Economy in Meso-America," *Agricultural History* 64:1 (winter 1990), pp. 1–17; see also Dawn Keremitsis, "Del metate al molino: La mujer mexicana de 1910 a 1940," *Historia Mexicana* 33:2 (October–December 1983), pp. 285–302.

60. "Memorandum relativo a las exisistencias y abastos de maíz en la república," September 28, 1950, AGN-MA 512/4436.

61. The first corn flour plant was Molinos Aztecas, S.A. (MASECA), founded by Roberto M. González in Nuevo León months earlier. See Nacional Financiera, S.A., *La industria de la harina de maíz* (México, 1982); and Jeffrey M. Pilcher, *¡Qué vivan los tamales! Food and the Making of Mexican Identity* (Albuquerque: University of New Mexico Press, 1998), p. 105.

62. *Últimas Noticias*, October 25, 1949; Nacional Finaciera, S.A. *La industria de la harina de maíz* (México: NAFINSA, 1982), p. 14.

63. See Douglas Bennett and Kennth Sharpe, "The State as Banker and Entrepreneur: The Last Resort Character of the Mexican State's Economic Intervention, 1917–1970," in Sylvia Ann Hewlett and Richard S. Weinert, eds., *Brazil and Mexico: Patterns in Late Development* (Philadelphia, Pa.: Institute for the Study of Human Issues, 1982), pp. 169–211.

6

Social Welfare and the
State Food Agency, 1952–1958

If the State Food Agency during the Alemán presidency tended toward liberalization and reluctant intervention, under Adolfo Ruiz Cortines (1952–1958), it was a vibrant activist agency that renewed its status as the premier social welfare agency on the national scene. Alemán's austerity programs and his general lack of attention to social issues sparked political pressure from a wide variety of new urban groups. Such rancor was displayed in the election of 1952, where the strongest challenger to Ruiz Cortines based much of his campaign on the necessity for government actions to alleviate poverty.

The State Food Agency became the primary vehicle that President Ruiz Cortines used to maintain political and social order. In its effort to meet the demands of the city, the Agency not only opened up more stores in newly settled neighborhoods, but it sought to coordinate its actions in the countryside. Its rural plan involved revamping its guaranteed price system and constructing a large number of warehouses earmarked for basic grains. The attention that the Agency afforded both the city and the countryside under Ruiz Cortines was unprecedented. This chapter analyzes the various factors surrounding the Agency's expanded intervention in both rural and urban areas.

The Urban Challenge

Ruiz Cortines inherited a Mexico that was rapidly industrializing and urbanizing. Its real GDP had more than doubled between 1940 and 1952.[1] The primary beneficiary of this expansion was the industrial sector, whose share of GDP increased as agriculture's share plummeted. The dynamic urban-based industrialization attracted a large flow of people seeking industrial jobs. Even though the majority of the Mexican population still lived in rural areas in the 1950s, this new influx into cities had created a number of pressures on the country's infrastructure, especially transportation and food distribution. Mexican cities had grown dramatically larger by 1950. Between 1921 and 1950, the number of people living in cities of 100,000 people or greater more than tripled from 5.3 to 17.8 percent. Although in 1921 only Mexico City and Guadalajara had populations greater than 100,000, by 1950 there were seven cities with at least that many people.

The metropolitan area of Mexico City alone nearly quintupled between 1921 and 1950 to over 3 million inhabitants. This trend continued throughout the 1950s, such that by 1960 some 23 percent of the population lived in cities of 100,000 people or greater.[2] Throughout the 1950s there was a growing preoccupation that unless dramatic steps were taken, Mexico City would be unable to absorb the influx of peoples from the countryside. Despite the fact that public works projects had been initiated under Avila Camacho and Alemán, infrastructure needs became obvious, and newspaper articles and studies of the situation became almost alarmist in tone.[3]

As urban areas became more concentrated, purchasing power for Mexico City's working classes declined. The last three years of the Alemán administration experienced growing price increases, with consumer prices increasing by approximately 32 percent.[4] The drop in urban purchasing power after 1949 helped to spark a growing tide of discontent among consumers. The Alemán government responded with increased intervention, stressing the enforcement of price controls. Such action served to keep some prices stable but did not resolve the problem.

The presidential election of 1952 gave workers, peasants, and some sectors of the military an opening to complain about the government's emphasis on industrial expansion at the expense of socially oriented programs. Many of these various groups united to support the dissident candidate General Miguel Henriquez Guzmán. One of the more prominent issues that Henriquez Guzmán brought to the fore of the national debate was the declining real wages of workers and the government's lack of ability, or unwillingness, to halt the erosion of purchasing power.[5]

Cost of living and food prices became issues that Ruiz Cortines had to address. Adopting much of the language used by Henriquez, Ruiz Cortines made numerous populist overtures. At the same time, he not only berated speculators but echoed his predecessor in promising to combat the high cost of basic foodstuffs by stimulating increased agricultural output. In a situation of abundant grain production, Ruiz Cortines argued that intermediaries would not be able to effectively hoard grain and create or exacerbate shortages.[6]

Despite Ruiz Cortines's attempts to win wide support, Henriquez Guzmán struck a chord with the urban populace and with a growing number of small producers, who gave him 17 percent of the vote. The outcome of the presidential election of 1952 demonstrated the vulnerability of Mexico's ruling party in urban areas. Although Ruiz Cortines was officially elected president of Mexico on July 1, 1952, he had won by a smaller margin than had any other official candidate in the past twenty years: 74 percent to Henriquez Guzmán's 17 percent. In the Federal District, however, he fared much worse, garnering about 50 percent of the vote. Henriquez Guzmán received 28 percent; the candidate of the conservative Partido de Accion Nacional (PAN) won 16 percent; and minor candidates, such as the labor leader Vicente Lombardo Toledano, the remainder.[7] The election reflected the relative unpopularity of the past administration, especially in Mexico City where pressures were more concentrated.

Once president, Ruiz Cortines attempted to win back the support of disaffected workers and peasants by emphasizing socially oriented programs aimed at reducing the cost of living. As Ramón Beteta, secretary of the treasury under Alemán, remarked, "the Ruiz Cortines government had very different ideas than ours, at least in theory. Cortines thought that in the so-called prosperity of the Alemán years . . . 'the rich got richer and the poor got poorer.' Consequently, Cortines had the idea of changing this completely."[8] Ruiz Cortines's changes in policy can be seen in the activities of the State Food Agency, which became the primary mechanism to win back the urban population and to defuse other incendiary situations such as the political repercussions of the peso devaluation of 1954.

Expansion of the State Food Agency

With the government's popularity at a low point, Ruiz Cortines's first year was marked by antispeculator rhetoric reminiscent of the populist language used by Cárdenas over a decade earlier.[9] Ruiz Cortines's pro-consumer rhetoric climaxed in his first state of the union address when he brashly proclaimed that "the state will be inflexible with merchants who are inhumanely abusive with the food of the people."[10] His combative posture toward speculators and price increases was reflected in his vision for the State Food Agency. Unlike Alemán, who used it to stimulate large-scale production and facilitate distribution and then hoped to dismantle it, Ruiz Cortines sought from the outset to give it prominence. He appointed a politician, Tomás Valles Vivar, who had some public exposure as a federal deputy and bureaucrat in other decentralized agencies, and he increased the amount of federal subsidies and grants targeted for the Agency.[11]

Valles took command of an agency that had been subordinate to other agencies; it was his task to build it into an effective, high-profile organization. In accordance with presidential rhetoric, the State Food Agency worked with the DGP to help enforce official prices. The DGP, part of SEN, levied over 16,000 fines on merchants during the first year of the Ruiz Cortines administration, a 51 percent increase over the year before.[12] These fines were announced with much public fanfare and helped create the image that government was doing something for consumers. A large percentage of these fines were voided on appeal, but such action rarely made the newspapers. Nevertheless, data on the total amount of fines collected still show a 19 percent increase between 1952 and 1953.[13]

Despite the increase in fines imposed, the enforcement of price controls continued to be a problem for the Ruiz Cortines administration. During the first year of his administration in 1953, he faced consumer complaints charging that merchants were hiding beans or not selling at the prices that were posted. State Food Agency inspectors were said to have made visits to stores, but they did not regularly check to see if merchants were selling the goods at the official price.[14] One of the most damning complaints came from an official who stated that his Agency's own stores were selling food to independent merchants instead of directly to consumers. This official discovered that many stores engaged in selling to merchants ran out of foodstuffs by 10 A.M. He also found that only a portion of the goods at many Agency stores sold at the official price; many items sold for much higher.[15] The agency itself fueled the black market.

Although it is difficult to gauge the opinions of unorganized consumers, qualitative evidence for the period demonstrates that grumbling grew louder when price inspectors did not enforce controls and when shortages inconvenienced consumers. The public leveled numerous charges against price inspectors for receiving and extorting bribes from merchants who did not comply with the official price. Popular frustration was reflected in the cartoons of Eduardo del Río, known as Rius, who laid much of the blame for increasing prices on price inspectors who demanded and accepted bribes.[16] The State Food Agency acknowledged graft and sought to counteract these charges with high-profile inspection campaigns. Nevertheless, the political will did not exist to fully eradicate graft or the black market.

The initial increase in the State Food Agency's operations and its enforcement of controls was financed by a substantial augmentation in the amount of credit and subsidies it received. The first infusion in the Agency's budget came from BANCOMEXT. In 1953, the amount of funds allotted to the Agency increased by nearly 20 percent after adjusting for inflation, making it the major recipient of the BANCOMEXT funds. Throughout Ruiz Cortines's term, more than 61 percent of bank credits went to the Agency to regulate prices (see Table 6-1). In real terms the amounts surpassed the historical peak of 1944. In addition, the amount of federal government subsidy to the Agency increased by 16 percent during the Ruiz Cortines administration (Table 6-2). These grants by the federal government were aimed at covering the operating costs of the Agency, including administrative costs such as salaries, office equipment, and supplies.

Table 6-1. Real BANCOMEXT Credits Allotted for Price Regulation, 1952–1958

Year	Credit Extended (thousands of 1950 pesos)	Credit Extended for Price Regulation as a Percentage of Total Credit
1952	657,735	54.9
1953	778,550	69.7
1954	709,890	60.3
1955	486,071	57.2
1956	613,404	62.3
1957	610,829	57.7
1958	646,818	61.7

Source: Calculated from BANCOMEXT, *Informe del consejo* (various years). Deflated using the wholesale price index in James W. Wilkie, "From Economic Growth to Economic Stagnation in Mexico: Statistical Series for Understanding Pre- and Post-1982 Change," in James W. Wilkie, David Lorey, and Enrique Ochoa, eds., *Statistical Abstract of Latin America*, vol. 26 (Los Angeles: UCLA Latin American Center Publications, 1988).

Table 6-2. Real Federal Government Subsidies to the State Food Agency, 1954–1958

Year	Nominal Subsidies	Real Subsidies (1950 pesos)
1954	223,900,000	153,777,473
1955	180,000,000	107,142,857
1956	326,400,000	183,062,255
1957	330,000,000	174,326,466
1958	352,000,000	177,777,778

Source: Ramón Fernández y Fernández and Ricardo Acosta, *Política agrícola: Ensayo sobre normas para México* (México: Fondo de Cultura Económica, 1961), p. 214. Deflated using the wholesale price index in James W. Wilkie, "From Economic Growth to Economic Stagnation in Mexico: Statistical Series for Understanding Pre- and Post-1982 Change," in James W. Wilkie, David Lorey, and Enrique Ochoa, eds., *Statistical Abstract of Latin America*, vol. 26 (Los Angeles: UCLA Latin American Center Publications, 1988).

The amount of money invested in the State Food Agency under the Ruiz Cortines administration rivaled and surpassed federal government investment in high profile ministries. For example, the State Food Agency received (through BANCOMEXT), more than double the amount of money given to the secretariat charged with developing irrigation works, Secretaría de Recursos Hidráulicos (SRH), and several times the amount that the federal government invested in agricultural credit (Table 6-3).

Table 6-3. Comparison of State Food Agency Funds from BANCOMEXT with Federal Investment in Irrigation Ministry and in Agricultural Banks, 1953–1958 (millions of pesos)

Year	A^a State Food Agency	B^b Secretaría de Recursos Hidraulicos	C^c Agricultural Banks
1953	1,028.9	573.7	71.3
1954	1,006.2	619.4	29.5
1955	816.6	643.2	80.0
1956	1,093.7	601.7	80.0
1957	1,156.3	641.5	80.0
1958	1,280.7	657.3	80.0

[a]Calculated from BANCOMEXT, *Informe del consejo* (various years).
[b]Martin Harry Greenberg, *Bureaucracy and Development: A Mexican Case Study* (Lexington, Mass.: D.C. Heath, 1970), p. 40.
[c]James W. Wilkie, *The Mexican Revolution: Federal Expenditure and Social Change since 1910* (Berkeley: University of California Press, 1970), p. 139.

The increase in investment and in government intervention came at times of political crisis. The first infusion of capital in the

State Food Agency came after the election of 1952, and the second followed the 44 percent devaluation of the peso in April 1954. The devaluation of the peso, announced during Mexico's "Holy week" when most Mexicans vacation, unleashed large-scale panic purchasing. Although the devaluation was timed for stores being closed on Easter Sunday, panic buying ensued nevertheless, and consequently, prices soared. Between March and May, the consumer price index jumped from 3.8 percent to 9.8, and by June it was at 11.6 percent.[17] Officially, PRI-controlled unions supported the devaluation but called for wage increases to cover their further decline in purchasing power. Nonofficially, workers threatened to strike, and some unions actually did go on strike.[18]

Following the devaluation, Ruiz Cortines publicly instructed the federal government and the State Food Agency to stabilize prices. The DGP vigorously enforced price controls during the months following the devaluation. The Federal District added 1,000 new inspectors to its payroll, and many more were hired by individual states. The number of fines given for selling foodstuffs above the official prices doubled between April and May 1954. Several large companies, such as Anderson-Clayton and Nestlé, received fines in highly publicized cases.[19] Ruiz Cortines also ordered the Agency to sell extra goods at fixed prices in its stores and directly to consumers in its "mobile stores," as well as to local merchants.[20]

Although the State Food Agency had been gradually shifting its policy to purchase more national grain, during times of crisis, such as during the aftermath of the devaluation of 1954, it imported substantial amounts of grains to provide immediate relief. When a decision had to be made regarding importing inexpensive grain or stimulating national production by raising prices, the former generally won out, as policymakers sought rapid solutions to growing urban problems. One of the most visible examples of this conflict can be seen in a conflict that arose in the cabinet in 1956. Because the Agency had been criticized for not halting the rising cost of living, a conflict arose. One side sought to increase imports of foodstuff from the United States, which had substantially reduced its price as it sought to get rid of surplus holdings. The other major argument, supported by General Manager Valles, held that Mexico was nearly self-sufficient in basic grains, and if it just rode out this latest crisis it would have an abundant national harvest next year.[21] However, political pressure from the urban sector proved too strong a force, and Valles was compelled to resign.[22]

Valles's successor, a former senator and governor from Nuevo León, José Vivanco, gradually increased the importation of corn despite increases in national production. During his tenure as the State Food Agency's general manager, he faced labor unrest from major sectors such as the railroad workers and teachers. Although the government increased the guaranteed price of basic grains to stimulate production in 1957, overproduction in the United States depressed prices, so that by 1958 it was 33 percent cheaper to purchase corn in the United States than in Mexico. Increasing political pressure in Mexico coupled with declining prices in the United States made importation a quick and attractive means by which to supply the cities with abundant inexpensive grains.

The State Food Agency's expanded activities attracted much debate from various sectors of society, the most vociferous dissent coming from merchant organizations. Ruiz Cortines and the Agency's initial hard line on lowering the price of basic foodstuffs especially alienated CONCANACO.[23] When it and the Agency had frequent conflicts in the past, most recently in 1949–1950, the government had generally mediated the conflicts.[24] CONCANACO's principal complaint against the State Food Agency was philosophical: government should not intervene in the marketplace. On a more routine level, the Confederación protested fines that its members received and won reductions in many. It also vigorously fought to ensure that the Agency did not replace private merchants completely, as had often been proposed by more radical elements within the PRI. The merchant organization's pressure, then, served to reduce the bite of government rhetoric, if not the bark.

CONCANACO's attacks on the State Food Agency raged throughout the first two-thirds of the administration, until a conscious effort was made by Vivanco to reach a truce. In 1956, a government-commissioned report constructively criticized the operations of the Agency, demonstrating that it operated inefficiently yet not without efficacy.[25] Once the Agency acknowledged its shortcomings, it actively sought the support of CONCANACO, winning implicit approval in late 1956. A formal accord was signed in 1960.[26]

Reorganizing the Countryside to Meet Internal Food Demands

In an effort to keep food prices low in urban areas, President Ruiz Cortines used the State Food Agency to better organize the resources of the countryside to feed the city. The new administration contin-ued Alemán's efforts to increase agricultural production, but it was more vigorous in its actions to increase storage capacity and to use price supports to stimulate production. Similar to Alemán, Ruíz Cortines privileged larger producers over *ejidatarios* and small pro-ducers. However, over time he would be forced to provide some direct support to the latter as rural militancy was renewed.

In order to increase the production of basic grains, Ruiz Cortines set the stage for more land to be cultivated, especially by seeking to spread ideas about modern farming practices developed by the Rockefeller Foundation. By the end of the Ruiz Cortines presidency, 44 percent more land was cultivated for corn production than when Alemán left office. Despite the best efforts of the Rockefeller's corn breeder Wellhausen and his assistant Efrain Xolocotzi, by the mid-1960s only 14 percent of Mexico's corn acreage was planted with hybrid seeds, and the new seeds had not reached small farmers.[27] Nonetheless, use of the seeds did lead to an increase in corn out-put. Bean production, similar to corn, did not fare as well as was expected under the Rockefeller programs. One scholar was unable to establish the extent to which improved bean seeds had been dis-tributed to small farmers.[28] Land under cultivation, then, was prob-ably just as important as yield in production of corn and beans.

In contrast to the corn and bean situation during the 1950s, gains in wheat production appear to have been caused by productivity gains made under the Rockefeller Foundation program. Because most wheat was grown in large-scale agriculture on irrigated lands and in fewer states than corn, wheat was ideal for the Rockefeller Foundation programs. The foundation could easily manage the cultivation of wheat because the growers were usually medium to large commercial farmers who could purchase the recommended fertilizers and insecticides.[29] Wheat cultivation was so successful that by 1951 new seed varieties constituted 70 percent of total acre-age.[30] The amount of land under wheat cultivation increased by 25 percent between 1952 and 1958, but the overall wheat output increased by 127 percent. The increase in production, then, can be attributed to the modernization of farming practices, such as the widespread use of improved seeds and increased irrigation and fertilizer use.

The State Food Agency's policies toward wheat complemented the expansion in wheat production, making Mexico self-sufficient in wheat production. Wheat producers, already a fairly strong and coherent group, were successfully able to pressure Agency officials to limit the imports of wheat to benefit producers. Between 1954 and 1958, the Agency purchased an average of 38 percent of the national production and no longer had to import wheat regularly (Table 6-4).[31]

Table 6-4. State Food Agency Purchases of Beans, Corn, and Wheat as a Percentage of National Production (P) and Total Supply (S), 1952–1958

Year	Bean		Corn		Wheat	
	P	S	P	S	P	S
1952	ND	ND	ND	0.8	ND	45.6
1953	2.2	16.2	ND	9.6	5.7	30.5
1954	ND	ND	16.9	19.4	33.7	37.8
1955	19.2	21.2	16.0	16.2	37.9	39.4
1956	ND	ND	8.4	10.9	30.1	35.3
1957	10.0	10.1	3.6	13.2	48.3	47.7
1958	ND	ND	9.7	16.1	41.8	41.7

Source: Data calculated from CONASUPO, *El mercado de las subsistencias populares*, 2 vols. (México, 1988); and Aída Mostkoff and Enrique C. Ochoa, "Complexities of Measuring the Food Situation in Mexico: Supply versus Self-Sufficiency of Basic Grains, 1925–86," in James W. Wilkie, ed., *Society and Economy in Mexico* (Los Angeles: UCLA Latin American Center Press, 1990).
Note: ND = no data.

Due to a variety of factors, per capita agricultural output had been expanding since the mid-1940s and continued throughout the 1950s. During the Ruiz Cortines years, per capita production of three of the four basic staples showed increases over output during the Alemán administration. Bean production per capita was 56.5 percent greater during the Ruiz Cortines administration, wheat was 46 percent greater, and corn was 6.3 percent greater. To deal with the increase in output and with the expected increase as technical expertise improved, the State Food Agency sought to better coordinate production and consumption.[32]

From 1952 to 1958, the State Food Agency improved its influence in the countryside. Upgrades of transportation throughout the country linked relatively isolated regions to national markets. The incorporation of new producers, planting of more land for basic grains, and use of improved seed varieties for wheat led to increased production and the ever-present need for improved storage facilities. The State Food Agency purchased an average of 38 percent of the wheat supply between 1954 and 1958 and an average of 12 percent of the yearly corn supply. To a lesser extent, the Agency was involved in the bean market, controlling up to 19 percent throughout the *sexenio* (see Table 6-4).

Careful analysis of BANCOMEXT's allotment to the State Food Agency reveals the extent to which the government focused on grain purchases. The amount of funds targeted for the purchase of corn and wheat generally averaged over 70 percent of the total loans destined for price regulation. Throughout the *sexenio* corn surpassed wheat in receiving the bulk of the credits for price regulation (Table 6-5). Beans received an increasing share throughout the administration, culminating at 18 percent in 1956.

Table 6-5. The Percentage of BANCOMEXT Credits to the State Food Agency, by Product, 1950–1957

Year	Beans	Corn	Wheat	Eggs	Other
1950	2.6	21.2	63.6	0.3	12.3
1951	1.1	30.1	50.7	2.6	15.5
1952	4.8	26.4	47.3	3.2	18.3
1953	8.8	51.3	23.4	5.0	11.5
1954	8.2	52.1	19.9	3.9	15.9
1955	12.7	59.9	5.1	0.5	21.8
1956	18.4	43.6	28.2	1.3	8.5
1957	6.9	32.9	37.5	0.4	22.3

Source: Adapted from BANCOMEXT, *Informe del consejo* (1952–1958).

Under Ruiz Cortines, the State Food Agency purchased increasing quantities of basic grains. Whereas in 1953 it imported 25 percent of the national supply of wheat and purchased 5.7 percent of national production, five years later the ratios shifted to zero imports and 42 percent of national production. Its operations in corn also showed signs of increased national purchases, yet not to the same degree as with wheat. During the first half of the administration (1952–1955), the amount of national corn that the Agency purchased reached unprecedented heights—17 percent in 1954. The initial push for the purchase of national corn and then a return to greater corn imports is reflected in loans extended by foreign trade banks. During periods of greater national purchases, corn received a larger share of the State Food Agency's attention; the opposite was true when increased imports affected the amount of credit contracts (Tables 6-4, 6-5).

Part of the reason for the massive importation of corn during this period can be attributed to the Agency's own pricing policy. One of Ruiz Cortines's major contributions to the Agency's operations was the establishment of a uniform guaranteed price for the basic grains.[33] Although there had been a guaranteed price system since 1937, it operated erratically and was not announced until after the harvest, thus reducing the impact it had on stimulating crop production. Another major shortcoming of the old pricing system was that it was poorly publicized, which resulted in the relatively infrequent selling of grains to the Agency by smaller producers.

In his 1954 state of the nation address, Ruiz Cortines announced that the guaranteed price would be publicized prior to planting.[34] This explicit emphasis on the announcement of guaranteed prices allowed it to be used to stimulate agricultural production. The new guaranteed price system was well publicized, and the State Food Agency made a greater effort than in the past to coordinate with agricultural banks and the secretary of agriculture to set the guaranteed price and to purchase from more producers. Although the exact nature of the process that was used to establish the guaranteed price is unclear, it appears that it was set in response to political realities. During the first year after the establishment of the new pricing system, guaranteed prices rose for beans, corn, and wheat. Then the prices fluctuated greatly, plummeting for beans and wheat by 1958 and rising for corn (Table 6-6).

Table 6-6. Real Average Guaranteed Prices, 1953–1958 (1950 pesos/ton)

Year	Beans	Corn	Wheat
1953	925	370	614
1954	1,030	378	627
1955	893	327	543
1956	841	315	512
1957	792	359	482
1958	758	404	461

Source: CONASUPO, *El mercado de las subsistencias populares*, 2 vols. (México, 1988). Deflated using the wholesale price index in James W. Wilkie, "From Economic Growth to Economic Stagnation in Mexico: Statistical Series for Understanding Pre- and Post-1982 Change," in James W. Wilkie, David Lorey, and Enrique Ochoa, eds., *Statistical Abstract of Latin America*, vol. 26 (Los Angeles: UCLA Latin American Center Publications, 1988).

Despite declines in real guaranteed prices during most years of the Ruiz Cortines administration, producers were largely protected from the world market as guaranteed prices were maintained above world prices. By the end of the Ruiz Cortines administration, the guaranteed price for corn was 35 percent above the world price, whereas the guaranteed price for wheat was 3 percent above the world price (Tables 6-7, 6-8). Since wheat production was a much more commercial venture than that for corn and producers tended to be larger and better equipped to take advantage of economies of scale and technological innovation, wheat producers were able to obtain better yields than corn growers. Thus the seemingly low rate of protection of 3 percent afforded to wheat was not as disadvantageous as it might appear (Table 6-8).

Table 6-7. Corn's Implicit Rate of Protection from the World Market, 1953–1958 (pesos per ton)

Years	A^a U.S. Wholesale Price	B^b Nominal/Mexico Guaranteed Price	C^c Transfer to Producer	D^d Transfer to Producer (%)
1953	519.0	500	-19.0	-3.7
1954	657.7	550	-107.7	-16.4
1955	612.5	550	-62.5	-10.2
1956	650.0	680	30.0	4.6
1957	600.0	800	200.0	33.3
1958	600.0	800	200.0	33.3

[a]United Nations Food and Agricultural Organization, *Production Yearbook* (various years).
[b]From Table 6-6.
[c]C = B - A.
[d]D + C / A.

Table 6-8. Wheat's Implicit Rate of Protection from the World Market, 1953–1958 (pesos per ton)

Years	A^a U.S. Wholesale Price	B^b Nominal/Mexico Guaranteed Price	C^c Transfer to Producer	D^d Transfer to Producer (%)
1953	717.9	830	112.1	15.6
1954	941.2	913	-28.2	-3.0
1955	1,025.0	913	-112.0	-10.9
1956	1,012.0	913	-99.0	-9.8
1957	987.5	913	-74.5	-7.5
1958	887.5	913	25.5	2.9

[a]United Nations Food and Agricultural Organization, *Production Yearbook* (various years).
[b]From Table 6-6.
[c]C = B - A.
[d]D + C / A.

Although at first glance corn producers seemed to be in a privileged position because the guaranteed price of domestic corn was greater than the import price from 1956 to 1958, this was not the case. The surplus of corn in the United States depressed prices and the United States sought various means of selling corn cheaply to neighboring countries.[35] The relatively low price proved tempting for the State Food Agency officials in Mexico City, who sought to flood the market with inexpensive corn to lower its price to consumers.

Nonetheless, the State Food Agency made a number of attempts to expand its purchasing operations throughout the country. It worked closely with the agricultural banks, the secretary of agriculture, and ANDSA. During the early years of the Ruiz Cortines administration, the most important agricultural bank, the BNCE, began to ask the Agency to establish agencies in various regions to aid them in the purchase of crops so that the BNCE would be better able to control the harvests of its clients. As a result of such lobbying, by 1958 some fifty-nine Agency offices were established throughout the country, employing 506 persons.[36]

With regard to credit, the BNCE sought to increase controls over debtors to ensure that loans were repaid. BNCE officials were especially concerned with the loans to corn and bean producers because the bank traditionally had difficulty in getting these producers to repay their loans. Although loan recuperation was relatively high for the lucrative commercial crops, such as cotton and coffee (83 and 95 percent, respectively), the rate for most crops was 75 percent, worse for corn. Recuperation for corn was extremely low—hovering just over 50 percent.[37] In fact, analysis of the bank's operations reveals that when it financed smaller amounts of corn, it lost less money, and conversely, the more it funded the more it lost. The two years that the bank saw profits (1943 and 1950) were years in which it financed only small amounts of corn production. By working with the State Food Agency, bank officials thought they would be better able to control the loans because they could force borrowers to sell to the State Food Agency, and thus the BNCE could recoup its loans.

Ejidatarios, however, resisted these coercive practices. To avoid repaying their bank loans, many *ejidatarios* sold their crops to local merchants at prices lower than the guaranteed price.[38] Often, small producers just did not deem the guaranteed price remunerative enough to sell to government agencies, especially if that meant they had to repay their loans. This was especially the case when the guaranteed price was only slightly higher than the local price. Because sellers had to transport the crop to the place of purchase, generally a designated railroad station or a government-operated storage facility, they often found it more convenient to sell to a local merchant and avoid transportation and handling costs altogether.[39] Because corn producers were generally not large-scale farmers but were often marginalized within the economic system, forced loan payments meant little money left for household expenditures.

Owing to improved roads and transportation, the State Food Agency was able to purchase more widely and more strategically penetrate new areas. To integrate the various regions of Mexico, Ruiz Cortines stepped up the expansion of the country's transportation infrastructure. Building upon the work of past administrations, many of the road and rail construction and improvement programs were continued, as total federal government expenditure on communications and public works reached an all-time high. In constant per capita figures, the Ruiz Cortines administration spent an average of 20.7 pesos a year, compared to 18.8 pesos spent under Alemán and 10.1 pesos under Avila Camacho.[40] One of the programs that Ruiz Cortines supported was expansion of the farm-to-market road program begun under Alemán. As we would expect, such roads aided in expanding the commercial possibilities of the countryside but led to an increased demand for more storage facilities.

That the State Food Agency began to purchase grains throughout the country made it even more imperative to increase storage capacity to maintain a regulating stock in various smaller urban centers. The government sought to expand Mexico's storage capacity for corn and beans. In doing so, the Agency worked closely with ANDSA.

Between the time of its creation in 1936 and 1956, ANDSA had been a relatively small and ineffective agency. Although various sectors of society had recognized that the expansion of state-owned agricultural warehouses was essential for the greater integration of various regions and to supply the expanding urban areas, little concrete action had been taken. Under Alemán, ANDSA and the State Food Agency undertook only a few large-scale projects such as the construction of grain elevators in the major ports and the building of Silos Miguel Alemán to store grains for Mexico City. It was not until the Ruiz Cortines administration, however, that there was any significant expansion of storage capacity in the states.

The emphasis that Ruiz Cortines gave to ANDSA's operations can be seen in the amount of capital that the federal government invested in it. During the *sexenio*, the fixed capital of ANDSA expanded more than eightfold in current pesos. In 1939, capital doubled from 5 million to 10 million pesos. Sixteen years later, in 1955, the fixed capital was augmented to 25 million pesos, and then increased twice more—in August 1956 it leaped to 65 million, and then in August 1957 it rose to 85 million pesos.[41]

Government studies during the period again demonstrated the need for an active state storage system. A 1954 study concluded that there was a lack of adequate storage capacity in at least forty-nine of the country's principal population centers. The study observed that the vast majority of warehouses were unevenly distributed, favoring urban over rural areas. Thus, ANDSA officials, in collaboration with secretary of agriculture and the State Food Agency, decided that it was essential to build more warehouses in rural areas. The agricultural valleys of Sonora and Sinaloa, Mexico City, Torreón, Saltillo, and Monterrey urgently needed increased storage capacity, even as the number of warehouses controlled by ANDSA and the total amount of storage capacity declined by 11 percent from the 1953 level.[42] In some cases, the lack of grain depositories in various regions led government agencies to use the local theater to store grain, as was the case in Ixtlahuaca in the state of Mexico in early 1955.[43]

To address the inadequate storage situation, ANDSA devised a plan in 1955 to build a network of eighty warehouses with a 400,000-ton capacity aimed at storing corn and beans in both urban and rural areas (Table 6-9).[44] The increase in the institution's social capital to 40 million pesos by 1956 was primarily targeted for the construction of these warehouses.[45] By building storage facilities in rural zones, the government was attempting to extend its operations to benefit producers who had long complained of the lack of storage facilities.

At the same time that ANDSA was expanding its storage capacity for corn and beans, so too was SAG. In 1954 and 1955, the agricultural secretariat was constructing thirty-eight warehouses in various regions with a capacity of 187,000 tons. The secretariat also purchased thirteen storehouses with a capacity of 27,889 tons. These forty-one new facilities, along with the nineteen already in possession of the secretariat, gave SAG a total of fifty-nine warehouses with a total capacity of 224,789 tons.[46]

With new warehouses, ANDSA and the SAG together had constructed a network of government storage facilities that spanned the Mexican republic. Warehouses were constructed in twenty-four different states and the Federal District, generally in the principal city within each state. Although some smaller agriculturally based towns, such as Ciudad Guzmán in Jalisco and Perote in Veracruz, also received several warehouses, the new warehouses were concentrated in urban areas, contrary to the recommendations of ANDSA's internal studies.

Table 6-9. ANDSA's National Network of Warehouses, Established in 1954

Site	State	Number of Warehouses	Capacity (tons)
Aguascalientes	Aguascalientes	3	15,000
Ciudad Guzmán	Jalisco	4	20,000
Chihuahua	Chihuahua	4	20,000
Culiacán	Sinaloa	3	15,000
Federal District	Federal District	12	60,000
Durango	Durango	3	15,000
Esperanza	Puebla	4	20,000
Guadalajara	Jalisco	9	45,000
Hermosillo	Sonora	2	10,000
Irapuato	Guanajuato	5	25,000
Mérida	Yucatán	3	15,000
Perote	Veracruz	8	40,000
Puebla	Puebla	2	10,000
Saltillo	Coahuila	13	65,000
	Baja California	2	10,000
Toluca	México	3	15,000
Total		80	400,000

Source: Almacenes Nacionales de Depósito, S.A. *Informe del consejo,* 1955.

With the addition of new storage facilities, which were completed by the end of the Ruiz Cortines administration, the State Food Agency became more active in seeking to ensure that urban centers had a reserve of grains. It had been the role of the Agency and its predecessors since the early 1940s to supply cities with grains as needed, but this role was enhanced with the expansion of roads and increased storage capacity. Enhanced infrastructure made it possible for the State Food Agency to flood cities with basic grains to stem "high" prices or shortages. For example, when in early 1953 merchants refused to sell corn and beans at official prices in Guanajuato, then State Food Agency director Tomás Valles Vivar that ordered ten railcars filled with corn and beans be sent to Guanajuato for immediate sale.[47] This type of relief action continued and increased throughout the Ruiz Cortines administration as the number of cities with Agency staff and improved storage and communication facilities rose throughout the republic.[48]

The State Food Agency was also used, to a greater extent than ever before, as a relief agency, providing foodstuffs to victims of natural disaster. This occurred first during torrential rains and floods in Veracruz and northern Hidalgo in late 1954 and continued throughout the administration.[49]

Expanding the Base of Urban Programs

The reorganization of the countryside to meet the needs of an expanding internal market meant that urban-based distribution programs would have to become more efficient and far-reaching. Throughout the Ruíz Cortines administration, the State Food Agency strengthened its marketing and distribution operations and began to involve itself in other markets, such as milk and eggs. Although it had gained much experience in selling grain and occasionally vegetable oil and salt, it had not delved much into the distribution of such items as milk and eggs. This movement into new markets complemented many of the Agency's traditional activities, including supplying mills with corn and wheat at subsidized prices and operating a network of stores throughout working class areas.

During the Ruiz Cortines administration, the State Food Agency expanded its program supplying grains to millers at subsidized prices. Once it purchased the grain, from national or foreign producers, it sold it to millers, especially those in the Federal District. During mid-1954, the Agency supplied all 743 *molinos de nixtamal* (corn mills) in the Federal District, with a total of 721.5 tons daily, to produce a million kilograms of tortillas.[50]

The retail marketing programs of the State Food Agency were strongest in Mexico City. By 1958, 460 Agency stores had been established and operated in over a hundred neighborhoods in all sections of the city. Aside from these stores, every Sunday and Monday mobile stores went to areas that did not have stores. Thirty different routes were covered, servicing forty-three different neighborhoods.[51] Also, by 1958 the Agency was supplying foodstuff to members and employees of fifty-three different unions and public sector agencies throughout the city. In the surrounding states of Mexico and Hidalgo the Agency operated forty-eight and five stores, respectively.[52]

As the urban programs of the State Food Agency continued to increase, the results of government intervention in the milling industry and in retail marketing seems to have kept the prices of staple goods below the general price level. The price of corn in Agency stores averaged some 50 percent below the market price in 1954.[53] For two-thirds of the Ruiz Cortines administration, the average price of tortillas in Mexico City was maintained at or below the wholesale price of maize.[54] Although we must be careful in attributing the entire "implicit subsidy" to the State Food Agency, it did sell grains to millers at prices lower than the purchase price, thus aiding the millers and shielding the consumer from increases in corn prices.

General prices in the Agency stores also seem to have been lower than the average prices of fourteen public supermarkets in Mexico City. Goods sold in the larger public markets of Mexico City were more expensive than those same items sold in Agency stores (Table 6-10). Although prices differed markedly, depending on the individual item, they ranged from anywhere from 7 percent cheaper for sesame seed oil to three times less for black beans.

Table 6-10. Comparison of Prices of Eight Items Sold in State Food Agency Stores with Items Sold in Private Stores in Mexico City, March 22, 1958

Item	Unit	Average Price in 14 Markets	Prices in State Food Agency Stores
Beef	Kg.	10.00	9.50
Pork	Kg.	14.75	12.50
Sesame seed oil	Liter	4.78	4.45
Black beans	Kg.	3.20	1.40
Beans	Kg.	4.49	1.40
Coffee with sugar	Kg.	2.85	2.50
Rice	Kg.	2.85	2.50
Eggs (fresh)	Piece	0.51	0.45

Source: CEIMSA, Departamento de investigaciones, "Estudio comparativo de precios de artículos del mercado libre segun datos del Departamento de Barometros Económicos y artículos CEIMSA," in CEIMSA, Acta del Consejo no. 698, March 24, 1958, CONASUPO-BAT.

Not all was rosy in the State Food Agency's retail operations, however. The two most glaring weaknesses were that the Agency favored Mexico City over other urban areas and the fact that it operated at a substantial financial loss. It gradually spread out much of its retail operations, but its stores continued to be overwhelmingly located in Mexico City. Also, the subsidies that millers in Mexico City received were greater than those received by provincial millers. Overall, by 1956, it was estimated that 75 percent of the Agency's operations were concentrated in Mexico City.[55] Such retail operations led to a mounting deficit. Between 1953 and 1959, it lost some 46 million pesos a year in its retail operations (not including subsidies granted for corn and wheat).[56] This sum translates into the equivalent of 20 percent of the federal government subsidies granted to the Agency during this period. These deficiencies in the retail operations were left to other administrations to resolve.

The State Food Agency continued to expand into the milk and egg markets. In both cases it responded to what it saw as potentially incendiary situations, sparked by decline in production of these two products and a resultant increase in prices. To protect consumers, it intervened to import these items and explore ways to prevent further shortages. To prevent prices from rising, the Agency intervened vigorously in the distribution of milk and eggs, which faced severe shortages throughout the 1950s. As milk prices rose with the general inflation of 1953 and 1954, due to the scarcity of milk triggered by hoof and mouth disease, the Agency expanded the milk programs initiated under the previous administration by increasing the amount imported and creating plants to recombine the milk. Similarly, as an outbreak of Newcastle Epitoozoa began to ravage the egg industry, the Agency responded by importing large quantities of eggs and then attempting to store them by bottling and freezing them.

Continuing to import powdered milk, the State Food Agency first sought to build more plants to recombine the milk in the wake of price increases and to gain more control over the milk trade. Its actions in the milk sector were highly criticized by cattle ranchers, who saw the government undercutting their price with inferior quality milk. During the early 1950s, after intense negotiations between milk producers and government officials, the producers agreed to allow the Agency to produce and sell 5,000 liters of bottled milk a day to supplement their production and to reach the poorer sectors of the urban population.

Shortly after the agreement, however, the producers realized that the State Food Agency was overstepping the accord by allowing the recombination of some 17,000 liters a day and selling it at stores near milk outlets. Producers demanded the reduction of powdered milk imports and greater protection of the milk industry.[57] In the Mexico City press, a virtual war erupted over the merits of pure milk versus recombined milk.

Ranchers met with Undersecretary of Health Gustavo Argil to defend their interests, and by 1953 an agreement was reached.[58] Ruiz Cortines's accord with ranchers made the State Food Agency the sole importer of powdered milk for supplementing production only. The federal government also committed itself to aiding ranchers in rebuilding the pure milk industry by restocking the cattle population through an artificial insemination program and by building stables.[59]

The cattle ranchers had legitimate concerns regarding the volatility of sales in their industry. Although by the 1950s pasteurized milk consumption in the Federal District began to increase, it did not keep pace with population growth. Pasteurized milk consumption in the Federal District more than tripled between 1932 and 1958, but the area's population nearly quintupled.[60] Per capita consumption of pasteurized fresh milk declined markedly during the first half of the 1950s, largely due to the decline in output caused by the hoof and mouth disease.[61] Of the fresh milk consumed in the Federal District during the mid-1950s, it was estimated that at least 28 percent was not pasteurized and evaded legal controls.[62] Coupled with the decline in milk production were problems in the distribution of milk. One study estimated the cost of distribution as accounting for some 40 percent of the consumer's cost. In Mexico City, for example, producers from the northern section of the city were selling their milk in the southern part of the city and vice versa.[63] The general lack of refrigerated transportation and storage facilities made the transportation of milk from the countryside to the burgeoning urban areas increasingly more difficult.

To alleviate the milk scarcity and resultant price increases, the State Food Agency stepped up its imports of powdered milk and became an important milk producer and supplier during the Ruiz Cortines administration. In 1954 imports surpassed their pre-1953 tonnage, with 8,222 being imported. By 1958 the amount of powdered milk imports tripled to over 25,000 tons.[64] The Agency began to operate its own milk recombination plants in 1953. Although it had been subsidizing other plants, such as Lechería Nacional, it saw the need for an increased role in the milk industry in large cities, especially in the ever-growing national capital. The first plant to open was at Tlalnepantla in the northern section of the Valley of Mexico. The physical location of this plant in the state of Mexico meant that it could supply the expanding capital city with sufficient milk at low prices, initially producing 35,000 liters of milk a day.[65] The recombined milk was bottled and sold in Agency stores primarily in the working-class districts of Mexico City, for as low as 53 percent of the price of fresh milk during the mid-1950s.[66]

As with other programs of the State Food Agency, however, intervention in the milk market created numerous problems.

Propaganda "milk wars" waged by cattle ranchers against recombined milk contributed to rumors that the Agency milk was an adulterated product causing illness, and indeed, its milk was adulterated, and the recombination plants used improperly treated water.[67] In 1958, inspectors of the Agency found a variety of irregularities in the operation of Lechería Nacional's milk recombination plant. The inspectors witnessed employees use the amount of powder needed to make 132,000 liters of milk to produce 139,000. The inspectors also found irregularities in the water treatment plant: the requisite amount of chlorine was not found in the water, and bottles were not being washed with chlorine. It was also found that the milk was not well refrigerated, being outside most of the day and transported on unrefrigerated trucks.[68]

Despite problems in the operation of recombined milk, the process was relatively simple and made milk more accessible to the working classes. Milk recombination plants were responsible for the production of over 200 million liters of milk during the Ruiz Cortines *sexenio*, equaling approximately 11 percent of the total milk consumed in the Federal District. Of the 11 percent, the recombination plants of the State Food Agency were responsible for over half.[69] According to the director Agency, its various programs accounted for 15 percent of the milk consumed in the Federal District by 1958.[70]

To stimulate milk production and reduce the importation of powdered milk from the United States, the Agency began construction of a plant to make Mexico's own powdered milk. This plant, constructed in cooperation with the United Nations Children's Fund (UNICEF) and the Food and Agriculture Organization (FAO) in Jiquilpan, Michoacán, was targeted for completion in mid-1958 but was delayed and did not begin operation until the López Mateos administration, when it produced 120,000 liters of milk per day.[71]

Despite the initial negative reaction by producers, they gradually came to accept the role of recombination, especially when the State Food Agency plant in Jiquilpan began to condense national milk. To overcome the milk industry's backwardness, the Agency took over even larger shares of milk production, especially because it sold milk to the poor sectors of the population.[72]

During the 1950s, the State Food Agency also entered the egg market. An outbreak of disease that decimated the hen population prompted the Agency to move beyond the importation of eggs to supplement declines in production. The operating fund of the Agency in the 1950s gave greater preference to eggs, with the board of directors raising the amount of subsidies targeted for eggs from

2 million pesos to 15 million pesos between 1955 and 1957.[73] As egg shortages grew worse, the Agency made an effort to bypass the high cost of importing eggs by making use of new technologies preserving eggs in liquid form, which was seen as an effective way to transport and store eggs as well as to maintain a reserve. The bold Agency policy on eggs brought new problems.

Egg production was primarily a local operation until the 1930s. Without refrigerated cars and effective packaging methods, distributing eggs throughout the country was difficult. Although the production price of eggs was generally considered low by international standards, it could not compete with imported eggs because rudimentary packaging led to large amounts of breakage. The eggs were generally transported by rail in variously shaped baskets and boxes wrapped in tissue paper. Many egg distributors were campesinos who, on a daily basis, brought relatively small numbers of eggs on foot from long distances, while producers in the United States would take advantage of economies of scale and more sophisticated handling and storage technology to export a cheaper product.[74]

Several attempts had been made to overcome the supply and distribution problems in the egg industry. A 1904 tariff exemption allowed rising importation of eggs to help overcome Mexico's shortfall of production and distribution problems. Gradually, however, greater import restrictions were imposed to protect the nascent industry, such as in 1922 when the tariff was set at 9 percent of import value. Throughout the 1920s yearly imports ranged from 3 to 7 million kilograms a year. This importation, however, came to a halt in December 1930 when the tariff rate for egg importation was set at 67 percent of import value.[75] The move to greater protection of the national egg market was seen as a way to increase national production. Although by 1950 egg production per capita in Mexico had doubled from forty-eight eggs per person to ninety-seven, consumption per capita was less than two eggs per week.

The relatively low per capita production of eggs further declined during the early 1950s. An outbreak of the disease Newcastle Epitoozoa reduced egg production by 13 percent, to 86 eggs per person.[76] Immediately, egg prices began to rise; retail price levels of eggs in Mexico City increased by 55 percent between 1949 and 1952. This increase was the most dramatic increase in egg prices since the height of wartime inflation in 1943–1945.[77]

Once disease was detected in hens in 1949, the State Food Agency began to import eggs, and the first shipment arrived from the United States in September. The eggs were sold in the various Agency stores for 30 centavos each, some 10–12 cents below the going rate for eggs in Mexico City.[78] The initial purchases of fresh eggs were in relatively small amounts. Yet by 1953, the amount of powdered eggs imported grew from 10,000 tons in 1949 to 374,000 tons.[79] Imports of fresh eggs continued at an increasing rate, while the BANCOMEXT and the Department of Agriculture devised a strategy to rebuild the crisis-ridden industry.

The State Food Agency devoted increasing amounts of money to importing eggs during the early 1950s. Most of these funds went to subsidizing prices at a financial loss.[80] By 1954, a small portion of the purchase was national, and this share continued to grow significantly, so that by 1958 over 95 percent of the powdered eggs purchased were nationally produced. By October 1958, the Agency was purchasing thousands of boxes of eggs at 9.60–9.70 pesos a kilogram, which it sold at a retail price of 9.50, some 50 centavos under the official price.[81] The major problem in selling eggs was the high rate of breakage. It was estimated that at least one-third, and usually more, of the eggs in boxes broke during the handling process.[82]

To resolve this problem and to find new ways to store the eggs, beginning in 1958 the State Food Agency began to process eggs, bottle them in liquid form, and freeze them to decrease the probability of breakage and spoilage allowing the government to store large amounts of eggs to be released on the markets in case of a shortage. Agency officials encountered numerous technical difficulties, many of which might have been avoided had market research been carried out. The processed eggs were not popular with consumers, and they did not catch on as a viable substitute for fresh eggs. Even when the price had dropped to 5 pesos per kilogram, 40 percent of the stored bottles spoiled.[83] There were also widespread complaints about the smell of the bottled eggs.[84] The eggs were difficult to sell for various reasons. Aside from the smell, they were only sold in 10-kilogram containers, much too large for the average family because the majority of working-class households did not have refrigeration. The bacteriological breakdown of the eggs was rapid, and because the eggs were not consumed immediately they spoiled quickly. State Food Agency officials concluded that their best option was to market this product for industrial use, such as enriching milk for use in schools, hospitals, and other public facilities.[85]

Because the advanced technological process required to liquefy and store eggs was not a viable solution for mass marketing eggs, the State Food Agency began to explore other operations for overcoming the shortfall in egg production and the distribution problems. Only the State Food Agency's investment in poultry raising would increase fresh egg production levels.[86]

The Agency's urban operations expanded with great speed during the Ruiz Cortines administration. It increased the number of stores that it operated in the urban areas and took active roles in the marketing of milk and eggs. Results in the milk and egg markets varied owing to differences in the industries: milk recombination gained more adherence due to the relatively simple and inexpensive process, whereas egg dehydration and recombination was a more arduous process that made increased production of fresh eggs more desirable.

Conclusion

During the presidency of Adolfo Ruiz Cortines, the State Food Agency was used as a "catch-all" agency to perform various types of social welfare functions. Cracks in the political system were beginning to appear with the elections of 1952; in the Federal District there were waves of consumer panic following the monetary devaluation of 1954. Both led the government to concentrate on relief efforts that sought to keep prices of staple goods down and to expand the State Food Agency's role by establishing stores throughout the city.

In the countryside, the Agency worked with the ANDSA to modernize storage and handling of basic grains. However, under Ruiz Cortines the Agency sought to reach out to a wider segment of the producer population, by expanding the number of grain reception centers and setting up a more stable and widely publicized guaranteed pricing system. These polices continued to benefit larger producers, especially wheat producers, who were able to convince the Agency to purchase large amounts of national production first and import wheat only when there were production shortfalls. Although small producers did not immediately flock to sell their goods to the Agency, due in part to their desire to circumvent repaying loans to the state agricultural banks, the mechanisms were put in place for the State Food Agency to reach more marginalized producers and incorporate them into the national market. These changes in the countryside would provide the basis for later reforms as the rural population begin to more actively struggle for greater federal government support under the administration of Adolfo López Mateos.

In its effort to keep the prices of basic goods low to supplement wages, the State Food Agency intervened in new markets and in new ways. With the outbreak of diseases that reduced the production of milk and eggs, the State Food Agency first imported foods and, then, realizing that the problems were greater than merely a low supply, began to process foods. Under Ruíz Cortines the State Food Agency became a major player in the milk market. Inexperienced moves into new and complicated industries created unintended problems for the State Food Agency but did provide relief from price increases during scarcity.

Notes

1. See Clark W. Reynolds, *The Mexican Economy: Twentieth-Century Structure and Growth* (New Haven, Conn.: Yale University Press, 1970), appendix D.

2. Calculated from Instituto Nacional de Estadística, Geografía, e Informática, *Estadísticas históricas de México* (México: Secretaría de Programación y Presupuesto, 1985), vol. 1, pp. 24–33.

3. See the series of articles on population and infrastructure in Banco Nacional de México, *Examen de la situación económica de México, 1925–1976*.

4. See Jeffrey L. Bortz, *Los salarios industriales en la ciudad de México, 1939–1975* (México: Fondo de Cultura Económica, 1988), p. 252. See also Table 6-2.

5. Although the election of 1952 has yet to be fully treated, good introductions to the subject can be found in Olga Pellicer de Brody, "La oposición en México; El caso del henriquismo," in *La crisis en el sistema político mexicano, 1928–1977* (México: El Colegio de México, 1977), pp. 31–45; and Carlos Martínez Assad, *El henriquismo, una piedra en el camino* (México: Martin Casillas editores, 1982).

6. See Ruiz Cortines's various statements on the increasing cost of living in *Ideario Ruíz-Cortinista*, bulletins 115 (April 28, 1952), 120 (May 6, 1952), 136 (May 24, 1952).

7. Jacqueline Peschard, in "Las elecciones en el Distrito Federal (1946–1970)," *Revista Mexicana de Sociología* 50:3 (July–September, 1988), pp. 235–236, reports that Ruiz Cortines garnered 49 percent of the vote. James W. Wilkie cites this figure at 51.4 percent, "New Hypotheses for Statistical Research," in James W. Wilkie, *Statistics and National Policy* (Los Angeles: UCLA Latin American Center Publications, 1974), p. 28.

8. "Ramón Beteta, político y haciendista," in James W. Wilkie and Edna Monzón de Wilkie, *Mexico visto en el siglo XX: Entrevistas de historia oral.* (Mexico: Instituto Mexicano de Investigaciones Económicas, 1969), pp. 48–49.

9. On February 5, 1953, the *New York Times* noted the shift in government slogans away from large-scale industrialization to the protection of the interests of peasants and workers.

10. See "La dura batalla," *Siempre*, September 12, 1953.

11. Roderic A. Camp, *Mexican Political Biographies, 1935–1981* (Tucson: University of Arizona Press, 1982), p. 307.

12. Olga Pellicer de Brody and Esteban L. Mancilla, *El entendimiento con los Estados Unidos y la gestión de desarrollo estabilizador, 1952–1960* (México: El Colegio de México, 1978), pp. 131–132.

13. Data on the amount of fines collected were calculated from Leopoldo Ortega Cruz, "El control de precios y su importancia en la economia del país," tesis de Licenciatura, México, UNAM, Escuela Nacional de Economía, 1965, p. 57.

14. These numerous complaints are located in AGN-ARC 521.8/3.

15. "Memo confidencial," to Ruiz Cortines from Captain Adrián Tiburcio González, January 8, 1953, AGN-ARC 521.8/3.

16. See Eduardo Rius, *Rius (1955–1958): Primeras porquerías* (México: Editorial Hereodoxo, 1973).

17. Data on the monthly cost of living are from Juan Moreno Pérez, "La economía mexicana desde 1900: Nuevas serias largas sobre producción interna bruta e inflación," unpublished manuscript, Los Angeles, 1992.

18. For discussion of the economic causes of the devaluation of 1954, see Dwight S. Brothers and Leopoldo Solís M., *Mexican Financial Development* (Austin: University of Texas Press, 1966), pp. 85–86. The impact of the devaluation on organized labor is treated in Olga Pellicer de Brody and José Luis Reyna, *Historia de la Revolución Mexicana: El afianzamiento de la estabilidad política, 1952–1960* (México: El Colegio de México, 1978), pp. 83–122.

19. Secretaría de la Economía Nacional, *Memoria*, January–December 1955, pp. 339–340; Pellicer de Brody and Reyna, *Historia de la Revolución Mexicana: El afianzamiento*, pp. 89–100.

20. *New York Times*, April 23, 1954.

21. *New York Times*, March 11, 1956.

22. *Siempre*, March, 1956; *New York Times*, March 11, 1956.

23. Pellicer de Brody and Luis Reyna, *Historia de la Revolución Mexicana: El afianzamiento de la estabilidad política*, p. 25.

24. See Robert J. Shafer, *Mexican Business Organizations: History and Analysis* (Syracuse, N.Y.: Syracuse University Press, 1973).

25. "Dictamen que rinde la comisión especial que suscribe, sobre la Compañía Exportadora e Importadora Mexicana, S.A." (August 21, 1956), in *Boletín del Archivo General de la Nación*, tercera serie, tomo VII, vol. I (22) (January–March, 1983), pp. 47–57.

26. Raymond Vernon, *The Dilemma of Mexico's Development: The Role of the Public and Private Sectors* (Cambridge, Mass.: Harvard University Press, 1964), p. 170.

27. E. C. Stakman, Richard Bradfield, and Paul C. Mangelsdorf, *Campaigns against Hunger* (Cambridge, Mass.: Belknap Press of Harvard University Press, 1967), p. 70.

28. Nicolás Ardito-Barletta, "Costs and Social Benefits of Agricultural Research in Mexico," Ph.D. diss., University of Chicago, 1971, pp. 16–17.

29. Ibid., p. 109.

30. Stakman, Brodfield, and Mangelsdorf, *Campaigns against Hunger*, pp. 7, 72–80.

31. See Hugo Azpeitia Gómez, *Compañía Exportadora e Importadora Mexicana, S.A. (1949–1958): Conflicto y abasto alimentario* (México: Centro de Investiganciones y Estudios Superiores en Antropología Social, 1994), chap. 5.

32. Calculated from Aída Mostkoff and Enrique C. Ochoa, "Complexities of Measuring the Food Situation in Mexico: Supply versus Self-Sufficiency of Basic Grains, 1925–86," in James W. Wilkie, ed., *Society and Economy in Mexico* (Los Angeles: UCLA Latin American Center Press, 1990).

33. Agustín Acosta L., "La política de subsistencias," *Cuestiones nacionales*, vol. 1 (México: Ediciones del Instituto Nacional de la Juventud Mexicana, 1964), pp. 81–82; Cynthia Hewitt de Alcántara, *La modernización de la agricultura mexicana, 1940–1970* (México: Siglo Veintiuno Editores, 1978), pp. 90–94; Ricardo Solís Rosales, "Precios de garantía y política agraria: Un análisis de largo plazo," *Comercio Exterior* 40:10 (October 1990), pp. 923–937.

34. BNCE, *Boletín de Estudios Especiales*, no. 19 (September 27, 1954).

35. For discussion of the U.S. Department of Agriculture's surplus grain disposal program, see *Hearing before the Committee on Agriculture, House of Representatives, Eighty-Fourth Congress*, May 27, 1955.

36. CEIMSA, "Acta de Asamblea," no. 693 (February 17, 1958), CONASUPO-BAT.

37. "Recuperación normal y de atraso por años sucesivos promedios de los ciclos 1949–50 a 1953–54," in BNCE, *Boletín de Estudios Especiales*, no. 46 (February 18, 1956), p. 295.

38. "La cosecha de maíz, tonamil en la agencia de Martínez de la Torre, Veracruz: Informe rendida por la agencia, invierno 1953–54," in BNCE, *Boletín de Estudios Especiales*, no. 22 (December 27, 1954); "Informe de la Agencia en Querétaro, Querétaro, 1954," BNCE, *Boletín de Estudios Especiales*, no. 28 (March 21, 1955), pp. 97–100.

39. Examples of this practice are described in the Secretaría de Agricultura y Gandería, *Boletín Mensual de la Dirección General de Economía Rural*, no. 347 (April 1955).

40. Calculated from James W. Wilkie, *The Mexican Revolution: Federal Expenditure and Social Change since 1910* (Berkeley: University of California Press, 1970), pp. 144–145; see also Raymond Vernon, *The Dilemma of Mexico's Development*, p. 111. For a contrasting treatment of the transportation sector during this era, see Pellicer Brody and Mancilla, *El entendimiento con los Estados Unidos y la gestión del desarrollo estabilizador*, pp. 248–252.

41. ANDSA, *Informe del consejo de administración a la XVIII asamblea general ordinaria de accionistas Ejercicio 1969–1970* (Mexico, 1971), p. 2.

42. ANDSA, *Informe del consejo de administración 1954*, p. 4.

43. Secretaría de Agricultura y Ganadería, *Boletín Mensual de la Dirección General de Economía Rural*, no. 346 (March, 1955), p. 148.

44. ANDSA, *Informe al consejo de administración 1955*, pp. 5–7.

45. To President Ruiz Cortines from Raúl Ortiz Mena Secretaría de Hacienda y Crédito Público August 30, 1956, AGN-ARC 506.1/168; ANDSA, *Informe al consejo de administración 1955*, pp. 5–7.

46. Secretaría de Agrícultura y Ganadería, *Resumen del informe de labores de la Secretaría de Agrícultura y Ganadero del 1° de septiembre de 1953 al 31 de agosto de 1954* (México: Talleres Gráficos de la Nación, 1954), p. 40.

47. *La Prensa*, February 5, 1953.

48. The Secretaría de Agricultura y Ganadería, in *Boletín Mensual de la Dirección General de Economía Rural*, chronicled the state of the grain supply throughout Mexico, detailing the cities and situations in which CEIMSA intervened to supply the city with grains.

49. *Excelsior*, October 16, 1954; also see the various news clippings in the personal papers of the Secretaría de Recursos Hidraulicos under Ruiz Cortines, Eduardo Chávez, AGN-EC.

50. Joaquín de la Peña, José Crowley, Santos Amaro, and Héctor Calles, *El maíz en México: Datos y apreciaciones* (México: EDIAPSA, 1955), p. 78.

51. *Excelsior*, September 9, 1958.

52. Ibid.

53. de la Peña et al., *El maíz en México*, p. 61.

54. Secretaría de la Economía Nacional, Dirección General de Estadísticas, *Compendio estadístico*, various.

55. "Dictamen que rinde la comisión especial que suscribe, sobre la Compañía Exportadora e Importadora Mexicana, S.A." (August 21, 1956), in *Boletín del Archivo General de la Nación*, tercera serie, tomo VII, vol. I (22) (January–March, 1983), pp. 47–57.

56. CONASUPO, *Informes al consejo de administración*, vol. 33, acta 14, October 18, 1964,

57. Letter to President Alemán from Lic. Alfredo Pino Cámara, Asociación de Productores de Leche Pura, and Mario Rabell, president of Plantas Pasteurizadoras, May 8, 1951, AGN-MA 368/9858.

58. *Últimas Noticias*, July 1, 1952.

59. Secretaría de Agrícultura y Ganadería, *Resumen del informe de labores de la Secretaría de Agrícultura y Ganadería del 1° de septiembre de 1953 al 31 de agosto de 1954* (México: Talleres Gráficos de la Nación, 1954).

60. Calculated from INEGI, *Estadísticas históricas de México*, vol. 1, p. 24.

61. From Secretaría de la Economía Nacional, *Compendio estadístico*, 1954.

62. Acosta L., "La política de subsistencias," p. 125.

63. Ibid., p. 125.

64. CONASUPO, *El mercado de las subsistencias populares: Cincuenta años de regulación* (México, 1988).

65. *El Universal*, July 30, 1953; Agustín Acosta L., "La política de subsistencias."

66. Oscar Lewis, *Five Families: Mexican Case Studies in the Culture of Poverty* (New York: John Wiley and Sons, fourth printing, 1964) 1959, p. 222.

67. Ibid., p. 222.

68. Letter to Lechería Nacional from Sr. Sánches del Moral Sub-gerente de Servicios Industriales, CEIMSA, September 29, 1958. Documents related to "Acta de asamblea," no. 720, Sept. 29, 1958, CONASUPO-BAT.

69. CEIMSA, "Acta de asamblea," no. 714 (August 4, 1958), CONASUPO-BAT; see also Agustín Acosta L., "La política de subsistencias," p. 130.

70. Julián Rodríguez Adame, *La CEIMSA: Su función económica y social* (México: Editorial La Justicia, 1958), p. 10.

71. Letter to governor of Michoacán from CEIMSA, February 8, 1958. Documents related to "Acta de asamblea," no. 720, Sept. 29, 1958, CONASUPO-BAT; CEIMSA, "Acta de asamblea," no. 725, November 10, 1958, CONASUPO-BAT.

72. Leonardo Martín Echeverría, *La ganadería en México* (México: Banco de México, 1960).

73. "Fondo de operación," January 10, 1955, CEIMSA, "Acta de asamblea," no. 634; memorandum from José Vivanco to the board of directors, January 31, 1957, in documents related to CEIMSA, acta de Consejo, CONASUPO-BAT.

74. Secretaría de Agricultura y Fomento, "Analisis económico del comercio del huevo," mimeo (ca. 1934), AGN-LC 522/1.

75. Secretaría de Agricultura y Fomento, "Analisis ecónomico del comercio del huevo." For Mexico's broader tariff policies, see Daniel Cosio Villegas, *La cuestión arancelaria en México* (Mexico, 1932), and M. T. de la Peña, "La industrialización de México y la política arancelaria," in *El Trimestre Económico* 12:2 (July–September 1945), pp. 187–218.

76. Paul Lamartine Yates, *Mexico's Agricultural Dilemma* (Tucson: University of Arizona Press, 1981), p. 101.

77. Calculated from SEN-DGE, *Compendio estadístico*, various issues.

78. *El Universal*, September 7, 1950.

79. CONASUPO, *El mercado de las subsistencia populares: Cincuenta años de regulación* (México, 1988), vol. 1.

80. CEIMSA, "Acta de asamblea," no. 715 (August 11, 1958), CONASUPO-BAT.

81. CEIMSA, "Acta de asamblea," no. 693 (February 17, 1958), CONASUPO-BAT.

82. CEIMSA, "Acta de asamblea," no. 715 (August 11, 1958), CONASUPO-BAT.

83. Ibid.

84. CEIMSA, "Acta de asamblea," no. 693 (February 17, 1958), CONASUPO-BAT.

85. CEIMSA, "Acta de asamblea," no. 725 (November 10, 1958), CONASUPO-BAT.

86. Yates, *Mexico's Agricultural Dilemma*, p. 229.

7

Rural Crisis and
the Creeping Hand of the State
in the Countryside, 1958–1970

By the late 1950s the State Food Agency had evolved into an important organization that provisioned cities with inexpensive foodstuffs for the mass of workers experiencing a real decline in their wages. The rural poor, however, did not receive the same attention. Instead the countryside was seen as a means to provision the cities. The majority of the Agency's resources in the countryside was not used to benefit *ejidatarios* and small producers, and those that it did benefit tended to live near government-controlled warehouses or near railroad stations. Although state policy did increase government presence in the countryside, small producers often found state policy obtrusive as the state sought to further integrate small producers into the market. Such impact on the countryside typified the government's lack of support for small producers and *ejidatarios* and unwillingness to listen to their complaints. Consequently, throughout the administrations of Presidents Adolfo López Mateos (1958–1964) and Gustavo Díaz Ordaz (1964–1970), there were growing tensions in the countryside that manifested themselves in a number of ways, including the rise of independent peasant organizations that seized lands and demanded greater government action on their behalf. Unrest in the countryside would lead Díaz Ordaz to use the State Food Agency as an explicit tool of rural development strategy, substituting land reform and the extension of credit for increased peasant outreach by the Agency.

This chapter analyzes how and why the transformation in the State Food Agency policies occurred and seeks to explain some of the consequences of the policies for both the urban and rural

sectors. As we have seen in the past chapters, the various reorganizations of the Agency did not occur in a vacuum. Instead, restructuring and expanding have generally been responses to the political
and economic climate at the time the policy decision was made,
and the 1960s were no exception. However, the changes that took
place during these two *sexenios* were far-reaching in that they altered the legal status of the Agency, reflecting the growing reliance
of the federal government on it as a social welfare agency of last
resort.

The State Food Agency under López Mateos

The phenomenal growth of the Federal District during the 1950s
was concentrated in the various communities surrounding the core
area of Mexico City, and it placed increasing demands on the existing infrastructure. In the northern and eastern industrial sections
of the Federal District (including Azcapotzalco, Gustavo Madero,
and Iztapalapa) population increased at 10 percent a year. In
Tlalnepantla, for example, the average annual growth rate during
the 1950s was 11.4 percent, far ahead of the 2.3 percent of the core
of Mexico City.[1] Because the private market chains and public markets were located in established areas of the city, there was rising
pressure placed on the government to take action and provide affordable foodstuffs in the newly settled areas of the city.[2]

Urban tensions resulted not only from urban growth but also
from worker efforts to increase purchasing power and to growing
struggles for union democracy. Among the best examples of the
labor struggles during this period can be seen in the railroad sector, where between 1958 and 1959, the union mobilized workers
for higher wages. Gradually, the movement was transformed into
a struggle for union democracy, culminating in one of the most significant challenges to Mexico's labor bureaucracy. Upon the election of the insurgent leader, Demetrio Vallejo, to the head of the
union, dissident unionists challenged corruption and union collu-
sion with the government in other national unions.[3] Although the
democratic trade union movement would eventually be broken, it
brought to the fore the issues of the decline of purchasing power
and union democracy. The triumph of the Cuban Revolution in 1959
also served to help reinvigorate the socialist left by providing a
new model for revolutionary activity and social justice. The formation of the Movimiento de Liberación Nacional (MLN) in 1961, composed of a broad coalition of interests including the Mexican

Communist parties and progressive elements within the PRI, sought to defend the Cuban Revolution, revive land reform, free political prisoners, and fight for national economic sovereignty.[4]

Tensions in the countryside began to flare during the late 1950s and throughout the first half of the 1960s. Under the auspices of the Partido Popular Socialista (PPS) and the Union General de Obreros y Campesinos Mexicanos (UGOCM), Jacinto López led peasants in an invasion of the lands of the Greene family's Cananea Cattle Company in the wealthy agricultural regions of Sonora in 1958. Although they were expelled from the Greene's lands and jailed, a new wave of campesino militancy ensued with increased land invasions.[5] In Mexico's centrally located sugar-growing state of Morelos, Rubén Jaramillo took up arms to demand greater autonomy for sugar producers, greater democracy in the communal *ejidos*, and more land. Throughout the 1950s Jaramillo had been a thorn in the side of local and federal officials. Although he worked with the government on several occasions, especially after López Mateos had granted him amnesty in 1958, his independence led him to take matters into his own hands and seize lands.[6] Such rural unrest broke with the relative peace of the countryside that had existed since the Cárdenas land redistribution, pressuring the federal government to respond.

Although President Adolfo López Mateos is often seen as a president "on the left of the constitution," most discussions of his presidency fail to examine the social context in which he took office. The growing social unrest and the increasing mobilization of diverse segments of the population forced López Mateos's hand. As secretary of labor during the previous administration, he had become adept at attempting to maintain social peace. As his biographers have stated, "To avoid labor conflicts, López Mateos placed special emphasis on improving the living conditions of workers."[7] It is in this context that he sought to expand the social welfare functions of the Mexican government. Especially notable were his policies directed at the working classes, including his expansion of the number of people covered by the Instituto Mexicana de Seguro Social (IMSS) and the creation of the Instituto de Seguridad y Servicios Sociales para los Trabajadores del Estado (ISSSTE),[8] his implementation of a profit-sharing law,[9] and the expansion of the State Food Agency.

By the end of the Ruiz Cortines's administration the State Food Agency was still not fully able to coordinate production and consumption of foodstuffs, primarily because it favored the demands of the urban sector, which often resulted in increased importation to the neglect of developing internal distribution networks. The problems of coordination persisted despite the expansion of storage facilities in the mid-1950s. In 1959, the director of the Agency estimated that 10 percent of the harvest was lost to poor handling techniques and a lack of storage depots.[10] The need for warehouses and better handling techniques became imperative as Mexico's grain output expanded in the 1950s when corn production increased by 78 percent, bean production by 132 percent, and wheat by 115 percent. Hence, while production increased, infrastructure for storage and distribution lagged.

Under the directorship of Roberto Amorós, the State Food Agency underwent a major reorganization in 1959. Through restructuring, the State Food Agency aimed to gain greater control over the crops it purchased, obtain greater efficiency in the retail operations of basic goods so as to benefit only the poorest sectors of the population, and decentralize many of its functions.[11] Because it was viewed as having overextended its operations in the city, Amorós attempted to limit its actions in much the same way as the Alemán administration had tried to do until 1949.

The main thrust of the State Food Agency's policy was to modify its traditional handling of grains. Central to this process was the creation of a Consortium made up of both agricultural banks and ANDSA. New guidelines called for *ejidatarios* and small landholders to be given priority in the sale of their grain to the state. Because middlemen had become accustomed to purchasing grain from small producers and selling it to the state, the Agency attempted to ensure that the amount of grain turned over by each producer did not exceed the amount that the land was capable of producing.[12] To better preserve grains, the Consortium established ANDSA as the sole receiver of grains, which would be graded prior to purchase to determine the amount to be deducted for loss in value due to humidity, rodents, or disease.

ANDSA, headed by the president's brother Mariano López Mateos, was one of the cornerstones of the new policy. Once all federal warehouses came under ANDSA control and some 200 new warehouses were constructed, the number of warehouses increased by a factor of eight, to 501, marking a 84 percent increase in capacity. In December 1960, the federal government increased ANDSA's fixed capital from 85 million pesos to 300 million pesos.[13]

The early implementation of this policy met resistance and criticism from small producers. Many provincial agents of the BNCE reported that the system of grain purchase deterred *ejidatarios* and many small farmers from selling to the state because the controls were too stringent. The BNCE representative in Cuernavaca, Morelos, complained that in the majority of cases, the Consortium deducted too much from the corn submissions. Credit societies in Jonacatepec resented the fact that ANDSA did not accept their products because they were more than 2 percent spoiled.[14] Other bank employees in the field echoed these complaints and argued that the peasants were being treated unfairly.[15]

Poor coordination between the various agricultural agencies served to discourage the sale of grain to the state. In Guerrero, a state with a large number of poor *ejidatarios*, the bank agent complained that there were not enough warehouses for the state to purchase and store corn because the few warehouses that existed still held much of the 1958 crop. This inability to sell to the state led many *ejidatarios* in Guerrero to sell to private merchants for 520 pesos per ton, 280 pesos less that the 800-peso guaranteed price.[16] BNCE representatives also noted the lack of employees and equipment such as scales to efficiently receive grain.[17] Such problems meant a steep decline in the State Food Agency's overall purchases in 1959, when corn purchases fell 65 percent (Table 7-1). This decline came at a time of abundant harvests, when small producers generally called for greater government support so that they were not forced to sell at the relatively low prevailing prices.

After its initial year of operation, the State Food Agency-led Consortium responded to the numerous attacks launched against it by relaxing many of its strict quality standards. Afterward, producers began to sell their grains in increasing quantity to the Agency. The resulting increase in the amount of grains available to the government was facilitated by a 62 percent increase in purchasing centers throughout the republic by 1962.[18] Further, the guaranteed prices of beans and corn were raised by approximately 17 percent in 1961 and 1963, respectively. At the same time inflation was low, yielding a substantial real increase in the guaranteed price.[19]

During the López Mateos presidency, then, State Food Agency grain purchases more than doubled. Following a decline in 1960, the percentage of national production of beans and corn that it purchased doubled between 1961 and 1965: from 6 to 11 percent for beans, and from 9.5 to 20.8 percent for corn (Table 7-1). Many of these purchases still benefited larger producers, but the expanding outreach of the Agency was affecting increasing number of smaller and *ejido* producers than ever before. Although the effort to increase national production and the coordination of production and consumption met some challenges, maintaining food prices remained a crucial function of the Agency.

Table 7-1. State Food Agency Purchases as a Percentage of National Production (P) and Supply (S), 1958–1970

	Beans		Corn		Wheat	
Year	*P*	*S*	*P*	*S*	*P*	*S*
1958	ND	ND	9.7	16.1	41.8	41.8
1959	.3	5.6	3.1	3.1	40.1	40.4
1960	.1	2.8	13.0	14.1	40.0	39.9
1961	6.0	6.6	9.5	9.5	53.5	53.2
1962	14.4	14.7	11.5	11.5	59.3	58.3
1963	12.3	12.8	12.7	11.9	69.5	70.6
1964	ND	ND	19.4	15.2	ND	ND
1965	11.0	11.2	20.8	24.5	67.9	98.8
1966	13.0	14.5	19.5	21.5	52.1	53.7
1967	10.2	10.8	22.2	26.0	51.9	59.7
1968	6.3	6.9	19.6	21.7	39.7	39.7
1969	6.5	7.8	17.4	19.7	51.4	57.6
1970	3.6	4.5	13.4	20.0	43.3	43.9

Source: Data calculated from CONASUPO, *El mercado de las subsistencias populares*, 2 vols. (México, 1988); and Aída Mostkoff and Enrique C. Ochoa, "Complexities of Measuring the Food Situation in Mexico: Supply versus Self-Sufficiency of Basic Grains, 1925–86," in James W. Wilkie, ed., *Society and Economy in Mexico* (Los Angeles: UCLA Latin American Center Press, 1990).
Note: ND = no data.

To combine the new rural focus of the State Food Agency with its traditional urban programs, on March 2, 1961, President López Mateos transformed CEIMSA into a new State Food Agency, changing its name to Compañía Nacional de Subsistencias Populares, S.A. (CONASUPO). According to López Mateos, the new agency was explicitly aimed at protecting the rural and urban poor. In his third state of the union address, the president explained that the fundamental objectives of the new agency were to increase the rural income through guaranteed prices for basic grains, maintain reserves of staple goods, and regulate the prices of basic goods in the retail markets.[20] The new agency signified a renewed populist emphasis on improving conditions for the rural poor that had been lacking since the early days of President Cárdenas. Instead of using the guaranteed price system mainly as a means of stimulating production, it was now aimed at raising the level of income of small producers and *ejidatarios*. Indeed, the basic name change indicated this shift: CEIMSA stressed importation and exportation and foreign trade, whereas CONASUPO stressed national purchases and basic foods.

CONASUPO began operating with a significant increase in federal support. As we have seen in previous chapters, the State Food Agency had been part of BANCOMEXT and received nearly half of the bank's operational credit, but the new State Food Agency was endowed with a 1 billion pesos investment and no longer was even theoretically dependent upon another agency for its existence.[21] Thus by design the new agency had to have its own budgetary resources.

Initially, the newly reformed State Food Agency was to coordinate the purchase of grains, but in response to labor militance it expanded its urban programs as well and continued to be a visible sign of the state's commitment to the working classes.[22] The Agency's organization included a number of subsidiaries. With the organization more defined, the various State Food Agency retail stores became part of the Compañía Distribuidora CONASUPO (CONDISUPO), and the powdered milk program fell under the Rehidratadora de Leche CONASUPO. Although each of these subsidiary agencies was directly controlled by CONASUPO, they had a certain amount of administrative autonomy.

The consumer focus of the State Food Agency was linked to López Mateos's social welfare aims, which were sparked by increasing political opposition. The rapid economic growth of the late 1940s and 1950s (5.8 percent) had not benefited all groups equally.[23] Although real wages in Mexico City's industrial sector climbed steadily throughout the mid-1950s and 1960s largely due to the low rates of inflation, not until 1968 did they reach their 1939 level. Studies on the distribution of income demonstrate that during the years of constant economic growth, the distribution of wealth became more skewed, with those in the lower deciles suffering the greatest decline in income.[24] A 1963 government study found that in the Federal District only 48.1 percent of the families interviewed ate meat daily and 66.3 percent consumed eggs. In the poorer areas of Mexico City, it was reported that many families could not afford to eat meat and eggs.[25] Although workers may have made some wage gains, they had not kept pace with the escalation in food prices during the past.

That the economic "miracle" did not equally benefit all groups was also the finding of the Instituto Nacional de Nutrición (INN).

The INN's own study of working-class diets concluded that chicken, eggs, and milk would be accessible to the population only if their prices were to decline by 67 percent of the official price or if wages were to increase by 300 percent.[26] Because such changes were highly unlikely, INN recommended that production of alternative inexpensive nutritious foods be explored.

Fish and soybeans were the primary foods singled out by the INN for working-class consumption. Although fish had long been an item of luxury, the late 1950s saw an expansion in Mexico's fishing industry to the extent that the supply became more abundant. Mexico City's General Hospital was engaged in numerous experiments in search of a way to preserve fish without refrigeration and still be able to keep the price within reach of the working classes. The emphasis on expanding fish consumption coincided with the campaign by the secretary of industry and commerce to stimulate the fishing industry and to sell fish at an accessible price in Mexico City.[27] With regard to soybean products, the INN determined them to have a greater nutritive value than the tortilla. It was hoped that they could be introduced to the Mexican diet so as to add the protein that was greatly lacking in working-class diets.[28]

The State Food Agency and INN worked to explore ways to expand consumption of fish and soybeans. Together they initiated a program aimed at enriching foodstuff with vitamins and other nutritive additives. At the end of 1962, plans were formulated to initiate a new line of products that would be protein-enriched to supplement the dietary deficiencies of poor Mexicans. Dubbed "Super Alimentos," such vitamin-enriched foods included enhanced *atole*, Mexico's historic corn-based drink, calling it "Atole con Chocolate CONASUPO."[29] Despite such plans, the Super Alimentos project was short-lived, and major resources were not expended on the plan.

In its efforts to increase outreach, the State Food Agency expanded its traditional role as a retailer. In particular, the Agency responded to the demands for retail outlets requested by unions and private parties on the outskirts of Mexico City, in provincial cities, and in the countryside. During the 1960s the Agency quadrupled the number of its food stores, and the amount of its sales jumped nineteenfold in real terms between 1961 and 1970.[30] In 1961 a program was launched in Mexico City that, along with increasing the number of stores, aimed at selling fifty products each for the price of one peso (*todo a un peso*).[31] During the same year, the State Food Agency purchased a fleet of sixty trucks to function as mobile stores to sell to those living on the outskirts of the city.[32] By year's end some fifty-four trucks were making 326 daily stops benefiting an estimated 2 million inhabitants in over 200 working-class neighborhoods.[33] By 1963 the mobile stores increased to fifty-eight and added clothes, shoes, toys, and utensils to their inventory.[34] These trucks traversed the metropolitan area, making stops in most of the neighborhoods outside the center of the city. Several routes went to very remote settlements well outside of the city, and several stops were made in the state of Mexico.

Under López Mateos, the State Food Agency started a chain of rural stores to benefit the poor. "Tiendas Rancheras" were established in June 1961 to sell to the rural population goods that could not generally be purchased in the countryside. Nine months later "Tiendas Campesinas" were established to benefit the rural population of the Federal District.[35] Of the 113 rural stores established by 1963, eighty were located in the Federal District and the remaining thirty-three were in the *ejido* district of La Laguna.[36]

The State Food Agency also expanded its food-processing activities. In 1962 it acquired the NAFINSA-financed corn flour company, MINSA. Established in 1950 with a loan from Nacional Financiera, MINSA developed corn flour as a viable means by which to preserve corn for a long period of time and to better regulate sanitary conditions of tortilla making. MINSA increased the production of corn flour steadily at its one plant from 27,000 tons in 1962 to 92,000 in 1970, equalling approximately 30 percent of the market share (Table 7-2). Market share, however, began to decline steadily by 1965. In that year, the State Food Agency invested in the expansion of the corn flour operation, with plans to build plants in Arriaga in the state of Chiapas, Ciudad Guzmán in Jalisco, Rio Bravo in Tamaulipas, and Ciudad Obregón in Sonora.[37]

Meanwhile, milk recombination continued to be an important aspect of the State Food Agency's industrial operations under López Mateos and Díaz Ordaz. Beginning in 1961, the Agency created a subsidiary, Rehidratadora de Leche CONASUPO, to oversee powdered milk purchases and the milk recombination plants. The early years of the new subsidiary saw a substantial increase in federal government investment, but after 1962 funds declined until 1968 (Table 7-3). It is likely that much of the increase in government investment in 1962 went to operate the newly opened plants in the states of Michoacán and Jalisco (see Chapter 6). Although no new recombination plants were established between 1961 and 1970, the Agency maintained its active role in supplying milk to the cities, even as the government was stimulating the pasteurization of fresh milk. Small producers seemed to have shifted their complaints against the recombination plants, which preoccupied them during the previous decade, to the pasteurization plants.

Table 7-2. The State Food Agency's Corn Milling Operations, 1962–1970

Year	Corn Flour Production (tons)	Market Share (percent)
1962	27,000	37
1963	40,000	39
1964	38,000	37
1965	40,000	37
1966	41,000	34
1967	52,000	34
1968	56,000	31
1969	62,000	29
1970	92,000	29

Source: CONASUPO, *El mercado de subsistencias populares: Cincuenta años de regulación* (México: CONASUPO, 1988), vol. 2, pp. 258–259.

Table 7-3. Real Federal Government Investment in Milk Recombination Plants, 1961–1970 (1950 pesos)

Year	Federal Investment
1961	604,956
1962	1,407,371
1963	564,372
1964	349,774
1965	452,732
1966	1,026,130
1967	629,434
1968	3,952,965
1969	1,222,955
1970	934,795

Sources: Compañía Rehidratadora de Leche CONASUPO, *Informe de labores, 1970* (México, 1971). Deflated using the wholesale price index in James W. Wilkie, "From Economic Growth to Economic Stagnation in Mexico: Statistical Series for Understanding Pre- and Post-1982 Change," in James W. Wilkie, David Lorey, and Enrique Ochoa, eds., *Statistical Abstract of Latin America*, vol. 26 (Los Angeles: UCLA Latin American Center Publications, 1988).

In October 1964 the state of Puebla passed a law requiring the pasteurization of all milk sold in the city of Puebla, but the move toward increased pasteurization was not widely accepted, and local small dairy producers revolted. They were joined by university students in attacking milk pasteurization as involving the creation of a milk monopoly because only the governor's brother could afford the expensive pasteurization equipment. They attacked the milk trucks of big companies and dumped the milk into the sewers. These protests gained momentum and led to fifteen days of rioting, until federal troops intervened and the governor resigned.[38] Pasteurization of milk slowed, leading to a renewed emphasis on milk recombination, long accepted by ranchers as a supplemental measure.

Gustavo Díaz Ordaz and the State Food Agency's Geographic Expansion, 1964–1970

Although Díaz Ordaz did not do much to alter the State Food Agency's organization, he did in fact shift many of its resources away from the city to cover the expenses of rural-based programs. Díaz Ordaz had realized early on in his electoral campaign that he would have to deal with rural tensions. In the North he encountered much peasant dissatisfaction as demands for land distribution increased. The discontent that Díaz Ordaz met with grew so intense that at a campaign rally in Chihuahua the presidential candidate was pelted with chunks of wood.[39] In an early effort to allay the fears of rural dwellers, many of whom felt that his conservative reputation would translate into further neglect of the countryside, he met with the leaders of the independent peasant confederation and convinced them of his commitment to reform in the countryside.[40]

However, dealing with the rural unrest would require a balancing act on the part of President Díaz Ordaz. He would not alter his political and economic project but instead would use the State Food Agency to carry out some social policies and deflect criticism. His agrarian policy rested on slowing land distribution and modernizing agriculture to benefit larger and more capitalized farmers and resorting to importing basic grains when necessary. Díaz Ordaz's strategy, therefore, for dealing with rural unrest would entail using the Agency more as a relief agency, while more fundamental reform was rejected.

Once in office, Gustavo Díaz Ordaz dealt with rural unrest by using the State Food Agency to target rural and urban consumers. In his first state of the union address, he proclaimed that "the action of the State is aimed to protect consumers in general, as well as to favor low income social groups, providing them with staple foods at a low price."[41] In keeping with his desire to provide inexpensive basic foods to consumers and modernize agriculture, he deemphasized the goals of self-sufficiency and announced that, in sharp contrast to previous administrations in the postwar period, "no country is self-sufficient. Therefore it is preferable to import grains and save the country many millions of pesos. . . . From now on we will follow this policy, renouncing the satisfaction of announcing that we do not have to import grain."[42]

Díaz Ordaz could make such a proclamation because the Green Revolution's increased productivity in certain areas and crops had led to the appearance of self-sufficiency. In reality this self-sufficiency was but an aberration in recent Mexican agricultural history.[43] During this brief interlude, a shortage of warehouses to store excess grain for future use meant that Mexico had to resort to exporting large amounts of grain, at relatively low prices, for one of the first times in its history. For wheat the amount exported reached as high as 20 percent of production, whereas for corn and beans the amount hovered at 10 percent.[44]

Because he did not see the need to boost agricultural production, Díaz Ordaz did not ask the State Food Agency to raise guaranteed prices. If we view the guaranteed price as a producer minimum wage, as López Mateos argued that it should be, producers faired poorly under Díaz Ordaz. In addition to the decline in price incentives for boosting production, real guaranteed prices of all basic grains fell 25 percent between 1964 and 1970. Real loans to *ejidos* dropped sharply during the first half of the administration.[45]

The result of such government policy was that basic grain production began to fall after 1966, and this decline in production led to what many scholars have referred to as Mexico's loss of self-sufficiency.[46] Guaranteed prices dipped sharply under Díaz Ordaz, but this was part of a long-term steady decline in real guaranteed prices: almost from the time of their establishment in 1953, they had showed a yearly downward trend, with only a few exceptions.[47] As rural producers were being squeezed, the more fortunate were able to migrate to the city or to the United States to supplement their family income. In many regions, *ejidos* were illegally rented out by the parcel. In one region the mid-1960s marked a peak in *ejido* parcel rentals.[48]

To offset this decline, the State Food Agency embarked on a plan of rural development aimed at integrating peasants into its operations. Despite the Agency's effort to increase its outreach to remote regions during the presidency of López Mateos, most regions had not directly benefited from its purchasing operations. Instead, purchases tended to concentrate in certain areas. This had been especially true of Agency wheat operations, in which approximately 80 percent of the wheat purchased came from the state of Sonora. Although not as pronounced as the geographic concentration of wheat operations, corn purchases also tended to be disproportionately confined to a small number of states.

To increase and deconcentrate storage capacity throughout the country, Díaz Ordaz established a program to build storage facilities in cooperation with agricultural communities and *ejidos*. "Graneros del Pueblo" (people's granaries) were built on the model of the Sonoran wheat growers who had their own warehouses, scales, and laboratories, and who trained their families how to run these facilities so as to eliminate the need for other intermediaries.[49] These new warehouses were built to meet local needs; thus they were much smaller in scale than many ANDSA warehouses. Between 1965 and 1969, the number of warehouses where the State Food Agency purchased corn nearly tripled, from 772 to 2,272, largely due to the construction of almost 1,300 Graneros del Pueblo.[50]

The cone-shaped granaries became a visible symbol of the first major effort to integrate many regions in the operations of the State Food Agency. As we have seen in previous chapters, even when the government had the best intentions of increasing the guaranteed price of corn, the majority of producers was unable to take advantage of high prices due to their relative distance from reception centers. Because the popular granaries were built with great speed, a number of problems arose that compromised their operation. The poor planning of the location of the granaries and dishonest grain handling has led one scholar to conclude that "so great were the deficiencies that the majority of the warehouses had to be closed or used for other purposes. In 1971, only 15 percent of them were operating and 'none of these efficiently or with adequate controls.' "[51] Although the granaries accounted for more than half of the reception centers, they stored only 13 percent of the total corn purchased by the Agency. In the few that operated, several complaints were lodged against local officials of the Agency by peasants who charged that they had to pay bribes to have their crops accepted or to expedite the purchasing process.[52] These charges were acknowledged by the Agency's general manager, Carlos Hank González, but would not be fully investigated until the next administration.[53] Despite the numerous problems that plagued the efficient operation of the granary program, the conical monuments of the Agency dotted the landscape and served as a constant reminder of the willingness of the state to intervene and at least attempt to address social and economic problems.

To address the poverty-stricken plight of many of Mexico's rural dwellers, the State Food Agency under Díaz Ordaz began to step up its program of rural retail operations. Data for this period are sparse, but it seems that the State Food Agency stores increased the total amount of goods it sold in rural areas sixfold during the *sexenio*, a slightly more accelerated rate than the amount of the increase of sales in the urban areas. In fact, the share of rural store sales of total Agency retail sales increased from 35 percent in 1964 to 40 percent in 1970.[54]

While the State Food Agency was increasing its presence in the countryside in the form of retail outlets and silos, in the urban areas many of the previous administration's stores were expanded. The number of retail outlets continued to grow from 436 in 1964 to 1,449 in 1970, and this expansion was reflected in the sustained growth of the retail subsidiary's deficit, which grew from 21,024,000 pesos in 1964 to 65,099,000 in 1970.[55]

As the number of stores in urban areas continued to grow, subsidies to corn millers began to fall off. The amount of corn that the State Food Agency sold at reduced prices remained the same, while its total sales doubled (Table 7-4). Thus, the amount of the subsidized sales as a percentage of total Agency sales fell by nearly 50 percent during the last five years of the *sexenio*. Despite the apparent expansion of urban operations, especially when one looks at the proliferation of the number of retail stores, the amount of subsidies channeled to consumers of corn remained the same.

Table 7-4. State Food Agency Subsidized Corn Sales, 1966–1971 (tons)

Year	Total Sales	Subsidized Sales	Percentage of Sales Subsidized
1966	676,625	398,893	58.4
1967	818,784	387,285	47.3
1968	900,215	391,593	43.5
1969	1,079,462	391,845	36.3
1970	1,376,871	386,901	28.1
1971	1,335,110	387,182	29.0

Source: CONASUPO, "Manual de información estadística" (mimeo, n.d.), CONASUPO=BAT.

By the end of the Díaz Ordaz administration, the State Food Agency came under sharp attack. There was a growing perception that the Agency's activities were merely thinly veiled attempts by the government to buy political support from the rural and urban poor. The left-of-center magazine *¿Por qué?* launched one of the most scathing critiques of the Agency's operations. It alleged that the real motives of the Agency were political and not economic, citing instances where peasants were forced to pay bribes in order to sell grain without deductions for poor quality. Examples of waste and inefficiency within the Agency were documented, such as the destruction of stored grain that had spoiled before it was sold. Scholars and students of the Mexican countryside also began to write more about the political aspects of Mexico's agricultural policy.[56]

The political uses of the State Food Agency were especially evident in the construction of the grain silos in small agricultural communities throughout the country. Agency attempts to penetrate deep into isolated regions of the country coincided with the spread of rural discontent, which in a number of communities led to outright rebellion. To address the concerns of peasant groups dissatisfied with the situation in the countryside, Díaz Ordaz stated prior to his election that land reform would no longer be used to meet their demands, and instead he embarked on a program of "rural development" that relied on silos for peasants to store their grains in and retail stores to give them access to consumer items at low prices.

The attacks against the State Food Agency reflected growing general disillusion with the federal government and the official party, which increased after the massacre of student demonstrators at the Plaza of the Three Cultures on October 2, 1968. The government's use of force against the peaceful demonstration called its legitimacy into question. As a result, succeeding governments have actively sought to win over many of the disaffected sectors of the population, both in the countryside and in the city. As we will see in Chapter 8, in reshaping the role of the government to recoup support the State Food Agency played a crucial role.

Conclusion

Under the administrations of Adolfo López Mateos and Gustavo Díaz Ordaz, the State Food Agency expanded and upgraded its administrative status. López Mateos reformed the Agency to enable it to more efficiently purchase and handle grains. When the strict grading standards for grain caused many producers to complain, the Agency lowered the requirements. López Mateos raised the guaranteed price to elevate the rural standard of the peasantry, and at the same time he established state food stores in the countryside and in the more marginal areas of the city.

Under Díaz Ordaz, the Agency expanded its rural focus to a greater extent than it had in the past. Driven primarily by unrest in the countryside, he looked for ways other than land reform to address the demands and concerns of peasants and of various peasant organizations. Díaz Ordaz used the Agency to expand the storage infrastructure in the countryside by targeting small and *ejido* producers, who generally had been neglected by past Agency activities and who comprised an important bloc of growing opposition to the government.

Despite these efforts, all evidence regarding the standard of living in the countryside seems to indicate that the State Food Agency's policies did not significantly enhance the lot of the peasant. Guaranteed prices, if we use them as a measure of minimum wages for producers as López Mateos, were raised only once for corn and beans during both *sexenios*, and wheat producers received no price increases. In general, the real guaranteed price of beans and corn fell by slightly more than 23 percent.

With regard to market access, smaller and more isolated producers did gain through the construction of small-scale silos. Although only some 15 percent of these silos were actually used, the presence of the State in certain areas of the countryside did or soon would provide producers with another alternative for selling their surplus. Despite the efforts of both administrations to use the State Food Agency to attempt to balance the demands in both the city and the countryside, neither area was pacified by these policies. Political and social unrest continued throughout Mexico during the late 1960s and presented a major challenge to President Luis Echeverría Alvarez as he prepared to take office.

Notes

1. Luis Unikel, Crescencio Ruíz Chiapetto, and Gustavo Garza Villarreal, *El desarrollo urbano en México: Diagnóstico e implicaciones futuras* (México: El Colegio de México, 1976), p. 136.

2. "Distribution of Foodstuffs in Mexico City," BANAMEX, *Review of the Mexican Economic Situation*, no. 454 (September 1963), pp. 9–10.

3. Barry Carr, *Marxism and Communism in Twentieth-Century Mexico* (Lincoln: University of Nebraska Press, 1992), chap. 6. For an in-depth discussion of the railroad workers' struggle, see Antonio Alonso, *El movimiento ferrocarrilero en México, 1958/1959: De la conciliación a la lucha de clases* (México: Ediciones ERA, 1972).

4. Carr, *Marxism and Communism*, pp. 232–234.

5. See Steven E. Sanderson, *Agrarian Populism and the Mexican State: The Struggle for Land in Sonora* (Berkeley: University of California Press, 1981), p. 157; Armando Bartra, *Los herederos de Zapata: Movimientos posrevolucionarios en México* (México: Ediciones ERA, 1985), pp. 81–83.

6. For overviews of Rubén Jaramillo's activities, see Hubert C. de Grammont, "Jaramillo y las luchas campesinos en Morelos," in Julio Moguel, ed., *Historia de la cuéstion agraria mexicana: Política estatal y conflictos agrarios 1950–1970* (México: Siglo Veintiuno Editores, 1989), pp. 261–276; Donald C. Hodges, *Mexican Anarchism after the Revolution* (Austin: University of Texas Press, 1995), chap. 3.

7. Marta Baranda y Lia García Verástegui, *Adolfo López Mateos, estadísta mexicano* (Toluca: Gobierno del Estado de México, 1987), p. 239.

8. Carmelo Mesa-Lago, "The Case of Mexico," in Mesa-Lago, *Social Security in Latin America: Pressure Groups, Stratification, and Inequality* (Pittsburgh, Pa.: University of Pittsburgh Press, 1978); and Enrique C. Ochoa, "Instituto Mexican de Seguro Social," in Michael S. Werner, ed., *Encyclopedia of Mexico: History, Society and Culture* (Chicago, Ill.: Fitzroy Dearborn Publishers, 1997), vol. 1, pp. 708–711.

9. Susan Kaufman Purcell, *The Mexican Profit-Sharing Decision: Politics in an Authoritarian Regime* (Berkeley: University of California Press, 1975).

10. Roberto Amorós, "La política de distribución y la intervención marginal del sector público," in *Nuevos aspectos de la política económica y de la administración pública en México, conferencias de invierno 1960* (México: Escuela Nacional de México, 1960), p. 88.

11. *Nuevo Sistema para la compra, recepción, y almacenamiento de maíz, frijol, y trigo* (México: CEIMSA, ANDSA, BANJIDAL, BANGRICOLA, 1959), pp. 9–10; Amorós, "La política de distribución," pp. 89–90.

12. Ibid.

13. Almacenes Nacionales de Depósito, S.A., *Informe del consejo de administración a la asamblea general ordinaria de accionistas, ejercico, 1969–70* (México, 1971), pp. 8–10; Adolfo López Mateos, *Informe que rinde al H. congreso de la union el C. presidente de la república Adolfo López Mateos del 1º septiembre 1960 al 31 de agosto de 1961* (México: Secretaría de Gobernación, 1961), pp. 44–45; López Mateos, "El Licenciado Adolfo López Mateos, al abrir el congreso sus sesiones ordinarias, el 1º de setiembre de 1962," in Luis González y González, ed., *Los Presidentes de México ante la nación: Informes, manifiestos, y documento de 1821 a 1966* (México: Cámara de Diputados, 1966), p. 787.

14. "Agencia en Cuernavaca, Morelos, 1959," in BNCE, *Boletín de Estudios Especiales*, no. 200 (August 10, 1960), pp. 358–359.

15. "Agencia en Pachuca, Hidalgo 1959," in BNCE, *Boletín de Estudios Especiales*, no. 204 (October 17, 1960), pp. 583–587; "Agencia en Córdoba, Veracruz, 1959," in BNCE, *Boletín de Estudios Especiales*, no. 200 (August 10, 1960), p. 337–338; "Jefatura de zona directa de Chetumal, Quintana Roo, 1959," in BNCE, *Boletín de Estudios Especiales*, no. 200 (August 10, 1960), p. 336–337.

16. "Agencia en Iguala, Guerrero, 1959," in BNCE, *Boletín de Estudios Especiales*, no. 200 (August 10, 1960), p. 349.

17. "Agencia en Pachuca, Hidalgo 1959," in BNCE, *Boletín de Estudios Especiales*, pp. 583–587; "Agencia en Cuernavaca, Morelos, 1959," in BNCE, *Boletín de Estudios Especiales*, pp. 358–359.

18. CONASUPO, *Informe anual 1962*, p. 125.

19. See Enrique C. Ochoa, "The Politics of Feeding Mexico: The State and the Marketplace since 1934," Ph.D. diss., UCLA, 1993, tables A-14 and A-16.

20. López Mateos, *Informe que rinde al H. congreso de la union el C. presidente de la república Adolfo López Mateos del 1° septiembre 1960 al 31 de agosto de 1961*, pp. 43–45; Julio Moguel and Hugo Azpeitia, "Precios y política agrícola en dos décadas de desarollo agropecuario," in Julio Moguel, ed., *Historia de la cuéstion agraria mexicana: Política estatal y conflictos agrarios 1950–1970* (México: Siglo Veintiuno Editores, 1989), p. 29.

21. In their *Informe del consejo de administración a la XXV asamblea general ordinaria de accionistas* (México: Editorial CVLTVRA, T.G., S.A., 1962), the Banco Nacional de Comercio Exterior states that the federal government now devotes sufficient resources to price regulation and that, therefore, the State Food Agency no longer requires support from the bank (p. 43).

22. The reformist "pro-labor" stance of López Mateos manifested itself in other policies. For an interesting analysis of the implementation of profit sharing, see Purcell, *The Mexican Profit-Sharing Decision*.

23. Roger D. Hansen, *The Politics of Mexican Development* (Baltimore, Md.: Johns Hopkins University Press, 1971), p. 42.

24. Ifigenia Martínez de Navarrete, *La distribución del ingreso y el desarrollo económico de México* (México: Instituto de Investigaciones Económicos, Esceula Nacional de Economía, 1960).

25. Cited in Patricia McIntire Richmond, "Mexico: A Case in One-Party Politics," Ph.D. diss., University of California at Berkeley, 1965, pp. 159–166.

26. "Informe al Señor Presidente de la Junta Nacional para el Mejoramiento de la Alimentación" (August 1, 1959), AGN-ALM 606.3/122.

27. Secretaría de Industria y Comercio, *Memoria de Labores, 1959* (México, 1959), pp. 31–32; Secretaría de Industria y Comercio, *Estadísticas básicas de la actividad pesquera nacional, 1959–1965* (México, 1966).

28. Informe al Señor Presidente de la Junta Nacional para el Mejoramiento de la Alimentación (August 1, 1959), AGN-ALM 606.3/122; "The Soybean and Its Food Products," in BANAMEX, *Review of the Mexican Economic Situation*, no. 393 (August 1958), pp. 12–14.

29. CONASUPO, *Informe anual 1962*, pp. 24–25.

30. CONASUPO, *El mercado de subsistencias populares* (México: CONASUPO, 1988), vols. 1 and 2.

31. Secretaría de Industria y Comercio, *Memoria de labores, 1961* (México, 1961), p. 45.

32. AGN-ALM 568.2/34.

33. Secretaría de Industria y Comercio, *Memoria de labores, 1961*, p. 45.

34. CONASUPO, *Informe anual 1963*, pp. 190–192.

35. Moguel and Azpeitia, "Precios y política agrícola," p. 29.

36. CONASUPO, *Informe anual 1963*, pp. 140–142.

37. CONASUPO, "Acta number 14, October 18, 1964," in *Informes al Consejo de Administración, tomo XXXIII* (1964), CONASUPO-BAT.

38. "City under Martial Law Last Night," *Mexico City Times*, October 31, 1964; for the view of one of the leaders of the demonstration, see Ramón Danzós, *Ramón Danzós: Desde la cárcel de Atlixco* (México: Ediciones de Cultura Popular, 1974), pp. 108–114.

39. *New York Times*, April 12, 1964.

40. See Bo Anderson and James D. Cockcroft, "Control and Co-optation in Mexican Politics," in Irving Louis Horowitz, Josué de Castro, and John Gerassi, eds., *Latin American Radicalism: A Documentary Report on Left and Nationalist Movements* (New York: Random House, 1969), pp. 366–389.

41. Díaz Ordaz, Gustavo, *Primer 1° Informe que rinde al H. congreso de la union el C. presidente de la república Gustavo Díaz Ordaz del 1° septiembre 1965* (México: Secretaría de Gobernación, 1965), pp. 28–29.

42. Ibid.

43. Aída Mostkoff and Enrique C. Ochoa, "Complexities of Measuring the Food Situation in Mexico: Supply versus Self-Sufficiency of Basic Grains, 1925–86," in James W. Wilkie, ed., *Society and Economy in Mexico* (Los Angeles: UCLA Latin American Center Publications, 1990), p. 131.

44. Ibid.

45. John Williams Mogab, "Public Credit Institutions as Development Agencies: The Case of Mexico's *Ejido* Credit System," Ph.D. diss., University of Tennesse at Knoxville, 1981, chap. 8.

46. See, for example, David Barkin and Blanca Suárez, *El fin de la autosuficencia alimentaria mexicana* (México: Ediciones Océano, 1985).

47. See Mostkoff and Ochoa, "Complexities of Measuring the Food Situation in Mexico."

48. John Gledhill, *Casi Nada: A Study of Agrarian Reform in the Homeland of Cardenismo* (Albany: Institute for Mesoamerican Studies, SUNY, 1991), pp. 173–182.

49. "Testimonio de Carlos Hank Gonzalez," in CONASUPO, *El mercado de subsistencias populares*, vol. 2, p. 40.

50. Merilee Serrill Grindle, *Bureaucrats, Politicians, and Peasants in Mexico: A Case Study in Public Policy* (Berkeley: University of California Press, 1977). See also Gustavo Díaz Ordaz, *Cuarto informe que rinde al H. congreso de la union el c. presidente de la república Gustavo Díaz Ordaz del 1° septiembre 1968* (México: Secretaría de Gobernación, 1968), pp. 28; and Cynthia Hewitt de Alcántara, *La modernización de la agricultura mexicana, 1940–1970* (México: Siglo Veintiuno Editores, 1978), pp. 95–96.

51. Grindle, *Bureaucrats, Politicians, and Peasants in Mexico*, p. 74; According to Gustavo Esteva and David Barkin, in 1970, 12 percent of capacity was utilized. See *El papel del sector público en la comercialización y la fijación de precios de los productos agrícolas básicos en México* (México: CEPAL, 1981), p. 14.

52. See Kenneth F. Johnson, *Mexican Democracy: A Critical View* (Boston: Allyn and Bacon , 1971), pp. 98–107. Johnson's critique of CONASUPO policies is drawn largely from *¿Por Qué?* (April 10, 1968).

53. See Marvin Alisky, "CONASUPO: A Mexican Government Agency Which Makes Low-Income Workers Feel Their Government Cares," *Inter-American Economic Affairs* 27:3 (winter 1973–74).

54. Calculated from CONASUPO, *El mercado de subsistencias populares*, vol. 2, appendix.

55. CONASUPO, *Manual de información estadística* (mimeo, n.d. [1973?]) CONASUPO-BAT.

56. One such scholar was the American political scientist Kenneth Johnson, who wrote about corruption and inefficiency in general, and specifically in the case of the State Food Agency, in *Mexican Democracy*, pp. 98–107.

8

The Apogee of the
State Food Agency, 1970–1982

W hen Luis Echeverría Alvarez (1970–1976) assumed the presidency in 1970, Mexico was mired in a deep political and social crisis. A wave of student demonstrations called into question the political and economic policies of past administrations. The movement culminated several years of grumbling beneath the surface at growing inequality and political domination during the period of the economic "miracle." The Mexican government's response to such demonstrations, exemplified by the massacre of students at Tlaltelolco on October 2, 1968, further alienated large sectors of the middle class.[1] Growing disaffection with the Mexican system was manifested in a number of ways, including the emergence of a number of guerrilla organizations.

Facing a new wave of political alienation and growing social unrest, the government sought to address social issues through increased state spending. Under presidents Luis Echeverría Alvarez (1970–1976) and José López Portillo (1976–1982), Mexico witnessed unprecedented state intervention in various sectors of the economy: the number of parastatal agencies more than doubled to over 1,000. By 1982 parastatal agencies accounted for some 42.7 percent of total state income,[2] and nearly 19 percent of all employed Mexicans worked in the public sector.[3]

The State Food Agency became the showcase for government policies aimed at both the urban and rural poor. During this twelve-year period, the Agency doubled the volume of its operations and emerged as one of the largest corporations in Mexico and Latin America. Its retail and wholesale stores expanded at a phenomenal rate, sparking one commentator to call it "a Mexican agency which makes low income workers feel their government cares."[4] It also worked with several other agencies throughout the period to boost agricultural production. Although the top-down strategy of state intervention was reinforced in many cases, certain Agency programs sought to empower producers and consumers to market their own products and not necessarily rely solely upon the state.

Luis Echeverría, "Shared Development," and the State Food Agency

Mexican society on the eve of Luis Echeverría's ascension to the presidency in 1970 was plagued with contradictions. Economically, at least on the surface, Mexico was in the midst of a long-term boom: GDP was steadily increasing at an annual rate of approximately 7 percent. Politically, however, the PRI was facing major challenges to its legitimacy. Unrest in both the city and the countryside had been manifested in a number of large-scale demonstrations and land seizures.

The 1968 massacre of student demonstrators unleashed widespread criticism of the Mexican state from various sectors of society. It sparked debate on the nature of government policy and brought to the fore discussions of the impact that Mexico's "economic miracle" of the past three decades had had on income distribution. A number of studies by independent scholars of the period demonstrated that Mexico's model for development did not help the poorer sectors of the population. Among the most significant of these scholarly works were Ifigenia Martínez's studies on income distribution, in which she demonstrated that the bottom strata of Mexican society bore the brunt of Mexico's economic growth.[5] Top literary intellectuals also became very critical of the Mexican state, and a general tone of dismay was conveyed in their work.[6] Likewise, students of Mexico's countryside began to critically assess the impact that Mexico's agricultural modernization had on the peasantry. These studies ably demonstrated that most peasants had never benefited from government credit, agricultural extension, and irrigation.[7]

Outside the walls of the university and intellectual circles, the growing opposition to the PRI was manifested in a variety of other ways. In the presidential election of 1970, approximately 40 percent of eligible voters stayed away from the polls.[8] Mexicans were resorting to other forms of political action. In various parts of the country they stormed city halls and PRI offices, attacking the legitimacy of the government. Such overt assaults accompanied a growing rural and urban guerrilla movement. In the mountains of the southwestern state of Guerrero, the peasant leader Genaro Vásquez transformed his civic action group into a guerrilla force in 1971, establishing a would-be coalition of workers, students, and progressive intellectuals to achieve the "political and economic independence of Mexico" and to install a new social order for the benefit of the working majority of the country.[9] Vásquez was met by the Mexican army, which sent 15 percent of its troops to the mountains of Guerrero and found and killed him. But the guerrilla movement did not disappear. Also in Guerrero, a guerrilla force under the leadership of Lucio Cabañas carried out a series of hit-and-run attacks on the Mexican army stationed in Guerrero. Such tactics prompted the army to become suspicious of the peasantry, and it carried out widespread repression in the countryside to quell the insurgency. Cabañas's death in late 1974 finally caused the guerrilla movement to falter and then fizzle, but not before it had forced the government to take a number of measures to attempt to win over alienated sectors of the population.

In the city, guerrilla activities were not so easily defeated; waves of kidnappings were pervasive throughout the early 1970s. Following the government repression of 1968, a number of urban guerrilla movements sprang to life. They claimed responsibility for bombings throughout the country: twenty-three in 1972; two in 1973; twenty-four in 1974 ; thirteen in 1975; and eight in 1976. Urban guerrillas kidnapped a number of prominent officials, including former senator and the father-in-law of the president, and the U.S. consul in Guadalajara.[10] The growth of both urban and rural guerrilla movements increased the pressure placed on the government to achieve social peace and stability.

Disillusion with the PRI's official unions led to a period of vigorous independent union-organizing activity. Inspired by events of the 1960s to attempt to buck the corporativist official unions that kept workers in line, such as the CTM and the umbrella organization known as the Congreso de Trabajo (CT), workers began organizing independent unions, seeking to establish union democracy. Independent labor mobilizations increased throughout the Echeverría administration, with the number of strikes growing significantly, and the proportion of these strikes that were in support of union democracy grew from 14 percent to 36 percent throughout the Echeverría *sexenio*, peaking in 1975 with 53 percent.[11]

In order to regain legitimacy, President Echeverría, who as secretary of government under Díaz Ordaz was one of those responsible for the repression, responded to complaints against the government by using the stick and then the carrot. Because overt military repression had proven unpopular, the security forces undertook the use of terror against suspected guerrillas.[12] A variety of tactics was also used to quell independent union organizing, by the state as well as by companies, including physical violence by police and the use of strikebreakers against workers and union activists in general.[13]

President Echeverría used economic modernization and social justice as a carrot to rebuild national consensus.[14] In an attempt to respond to the critiques by intellectuals and academics, Echeverría invited many of them into the government or offered them advisory posts. To rebuild national consensus he called for a plan of "Shared Development," to redistribute wealth so that the poorer sectors of the population could "share" in Mexico's economic miracle.[15]

Although Echeverría's used social justice rhetoric during his campaign and early years of office, sharp increases in state spending aimed at the State Food Agency did not come until late in 1973. In the early years of the Echeverría administration, the amount of federal government transfers to the Agency remained relatively constant, accounting for approximately 26 percent of total federal government transfers to decentralized agencies (Table 8-1). Owing in part to increased government spending and worldwide inflation, by 1974 domestic inflation increased to 22 percent, up from less than 9 percent in the previous two years. The sudden rise in prices caused the urban sector to demand relief from government, and there were more strikes in 1974 than in any year since the early 1960s.[16] Even the official CTM threatened to strike if the government did not intervene to alleviate the impact of the rising cost of living.[17] The upper middle classes also felt the pinch of this inflationary wave and began exerting pressure on the government by threatening to withdraw their capital from the Mexican market.

To combat inflation, Echeverría not only imposed price controls on a variety of items but created a number of new agencies. Many of the programs that he initiated were aimed at compensating for the worker's eroding purchasing power. He established price controls for a number of consumer items as well as for inputs for national industry, created a national housing institute to grant credit to workers to help build their own houses,[18] and named commissions to monitor grain scarcity and hoarding.[19] These initial steps at combating inflationary pressure were similar in strategy to those of previous presidents, but the size and magnitude of state intervention was much greater than in the past.

President Echeverría's main weapon in the fight against inflation was the State Food Agency, which became his primary social welfare agency. Between 1973 and 1974 the amount of federal government transfers to the agency were augmented in real terms by 270 percent. As the size of the entity grew, so too did its place in the Mexican bureaucracy. By 1974, federal government operation transfers to the State Food Agency accounted for 46 percent of all federal government transfers to decentralized agencies, more than double the share it received in 1970 (Table 8-1).

Table 8-1. Real Federal Government Operation Transfers to the State Food Agency, 1970–1976

Year	Transfers to State Food Agency (thousands of 1950 pesos)	State Food Agency Transfers as a Percentage of Total Federal Government Transfers
1970	296,931	23.1
1971	343,750	33.3
1972	352,941	21.8
1973	286,011	25.6
1974	952,784	46.4
1975	1,098,499	46.5
1976	459,911	31.3
1977	505,406	32.6
1978	855,302	45.9
1979	936,924	52.1
1980	1,663,958	61.7
1981	2,381,317	59.8
1982	2,468,784	65.4

Source: Carlos Salinas de Gortari, *Tercer informe de gobierno: Anexo estadístico* (México: SPP, 1991).

Increased federal investment in the State Food Agency led to the growth of its subsidiaries to 16 in 1975, a threefold increase from the end of the previous administration.[20] At the same time, the number of employees working for its various branches increased from 1,079 to 9,259 between 1964 and 1974. While the central Agency bureaucracy grew by some 300 percent, the most dramatic growth occurred in the proliferation of subsidiaries. Far and away the sector with the greatest number of employees, nearly two-thirds in 1974, was the retail marketing subsidiary DICONSA (Table 8-2).

This sector's growth was largely attributable to the proliferation of retail stores in Mexico during Echeverría's presidency.

Table 8-2. State Food Agency Employees, by Subsidiary, 1964–1974

Subsidiary	Function	Number of Employees October 1964	ca. 1974
CONASUPO	Central office	336	1,283 (April 1974)
LICONSA	Milk recombination	129	650 (April 1975)
DICONSA[a]	Retail marketing	614	5,716 (November 1974)
ICONSA	Industrias CONASUPO, S.A.	0	n.d.
MICONSA[b]	Corn flour milling	n.d.	242 (June 1974)
TRICONSA	Wheat flour milling	0	164 (June 1973)
ARCONSA	Almacenes de Ropa CONASUPO	0	200 (October 1973)
BORUCONSA	Bodegas Rurales CONASUPO, S.A.	0	500
MACONSA	Construction materials	0	100
CECONCA	Centros CONASUPO de Captación	0	200
Promotora	Peasant outreach	0	200
Total		1,079	9,255

Sources: For 1964, "CONASUPO," Acta de Consejo 15," November 16, 1964, CONASUPO-BAT. For 1974 data, see Merilee S. Grindle, *Bureaucrats, Politicians, and Peasants in Mexico: A Case Study in Public Policy* (Berkeley: University of California Press, 1977), pp. 19–23.
[a]DICONSA was originally known as CONDISUPO.
[b]MICONSA was originally known as MINSA.
n.d. = no data.

In accordance with its pledge to keep basic goods accessible to the working classes, the State Food Agency expanded urban retail outlets by 44 percent between 1970 and 1975 (Table 8-3). Aside from establishing small stores in working-class areas, in 1975 the Agency began to establish large discount stores designed to compete with the big supermarket chains in Mexico City.[21] The Agency did make some gains against inflation. One study, conducted in the early 1970s, found that in a basket of thirty items, prices at the Agency stores increased at a slower rate than did the general consumer price index: between 1970 and 1974, general consumer prices increased by 35 percent, whereas Agency prices increased by 18 percent.[22] Aside from the price savings that consumers received from shopping at these outlets, another study found that the clientele of the stores generally did not own cars and that the location of Agency stores increased their use by lower income groups. Public perception of the social welfare function of the Agency's retail outlets was favorable by all income groups.[23]

Table 8-3. Number and Location of State Food Agency Stores, 1970–1982

Year	Urban Stores	Rural Stores	Total
1970	1,426	43	1,469
1971	1,729	74	1,803
1972	1,875	89	1,964
1973	2,074	479	2,553
1974	2,036	547	2,583
1975	2,957	899	2,957
1976	2,081	920	3,001
1977	2,125	751	2,876
1978	1,860	3,311	5,171
1979	1,880	4,780	6,660
1980	2,042	6,327	8,369
1981	2,047	8,424	10,471
1982	2,242	9,049	11,291

Source: CONASUPO, *El mercado de subsistencias populares*, vol. 2. (México, 1988).

The State Food Agency also began to intervene in the marketing of nonstaple consumer items. New subsidiaries were created to market construction materials (MACONSA), fresh fruits and vegetables (ACONSA), and clothing (ARCONSA). The primary motive behind such a move was to help urban dwellers cope with inflation, and in the midst of such populist policies, the Agency began to expand its definition of basic goods to include clothing and other nonedible items. Almacenes de Ropa CONASUPO (ARCONSA) was established in April 1973 "to help consumers with scarce resources to purchase good quality clothing, material, and shoes at low prices, thus increasing their purchasing power and economic capacity."[24] By June 1974, fifty-four ARCONSA stores were operating in various cities throughout the country, over 30 percent of which were located in the Federal District. The stores claimed to sell clothing at 15 percent below the price that it was sold for in the most important commercial centers in Mexico City. The value of sales expanded greatly during ARCONSA's initial months of operation and then declined steadily: between April and December 1973, total sales grew from 547,600 pesos to 14,571,400, but by June 1974 the amount fell to 6,213,000 pesos.[25] The decline in sales at ARCONSA stores coincided with the Agency's move to build a number of large multipurpose stores in large cities, hence closing

ARCONSA stores and transferring the sale of clothing to these department stores.

One of the most important areas in which the Agency expanded in the consumer market was in the area of food processing. Although it had been involved with milk recombination and milling operations since the 1950s, the production of these goods in the 1970s expanded notably, and a number of other food items began to be produced by the Agency. Between 1970 and 1976, the Agency's output of recombined milk increased by 67 percent, and the number of families that benefited from government programs more than doubled.[26] A similar expansion of output can be seen in the wheat-milling operations (TRICONSA), in which the amount of bread baked for the distribution and sale to government stores nearly doubled between 1973 and 1974.

The largest industrial undertaking by the State Food Agency during the presidency of Echeverría was the establishment of Industrias CONASUPO, S.A. (ICONSA). Founded upon the acquisition of plants from the industrial group Empresas Longoria, fourteen industrial plants began producing goods such as cooking oils, flour, crackers, cookies, and pastas. By the end of the Echeverría administration, ICONSA began to play a growing role in the various markets.[27] Many of the goods produced went to fill the shelves of the Agency's rapidly growing chain of stores.

While the State Food Agency's activities expanded in the city to help compensate for increases in the cost of living, it undertook a major attempt to reform its actions in the countryside. With both the production of basic grains declining and with rural discontent on the rise, it became imperative for the government to take action in the countryside. According to Echeverría and his director of the State Food Agency, Jorge de la Vega Domínguez, structural barriers prevented the peasant from participating fully in the national economy, and although the Agency had been designed to help the peasant sell his or her crop, this had not happened. As one Agency official during the period commented: "The traditional role of CONASUPO until this administration has been to protect [urban] consumers. The government's economic policy was to keep prices stable, especially in the urban areas, keeping salaries low and stimulating industry. That is why DICONSA has grown so greatly in urban areas and why corn was bought in the areas of highest production with little thought to the protection of producers."[28]

To expand opportunity for small producers and *ejidatarios* to store their crop and sell at their convenience, the State Food Agency created Bodegas Rurales CONASUPO, S.A. (BORUCONSA). To overcome traditional purchasing practices that were often harmful to peasants, BORUCONSA tried to include the peasantry in its operations. By training *ejidatarios* how to weigh and grade the grain, in the Centros CONASUPO de Captación (CECONCA), officials hoped to empower the peasants to give them more leverage over middlemen and to free them from government officials who would often defraud them. By 1974 some 1,483 *ejidatarios* had been trained to receive grains at the warehouses.[29] The number of reception centers offering diverse forms of technical assistance, such as fertilizer and improved seeds, also increased substantially. The most notable feature of BORUCONSA's expanding influence was in the share of total Agency purchases that were made at its reception centers: in 1971, 13 percent of the total national purchases were made through such centers; by 1972 that amount jumped to 42 percent; by 1973, 60 percent; and by 1974, 71 percent.[30]

Aside from being mere receptors of grain and dispensers of technological information, BORUCONSA sought to create a greater sense of community. The State Food Agency used the reception centers to disseminate information by having traveling theater brigades visit the various *ejidos*. A radio soap opera based on the lives and struggles of peasants was transmitted throughout the country, a monthly publication was distributed at the reception centers detailing the programs of the Agency, and a collaborative program between the IMSS and the Agency provided *ejidatarios* with medical consultation and treatment at BORUCONSA outlets.[31]

One of the most innovative moves by CONASUPO to help raise the consciousness of the peasantry and apprise them of their rights was the creation of the Teatro CONASUPO de Orientación Campesina (CONASUPO Theater of Peasant Training) in 1971.[32] Traveling theater companies performed short plays to give information on CONASUPO's programs to further the goals of breaking the control of local markets and helping peasants to participate fully in the marketplace. Over time peasants began to act in the plays, which were often pulled from their own experiences or were adapted from local indigenous plays. Many portrayed the struggles between merchants and peasants and demonstrated the ways that merchants took advantage of peasants. One improvised play, entitled "El Campesino y el Rico" (The peasant and the rich man), portrayed a man who sold his crop to a middleman at below the market price; the peasant's wife and daughter confront the middleman and get the money back.[33] During the four years that the theater operated (1972–

1976) fifty-two theater troupes gave approximately 6,000 perfor-
mances to an estimated audience of 3.25 million, educating many
about their rights and government programs designed to aid them.[34]

To further draw producers into the national market, the nominal guaranteed prices of basic grains saw their first increase since
the early 1960s. In 1973 the price of beans rose 180 percent, and
corn and wheat prices rose nearly 30 percent (Table 8-4). These gains
initially outpaced inflation, seemingly giving a major boost to
producers and an increased incentive to augment basic grain production. The increase in guaranteed price, however, did not auto-
matically result in the increase in production of basic grains. Much
of the corn that the State Food Agency purchased was from large-
scale producers grown on irrigated lands. Because the guaranteed

Table 8-4. Real Guaranteed Prices of Beans, Corn, and Wheat, 1970–1982
(1970 pesos)

Years	Beans	Corn	Wheat
1970	1,750.0	940.0	913.0
1971	1,657.6	890.4	864.8
1972	1,560.1	838.0	775.6
1973	1,694.4	945.7	945.7
1974	3,850.5	962.6	834.3
1975	2,635.9	1,054.4	971.1
1976	2,323.3	1,087.3	813.2
1977	1,781.3	1,033.1	730.3
1978	1,906.2	884.5	793.0
1979	1,965.1	882.4	760.7
1980	2,364.1	876.7	699.4
1981	2,478.2	1,014.5	712.5
1982	2,043.1	926.7	708.1

Source: CONASUPO, *El mercado de las subsistencias populares*, 2 vols. (México, 1988).
Deflated using the wholesale price index in James W. Wilkie, "From Economic
Growth to Economic Stagnation in Mexico: Statistical Series for Understanding Pre-
and Post-1982 Change," in James W. Wilkie, David Lorey, and Enrique Ochoa, eds.,
Statistical Abstract of Latin America, vol. 26 (Los Angeles: UCLA Latin American
Center Publications, 1988).

prices of crops such as sorghum increased much more than did corn
prices, large growers had a greater incentive to shift production to
the more lucrative crops. The guaranteed price of sorghum nearly
doubled between 1971 and 1974, and given its higher yield and
lower input cost, sorghum was much more attractive to large-scale
agriculture. Peasant agriculture, however, was in no position to pick
up the slack in corn production, as it had suffered from years of

low productivity and lack of access to resources.[35] Nonetheless, such steps did signal peasants that the government presence in the countryside was greater and that more resources were available to them.

As part of the continuing effort to reach out to more marginal producers, the Echeverría administration launched a short-lived program called the Programa de Apoyo a la Comercialización Ejidal (PACE) in 1975. PACE sought to provide marketing support to small corn producers and strengthen access to government reception centers. BORUCONSA took over the warehouse network of Graneros del Pueblo and worked to empower peasants to pressure their organizations to push for an increased government marketing support program. By 1976, 3,753 communities were enrolled in the program, but less than 10 percent actually participated.[36] Before the groundwork could be fully laid, however, the Echeverría administration witnessed a growing economic crisis that caused the suspension of many of these innovative programs.

Coupled with the program to incorporate the countryside into the national economy, the State Food Agency began to increase the number of rural stores, from a mere forty-three in 1970 to 899 in 1975. Many of the rural stores were initially planned for areas targeted by other government agencies. Primary among the agencies with which the Agency worked were the National Indian Institute, the state coffee agency, the state tobacco company, and various *ejidos*.[37] These stores were established in remote areas, oftentimes in communities where few or no stores existed. Local neighborhood stores, frequently run as monopolies, were now forced to compete with the Agency stores, which improved service to communities.

To meet the growing political crisis in both the city and the countryside, then, the government of Luis Echeverría increasingly relied on federal government spending to stimulate the economy and to promote social justice. The policy of shared development was most evident when the State Food Agency sought to increase production of grains and basic foods while at the same time increasing producer incomes and cushioning consumers from the impact of inflation. These policies were successful in expanding the reach of the state into small communities throughout the countryside, and in many regions this was the first real effort to integrate isolated areas into the national market since the rural school campaigns of the 1920s and 1930s.

Many of the programs, however, were not fully implemented due to an economic crisis at the end of the *sexenio* and the lack of continuity in the following *sexenio*.[38] Nonetheless, significant programs were attempted, some of which granted peasants greater control over their resources and included them in the decision-making process.

López Portillo and the State Food Agency

The prominence that the Agency had acquired under Echeverría's presidency continued throughout much of the administration of President José López Portillo. Although the first two years of López Portillo's administration saw an economic downturn, during which time the Agency remained approximately the same size as it was under Echeverría, by 1979 the economy was spurred by a petroleum boom, which led to increased spending and the expansion of the Agency. López Portillo, through the Sistema Alimentaria Mexicana (SAM), used petroleum receipts to expand the state's effort to increase peasant agricultural production, incorporate the countryside into the national economy, and raise the standard of living of the poorer rural and urban dwellers. In this effort, the Agency, being one of the most established institutions operating in both the countryside and the city, became a linchpin of López Portillo's rural development policies.

When President López Portillo took office in late 1976, Mexico faced an economic slump due, in part, to capital flight and the decline in world trade. Even though Echeverría had devalued the peso by 100 percent, the economy remained sluggish. To re-energize the economy, Echeverría negotiated a loan with the International Monetary Fund (IMF) at the cost of scaling back public sector spending. Although the pact with the IMF was not signed until López Portillo had taken office, Echeverría began to comply with many of the loan provisions in 1976,[39] and by the end of 1977 austerity measures had led to a real decline in the funds targeted for the Agency and in real wages.[40]

Beginning in 1978, however, the federal government began to tie the Mexican economy's growth to the exploitation of petroleum, which boomed from 1979 until mid-1982.[41] This good fortune allowed President López Portillo to renew the populist overtones of the Echeverría regime. Beginning in 1978, many of the receipts from the newfound petroleum wealth went to expand the operations of the State Food Agency in order to alleviate the effects of the austerity measures on workers. The amount of government transfers to the Agency increased sixfold, doubling its share of the total amount of federal government transfers between 1978 and 1980. Much of the increase in funds went to urban affiliates, such as the milling operations and the industrial plants, and was driven by urban demands that peaked with the 1977 austerity measures.[42]

By 1980 López Portillo added the revitalization of Mexican agriculture to his major policy objectives, creating SAM in order to unify the other agricultural bureaucracies. By drawing on the resources of a number of state agencies, including those of the State Food Agency, SAM attempted to make Mexico self-sufficient in corn and bean production and to address all the factors in the countryside that hindered peasant agriculture and perpetuated poverty. Thus, according to SAM planners, this integrated policy approach had to address questions of production, distribution, nutrition, and the general well-being of the rural dweller if the standard of living in the countryside was to be raised.[43]

Unlike, past approaches, SAM was implemented as an effort to redistribute income to poorer rural groups using market mechanisms to achieve agrarian reform. In contrast to what we have generally seen in policy implementation, it was a preemptive measure not directly sparked by peasant pressure; instead it was a move to "forestall a potential increase in social unrest."[44]

The primary role that the State Food Agency played in increasing agricultural production under SAM was through increasing the guaranteed price that it paid for grains, expanding grain storage and reception programs, and buying more corn and beans from national producers. Although inflation had cut into guaranteed prices, for example, and caused the real price of corn to fall by 16 percent, with the advent of SAM the guaranteed prices were augmented to stimulate the production of these grains (Table 8-4). The adjustment of the guaranteed prices in 1981 outpaced inflation for one of the few times in Agency history.

Another Agency effort, in concert with other SAM-affiliated agencies, involved increasing the capacity and efficiency of its storage facilities. Since the late 1960s the State Food Agency had created small-scale storage depots targeted for small producers and *ejidos* throughout the country, but these did not always operate at full capacity, due in part to the rather low priority that storage was accorded. However, under SAM the Agency's storage capacity increased by some 10 percent between 1979 and 1981, and more significantly, the amount of goods stored in the various warehouses jumped by 80 percent.[45] There was also renewed emphasis on programs aimed at supporting peasant and *ejido* marketing of basic grains.

The incentives that the state gave to producers to expand production of beans and corn, both the increased guaranteed price and the enhanced efficiency of small-scale warehouses, were reinforced with expanded state purchases of nationally produced beans and corn. The State Food Agency's purchases of national production had been steadily increasing since 1938, and by the 1970s, for corn, it hovered between 12 and 14 percent of the total national production. In addition, substantial imports of corn by the Agency increased its control over the national corn supply to well over 20 percent. During the SAM years, the Agency's purchases of national corn production shot to 32 percent by 1982, sharply reducing the amount of corn that it had to import.

As the State Food Agency worked closely with SAM to increase output and marketing conditions for small producers, it also sought to further integrate these producers into the national market by expanding rural Agency stores and increasing the nutritional content of food. Working in conjunction with López Portillo's rural development agency, Coordinación General del Plan Nacional de Zonas Deprimidas y Grupos Marginadas (COPLAMAR), the Agency devised a strategy to distribute goods that were most scarce and that would have the greatest impact on diet in the countryside.[46] The goal set for the end of the López Portillo administration was to establish stores in 14,000 sites with populations between 500 and 10,000 inhabitants, populations generally served by neighborhood stores that did not have competitive pricing.[47]

By 1978, the number of rural stores surpassed the number of urban stores for the first time: 3,311 of the State Food Agency's 5,171 stores were in rural areas, and at the end of the López Portillo presidency rural stores outnumbered urban stores by a ratio of 4.4 to 1 (Table 8-3). Although the goals set for the increase in the number of Agency stores were not completely met, this move into the rural areas was aimed to break a long cycle of control that a few wholesalers and a number of small retailers had on the countryside, one of the last areas in which these traditional commercial structures had not been challenged. The imbalance in price this monopoly caused was compounded by the fact that, even by 1980, some 40–50 percent of government subsidies destined for maize and for white bread went to Mexico City.[48] Under SAM, the Agency's retail marketing agency, DICONSA, was successful in bringing competition to the countryside.

Although much of the SAM strategy remained, as scholar Jonathan Fox has demonstrated, "more of the same" benefiting a relatively select group of producers, the rural food distribution policy established during this period was a significant departure from past policy.[49] Whereas in the past, CONASUPO stores were often granted through concession and, as we have seen, did not always substantially reduce the prices of basic foods due to manipulations by local caciques, CONASUPO-COPLAMAR stores mobilized community participation to oversee the operations of the stores to ensure that no such abuses would occur. As Fox demonstrated, community oversight provided a counterweight to local merchants and reluctant and often recalcitrant bureaucrats to shift the balance of the power in the marketing structure. The shift on the part of CONASUPO itself to using community mobilization made the reforms effective.[50]

To aid small wholesale merchants in obtaining their goods from sources other than the large oligopolistic wholesalers, the State Food Agency established the Impulsadora del Pequeño Comercio, S.A. de C.V. (IMPECSA), to set up wholesale distribution centers in various parts of the country in order to supply small merchants and consumer cooperatives with basic food items at a discount that could be passed on to consumers. By the end of its first year of its operation, IMPECSA had established seventeen branches in diverse regional centers. Within five years, in 1982, the numbers of branch outlets had jumped to 198.[51] Affiliates began to spread throughout the country. Each store affiliated with IMPECSA prominently advertised that fact on the building facade, helping to expand the Agency's distribution network in marginal areas of various towns and cities, as well as in more remote villages.

To supply the State Food Agency's ever-expanding retail operations with increasing amounts of low-cost goods, food processing operations also increased. In particular, output of a number of processed foods and vegetable oils was expanded as ICONSA gradually produced a greater share of the market of these products (Table 8-5). ICONSA's industrial operations were largest in the milling of corn flour, which the Agency had been milling since 1950. Along with the processing of more traditional foods, the Agency, through ICONSA, began to capture a sizable share of the cooking oil market and the noodle market. Cooking oils were produced to make their price more accessible to working families, so that they could gradually shift away from using animal lard, which was considered unsanitary and also tended to have greater price fluctuation owing to its unstable supply.

Table 8-5. ICONSA's Market Share of Selected Processed Foods and Oils, 1975–1982 (percent)

Year	Refined Cooking Oil	Corn Flour	Wheat Flour	Soup Noodles
1975	2.2	7.8	3.4	3.3
1976	9.1	15.6	7.9	5.9
1977	11.0	16.7	9.9	5.3
1978	12.9	14.6	8.8	5.7
1979	12.8	15.1	9.1	4.6
1980	15.8	15.8	9.3	6.1
1981	11.3	15.6	8.8	4.7
1982	13.1	13.8	7.3	5.6

Source: CONASUPO, *El mercado de las subsistencias populares: Cincuenta años de regulación* (México: CONASUPO, 1988), vol. 2, pp. 251–252.

Along with ICONSA's expansion, the State Food Agency's other industrial subsidiaries stepped up operations. Corn flour processing was also expanded by MICONSA, the subsidiary that had initially milled corn in 1950. Aside from the founding plant in Tlalnepantla, just north of Mexico City, MICONSA added smaller plants in Guadalajara, Los Mochis Sinaloa, Arriaga, Chiapas, and Jaltipan, thus decentralizing its operations. The subsidiary charged with the purchasing, recombination, and distribution of powdered milk, LICONSA, added four recombination plants to its founding plant in Tlalnepantla, just north of Mexico City, and by 1982 it had increased its number of pasteurization plants from one to five.[52]

The increased production of processed foods during the López Portillo years led to the marketing of milk and processed foods in stores throughout the country. The bulk of the items were sold through the State Food Agency's ever-expanding retail chains, under brand names such as "Nutri-leche" for milk and "Alianza" for products produced in the ICONSA plants. These products generally sold for less than did their competitors.

The expansion of the State Food Agency during the López Portillo years followed the trend established during the Echeverría administration of expanding operations in both the countryside and the city. In part, this strategy was aimed at addressing the various sectors of the population that had not benefited from previous

Agency actions. Rural and village dwellers were able to take advantage of the rural retail outlets of the Agency, and small producers and *ejidatarios* saw increased state aid in establishing public warehouses and marketing their goods. For the first time in the history of the State Food Agency, a large number of small producers were given the opportunity to free themselves from the traditional operation of the market, which in many cases was dominated by a small group of wholesale merchants.

State Food Agency activities came at a high cost. On a purely financial level, Agency operations during its heyday seem to have been highly inefficient and wasteful. Between 1970 and 1982, federal government subsidies accounted for a large share of the State Food Agency's income, and the debt of the agency continued to mount. Cost-benefit analyses of Agency operations in the corn market shows that in 1972, 61 centavos per peso invested was channeled to producers and consumers, but by 1983 the figure was 14 centavos.[53]

A bloated bureaucracy more than likely contributed to this increase in administrative and operational costs. However, although charges of corruption in the State Food Agency are legion, evidence of large-scale corruption has been well concealed. A survey of over 900 news articles on corruption between 1970 and 1984 found no major corruption in the Agency. Despite the fact that the amount of fraud committed in agriculture-related activities was relatively high, direct references to the Agency were not revealed.[54] Nonetheless, as demonstrated by recent charges against longtime Agency official Raúl Salinas de Gortari, this story remains to be told.

To analyze the growth of the State Food Agency's operations at exclusively a financial level, however, would be to miss the point of both the goals of the agency as well as the goals and aspirations of the Echeverría and López Portillo administrations. Regardless of financial loss and inefficient operations, it is difficult to overstate the political value of the Agency's operations. The political motivations for the expansion of the State Food Agency should not be underestimated; government revenues were used to regain popular support for the official party.

Conclusion

As the State Food Agency was used to counter popular discontent in the wake of the student uprisings and subsequent unrest in both the countryside and the city, its expansion was tentacular; it became the agency that dealt with all types of consumer shortages and sought to develop the rural economy. After a slowdown in its growth during 1976 and 1977, the Agency's retail operations, both urban and rural, began to grow rapidly, and by 1980 the State Food Agency played a pivotal role in both pricing policy and in storage of increased production. Agency stores provided larger sectors of the urban population with greater accessibility to inexpensive foodstuffs than ever before. Also, by the end of the López Portillo administration, Agency stores dotted the countryside. Grain silos, painted with the Agency colors (red and white) and logo, also could be seen in nearly all rural areas throughout the countryside, successfully making their presence, and the presence of the Mexican state, visible in even the most rural communities.

Notes

1. For an account of the student movement and its repression, see Elena Poniatowska, *Massacre in Mexico* (New York: Viking Penguin, 1975).
2. James M. Cypher, *State and Capital in Mexico: Development Policy since 1940* (Boulder, Colo.: Westview Press, 1990), p. 128.
3. James W. Wilkie, "The Six Ideological Phases of Mexico's 'Permanent Revolution' since 1910," in James W. Wilkie, ed., *Society and Economy in Mexico*. Los Angeles: UCLA Latin American Center Press, 1990, p. 28.
4. Marvin Alisky, "CONASUPO: A Mexican Agency Which Makes Low Income Workers Feel Their Government Cares," *Inter-American Economic Affairs* 27:3 (winter 1973–1974).
5. Ifigenia Martínez de Navarrete, *La distribución del ingreso y el desarrollo económico de México* (México: Instituto de Investigaciones Económicas, 1960).
6. See Octavio Paz, *The Other Mexico: Critique of the Pyramid* (New York: Grove Press, 1972). For other works, see Dolly J. Young, "Mexican Literary Reactions to Tlatelolco 1968," *Latin American Research Review* 20:2 (1985), pp. 71–85.
7. See, for example, Rodolfo Stavenhagen, Fernándo Paz Sánchez, Cuahtémoc Cárdenas, and Arturo Bonilla, *Neolatifundismo y explotación: De Emiliano Zapata a Anderson Clayton* (México: Editorial Nuestro Tiempo, 1968); and Arturo Warman, *Los campesinos: Hijos predilectos del régimen* (México: Editorial Nuestro Tiempo, 1972).
8. Barry Carr, *Marxism and Communism in Twentieth-Century Mexico* (Lincoln: University of Nebraska Press, 1992), p. 273.
9. Cited in Samuel Schmidt, *The Deterioration of the Mexican Presidency: The Years of Luis Echeverría* (Tucson: University of Arizona Press, 1991), p. 84; Donald C. Hodges, *Mexican Anarchism after the Revolution* (Austin: University of Texas Press, 1995), chap. 5.
10. Carr, *Marxism and Communism*, chap. 8; Schmidt, *The Deterioration of the Mexican Presidency*, pp. 82–87.
11. Enrique de la Garza Toledo, "Independent Trade Unionism in Mexico: Past Developments and Future Perspectives," in Kevin Middle-

brook, ed., *Unions, Workers, and the State in Mexico* (La Jolla: University of California at San Diego Center for U.S.-Mexican Studies, 1991), pp. 153–183.

12. Carr, *Marxism and Communism*, pp. 270–271; Schmidt, *The Deterioration of the Mexican Presidency*, p. 87.

13. De la Garza Toledo, "Independent Trade Unionism in Mexico," pp. 160, 164.

14. In *Mexico's Dilemma: The Political Origins of Economic Crisis* (Boulder, Colo.: Westview Press, 1984), p. 122, Roberto G. Newell and Luis F. Rubio, see the maintenance of political consensus as a primary motivating factor behind Echeverría's policies. In "Populism and Economic Policy in Mexico, 1970–1982," in Rudiger Dornbusch and Sebastian Edwards, eds., *The Macroeconomics of Populism in Latin America* (Chicago, Ill.: University of Chicago Press, 1990), pp. 223–262, Carlos Bazdresch and Santiago Levy analyze the political factors surrounding populist economic policies during this period.

15. For a discussion of housing policies during the Echeverría administration, see José A. Alderete-Haas, "The Decline of the Mexican State? The Case of State Housing Intervention (1917–1988)," Ph.D. diss., MIT, 1989.

16. Schmidt, *The Deterioration of the Mexican Presidency*, pp. 80–82, 174–175; Carlos Tello, *La política económica en México, 1970–1976* (México: Siglo Veintiuno Editores, 1979), pp. 102–103.

17. Jorge Basurto, *La clase obrero en la historia de México: En el régimen de Echeverría: Rebelión e independencia* (México: Siglo Veintiuno Editores, 1983), p. 112; Schmidt, *The Deterioration of the Mexican Presidency*, p. 81.

18. The decree establishing price controls is reprinted in Héctor Vásquez Tercero and José Luis Robles Glenn, *Control de precios* (México: Editorial Tecnos, S.A., 1976), pp. 31–53.

19. Carlos Tello, *La política económica en México, 1970–1976*, pp. 100–103.

20. Merilee Serrill Grindle, *Bureaucrats, Politicians, and Peasants: A Case Study in Public Policy* (Berkeley: University of California Press, 1977), p. 18.

21. Harye Tharp Hilger, "Consumer Perceptions of a Public Marketer: The Case of CONASUPO in Monterrey, Mexico," Ph.D. diss., University of Texas at Austin, 1976, p. 39.

22. Miguel Patiño Alvarez, "DICONSA como reguladora de artículos de primera necesidad," licenciatura thesis, Escuela Nacional de Economía, UNAM, 1974, pp. 90–92.

23. Hilger, "Consumer Perceptions of a Public Marketer," p. 189.

24. *Gaceta de CONASUPO* (September 1, 1974), no. 8.

25. Ibid.

26. CONASUPO, *El mercado de subsistencias populares*, 2 vols. (México, 1988).

27. According to Nora Lustig and Antonio Martín del Campo, "Descripción del funcionamiento del sistema CONASUPO," in *Investigación Económico* 173 (July–September 1985), p. 239, this amount hovered around 5 percent of market share in 1976 and slightly increased in 1982.

28. Cited in Grindle, *Bureaucrats, Politicians, and Peasants*, p. 75.

29. Ibid., pp. 114–115.

30. Ibid., p. 115.

31. Gustavo Esteva, "La experiencia de la intervención estatal regula-dora en la comercialiazación agropecuaria de 1970 a 1976," in Ursula Oswald, ed., *Mercado y dependencia* (México: Editorial Nueva Imagen, 1979), pp. 238–239; William P. Glade, "Entrepreneurs in the State Sector: CONASUPO of Mexico," in Sidney M. Greenfield, Arnold Strickon, and Robert T. Aubry, eds., *Entrepreneurs in a Cultural Context* (Albuquerque: University of New Mexico Press, 1979), p. 204.

32. Donald H. Frischmann, "Misiones Culturales, Teatro CONASUPO, and Teatro Comunidad: The Evolution of Rural Theater," in William H. Beezley, Cheryl English Martin, and William E. French, eds., *Rituals of Rule, Rituals of Resistance: Public Celebrations and Popular Culture in Mexico* (Wilmington, Del.: Scholarly Resources, 1994), pp. 290–296.

33. Ibid., p. 292.

34. Ibid., p. 296.

35. Kirsten A. de Appendini and Vania Almeida Salles, "Algunas consideraciones sobre los precios de garantía y la crisis de produción de los alimentos básicos," *Foro Internacional* 19:3 (January–March, 1979), pp. 402–428. For discussion of the substitution of corn for sorghum, see Billie R. De Walt, "Mexico's Second Green Revolution: Food for Feed," in *Mexican Studies/Estudios Mexicanos* 1:1 (winter 1985), pp. 29–60.

36. Jonathan Fox, *The Politics of Food in Mexico: State Power and Social Mobilization* (Ithaca, N.Y.: Cornell University Press, 1992), pp. 133–137.

37. "El programa de tiendas rurales," *Gaceta de CONASUPO*, no. 5 (August 1, 1974).

38. See Grindle, *Bureaucrats, Politicians, and Peasants*.

39. Cypher, *State and Capital in Mexico*, pp. 106–108.

40. Raúl Trejo Delarbe, *Crónica del sindicalismo en México (1976–1988)* (México: Siglo Veintiuno Editores, 1990), p. 31.

41. See Judith A. Teichman, *Policymaking in Mexico: From Boom to Cri-sis* (Boston: Allen and Unwin, 1988).

42. Calculated from José López Portillo, *Tercer informe de gobierno: Anexo programático II-A, 1978* (México, 1979); José López Portillo, *Quinto informe de gobierno: Anexo programático II-A, 1980* (México, 1981); and José López Portillo, *Sexto informe de gobierno: Anexo programático II-A, 1981* (México, 1982).

43. Cassio Luiselli, *The Mexican Food System: Elements of a Program of Accelerated Production of Basic Foodstuffs in Mexico*, Research Report Series 22 (La Jolla: Center for U.S.-Mexican Studies, University of California at San Diego, 1982); Mario Montanari, "The Conception of SAM," in James E. Austin and Gustavo Esteva, eds., *Food Policy in Mexico: The Search for Self-Sufficiency* (Ithaca, N.Y.: Cornell University Press, 1987), pp. 48–60; Celso Cartas Contreras and Luz María Bassoco, "The Mexican Food Sys-tem (SAM): An Agricultural Production Strategy," in Bruce F. Johnson, Casio Luiselli, Celso Cartas Contreras, and Roger D. Norton, eds., *U.S.-Mexico Relations: Agriculture and Rural Development* (Stanford, Calif.: Stanford University Press, 1987), pp. 319–332.

44. Fox, *The Politics of Food in Mexico*, p. 155.

45. James E. Austin and Jonathan Fox, "State-Owned Enterprises: Food Policy Implementers," in Austin and Gustavo Esteva, eds., *Food Policy in Mexico: The Search for Self-Sufficiency* (Ithaca, N.Y.: Cornell University Press, 1987), p. 78.

46. Luiselli, *The Mexican Food System*, pp. 11–12.

47. CONASUPO, *CONASUPO 1977–1982* (México: CONASUPO, n.d.), p. 41.

48. Much research remains to be done on Mexico's commercial structure. However, for a good general overview of the different distribution channels in Mexico City, see Cynthia Hewitt de Alcántara, "Feeding Mexico City," in Austin and Gustavo Esteva, eds., *Food Policy in Mexico: The Search for Self-Sufficiency* (Ithaca, N.Y.: Cornell University Press, 1987), p. 190.

49. Fox, *The Politics of Food in Mexico*, p. 1.

50. Ibid., chap. 6.

51. Enrique González Casanova, "1965–1982 CONASUPO, Organismo público descentralizado," in CONASUPO, *El mercado de la subsistencias populares: Cincuenta años de regulación*, vol. 2 (México: Compañía Nacional de Subsistencias Populares, 1988), pp. 14–131. The data on IMPECSA's operation come from the statistical appendix of the above volume, p. 270.

52. CONASUPO, *El mercado de las subsistencias populares*, vol. 2, statistical appendix.

53. Oscar H. Vera Ferrer, *El caso CONASUPO: Una evaluación* (México: Centro de Estudios en Economia y Educación, A.C., 1987), pp. 234–238.

54. Stephen D. Morris, *Corruption and Politics in Contemporary Mexico* (Tuscaloosa: University of Alabama Press, 1991), pp. 56–64.

9

Neoliberalism and the Dismantling of the State Food Agency after 1982

Beginning in 1982, Mexico plunged into its worst economic crisis since the 1930s. A sudden drop in the price of oil precipitated Mexico's inability to repay the huge debts it had incurred to fund the statist activities of the previous two presidents. The economic downturn and high rates of inflation sent real wages spiraling downward: between 1982 and 1988, GDP stagnated, and the real minimum wage fell by nearly 50 percent.[1] In response to the crisis, Presidents Miguel de la Madrid (1982–1988) and Carlos Salinas de Gortari (1988–1994) sought to stabilize prices, attract foreign capital, and open the economy to the world market. One of the foremost ingredients in the de la Madrid and Salinas recipe for pulling Mexico out of the crisis was to reduce the size of government by privatizing or liquidating much of the public sector. This action did not exclude the State Food Agency.

The manner in which the Mexican government dealt with the malaise of the 1980s was a major departure from past policies. After 1982 the government attempted to retreat from direct intervention in the economy and instead modified its role to that of a regulator. As a result the number of decentralized agencies declined from 1,058 in 1983 to 209 in 1993, and the public sector's contribution to GDP declined from 25.4 percent to 7.5 percent during the same time frame.[2] It is in this context that the State Food Agency saw a dramatic reduction in its operations. Whereas during the previous two *sexenios* the State Food Agency had experienced a proliferation in the number of subsidiaries and in the amount of government investment, under de la Madrid and Salinas it saw what amounted to a dismantling of many of its activities. However, the dismantling of the Agency followed a more gradual process than the streamlining of many other government programs, and indeed, during the early years of the economic crisis, it saw its operations expanded.

This chapter explores how policymakers dealt with the State Food Agency during Mexico's economic crisis. Although for years many observers had argued that to dismantle the Agency was to wreak political havoc on the official party, such political problems did not immediately occur in part because the dismantling of the State Food Agency was gradual and because a new catch-all social welfare agency, Programa Nacional de Solidaridad (PRONASOL), was created. By the end of the Salinas administration, however, growing social unrest began to occur in the countryside. Nevertheless, Salinas's successor, Ernesto Zedillo, has remained steadfast in his move to liberalize the economy.

Economic Crisis and the Expansion of the State Food Agency under Miguel de la Madrid

When Miguel de la Madrid took office on December 1, 1982, petroleum prices had plummeted, inflation reached nearly 100 percent for 1982, the rate of economic growth was -0.6 percent, and the country's debt was mounting. The combination of the economic crisis and the government's response to it placed a heavy burden on Mexican society. Wage earners felt the pinch almost immediately. The previous two decades had seen steady increases in real wages, but the onset of economic crisis saw these gains quickly reversed, with outcries for populism quickly forthcoming. Independent unions led protests against the austerity measures, the largest of which resulted in national strikes in October 1983 and in June 1984. The CTM also threatened the government with strikes, demanding greater government intervention in the distribution and marketing of foodstuffs.[3]

President de la Madrid's prescription for the economic crisis entailed limiting government expenditure and increasing revenues. Upon taking office, he replaced the more statist-oriented supervisors in government bureaucracies with those who advocated a great reduction in state intervention, in an attempt to transfer such power from the government to the private sector.[4] During the first three years of his administration, de la Madrid cut the number of the public sector agencies by 20 percent, reduced the government outlay to many of the remaining agencies, and laid plans for further cuts and reductions.[5] Although many in his cabinet and the IMF advocated deeper cuts at a more rapid pace, resistance from social actors within the government slowed the pace of reform.[6]

Because of the severity of the crisis and of the potential for social unrest, under de la Madrid the State Food Agency continued to serve as the primary relief agency during the initial years of the crisis. It was charged with maintaining a steady flow of basic foodstuffs at an affordable price to avoid public disturbances. The Agency boasted that at no time during the crisis was there a scarcity of basic grains.[7] To maintain the social peace of which the Agency was so proud, it had to import grains to supplement national shortfalls. To do so in an era of diminishing financial resources demanded that the Agency reorganize, decentralizing its decision-making powers.

During the early years of reorganization, the State Food Agency continued to receive large sums of money from the federal government and to expand its operations to cushion the impact of restructuring. After an initial decline in the real amount of federal government transfers targeted for the Agency, in 1983 real transfers to it rose 28 percent over the amount it had received at the height of López Portillo's statist policies (Table 9-1). During the

Table 9-1. Real Federal Government Transfers to the State Food Agency, 1977–1987 (millions of 1978 pesos)

Year	Real Transfer to State Food Agency	Share of State Food Agency in Total Transfers (%)
1977	6,455	16.6
1978	11,031	25.0
1979	11,644	23.0
1980	19,022	26.7
1981	24,491	25.3
1982	26,732	19.0
1983	20,597	34.7
1984	34,329	26.4
1985	29,167	26.4
1986	23,207	30.1
1987	14,627	24.3

Sources: Secretaría de Hacienda y Crédito Público, "Estadísticas de finanzas públicas: Cífras anuales, 1977–86"; Secretaría de Hacienda y Crédito Público, "Estadísticas de finanzas públicas: Cífras anuales, 1987," deflated using price index in Juan Moreno Pérez, "La economía mexicana desde 1900: Nuevos series largas sobre la producción interna bruta y la inflación," unpublished manuscript (October 1992).

first two years of the de la Madrid administration, much of the Agency's efforts were concentrated on importing basic grains and in expanding the network of retail stores. The number of Agency stores increased at a pace similar to that of the previous two *sexenios*: between 1982 and 1984 the number of stores rose by 39 percent, from 11,291 to 15,669.

To ameliorate the effects of inflation on the working classes, the State Food Agency worked with the official party's confederation of unions, CT. On May 1, 1983, the Agency inaugurated a program in which food packets containing 250 items were sold at a 40 percent discount in Mexico City, Puebla, and Toluca. Further, the Agency announced plans to extend this program to twenty-six other sites in thirteen states.[8]

As the number of retail outlets and urban-based programs increased, so too did the State Food Agency's industrial activities. The increase in the number of stores accelerated the demand for Agency products to fill store shelves. The number of employees in the Agency's various industrial activities swelled from 9,773 in 1982 to 14,916 in 1986.[9] Output of goods and market share increased for ICONSA, MICONSA, and LICONSA. ICONSA's market share of its major products, with one exception, increased between 28 and 100 percent, and the number of industrial plants increased from fifteen to nineteen during the four-year period (Table 9-2). LICONSA's

Table 9-2. Market Share of ICONSA's Processed Foods, 1982 and 1986 (percent)

Food Product	1982	1986
Refined oil	13.1	22.3
Vegetable lard	22.9	15.3
Wheat flour	7.3	9.6
Corn flour	13.8	20.3
Soup noodles	5.6	7.2
Cookies	0	6.9
Soap and detergent	0	2.2

Source: CONASUPO, *El mercado de subsistencias populares*, vol. 2 (Mexico, 1988), p. 232.

recombined milk output nearly doubled during the first four years of the de la Madrid administration: 788.2 million liters in 1982, compared to 1,404.4 million in 1986. A similar increase was also noted for MICONSA, with its participation in the corn flour market expanding from 29 percent in 1982 to 37 percent in 1986 and its overall production increasing by 36 percent. The one industrial enterprise that declined in output was the wheat flour and bakery subsidiary TRICONSA, which produced 255.8 million pieces of bread in 1982 but only 136.5 million in 1986.[10] The general expansion of these food industries in an effort to ease the working class's economic pain added to the fiscal burdens of the de la Madrid administration.

During this expansion the State Food Agency engaged in deficit spending on the same scale that it had during the final years of the López Portillo presidency. In 1981, it spent 39 percent more than it took in, an amount hitherto unheard of. During the first full year of the de la Madrid administration this amount fell slightly to 33 percent but nevertheless was high for an administration seeking to cut public sector expenditure.[11] To reduce its deficit and to more effectively provide relief to urban and rural poor, the Agency began to restructure its activities by reducing the foreign deficit, which by the beginning of 1984 had reached 2.8 billion dollars;[12] decreasing national purchases, thus allowing the private sector to buy more; canceling nonpriority programs and those not necessary for the regulatory function; decentralizing the administrative apparatus; reducing operation costs; and rationalizing or eliminating subsidies.[13]

As part of President de la Madrid's general effort to decentralize the public sector, DICONSA's decision-making power was refocused by expanding the number of regional companies from six in 1982 to nineteen in 1988. The number of Agency stores rose to 21,305 by the end of his administration, 18 percent in one year alone (1986–1987). Such decentralization meant that retail stores multiplied to reach poorer sectors of the population in the various states of the republic; the number of stores outside the Federal District more than doubled under de la Madrid. Of the 22,600 stores open in 1988, 70 percent were located in rural areas (Table 9-3). Thus Mexico City's share in the total sales fell from 30 percent in 1982 to 8.3 percent in 1988.[14]

Cutbacks came in the form of reduced subsidies to consumers, phased in gradually so as not to further heighten popular discontent. The first reductions came in 1983, when subsidies for bread and tortillas were slashed by 60 percent and 49 percent, respectively.[15] In June 1984, the State Food Agency began to selectively support lower income groups by reducing the price of tortillas and milk for them. In the target program (the national program of subsidized tortillas), tortillas were sold in government stores at approximately 75 percent of the official price.[16] At the same time the subsidy given to mills was gradually withdrawn, passing the savings directly on to the consumer and reducing public expenditures.[17]

Table 9-3. Regional Distribution of State Food Agency Stores, 1982–1988

States	1982	1983	1984	1985	1986	1987	1988
Aguascalientes	255	276	292	340	340	366	351
Baja California Norte	70	76	301	307	462	928	549
Baja California Sur	57	60	91	96	104	132	139
Campeche	105	110	187	213	207	255	276
Coahuila	175	180	200	225	191	395	662
Colima	220	227	275	314	340	373	258
Chiapas	800	827	923	1,071	1,075	1,129	1,226
Chihuahua	240	257	597	814	812	863	882
Durango	102	111	198	161	381	411	—
Guanajuato	310	366	374	433	437	518	517
Guerrero	340	415	577	635	736	785	937
Hidalgo	102	122	129	122	120	716	731
Jalisco	210	272	368	420	477	522	675
México	336	407	689	916	1,046	1,255	1,193
Michoacán	505	573	594	829	870	895	887
Morelos	150	183	218	288	292	320	325
Nayarit	230	257	310	358	442	444	465
Nuevo León	140	153	167	256	253	731	802
Oaxaca	798	802	928	1,050	1,169	1,454	1,677
Puebla	912	937	1,012	987	1,012	1,254	1,248
Querétaro	195	208	306	391	382	478	460
Quintana Roo	95	117	170	174	190	225	231
San Luis Potosí	105	110	122	232	194	595	646
Sinaloa	163	204	491	974	954	1,028	1,160
Sonora	150	178	662	806	736	861	855
Tabasco	452	627	655	669	632	—	—
Tamaulipas	130	154	178	271	248	636	628
Tlaxcala	30	45	50	162	170	193	184
Veracruz	1,082	1,167	1,237	1,273	1,352	1,639	1,685
Yucatán	199	242	297	358	372	396	431
Zacatecas	305	313	403	475	479	579	592
Total	8,409	9,792	12,886	15,643	16,292	20,978	21,083

Source: *Mexico: Desarrollo regional y decentralización de la vida nacional, 1982–88* (México: SPP, 1988).

The Agency refined its targeting in April 1986 by giving coupons for subsidized tortillas to families earning less than two times the minimum wage. Under this program, popularly known as *tortibonos*, each coupon allowed a family to purchase a kilogram of tortillas at 32 pesos, whereas the market price was 200 pesos per kilogram. The tortilla coupon program came under attack by many who charged that the official party was distributing coupons to obtain political support. Some charged that as families registered to vote for official candidates, they also received applications for the *tortibono* program, regardless of their eligibility.[18] Although it is not clear to what extent the coupon program was politically motivated, it reduced the number of people eligible to receive government food support, thus opening up the possibility of corruption or other nefarious dealings to become eligible for the program.

Milk subsidies were also targeted to reach the poorer sectors of the Mexican population under de la Madrid. Milk production had generally not maintained pace with population growth for several decades, and because the 1980s saw milk production stagnate and per capita output plummet to a new low,[19] the State Food Agency imported more powdered milk than ever before, expanded its output of recombined milk, and initiated a program that aimed at providing incentives for ranchers to expand milk production.[20] Between 1982 and 1988, the amount of recombined milk distributed by the Agency increased by 108 percent, and the number of families benefiting tripled to 1,829,000 (Table 9-4).

Table 9-4. Volume and Real Value of Subsidies for Milk and Tortillas, 1980–1990 (millions of pesos 1985)

Year	Milk T Liters Distributed Daily	Subsidy T Families Benefited	Program Value of Subsidy Daily	Tortilla Tons Distributed	Subsidy T Families Benefited	Program Value of Subsidy
1980	1,000	425	18,779	7,597	5,664	N.D
1981	1,000	536	21,602	7,769	5,792	N.D
1982	1,599	566	31,690	8,093	6,034	N.D
1983	1,734	742	28,099	9,208	6,865	N.D
1984	1,889	788	33,157	9,312	7,092	N.D
1985	2,241	1,029	38,886	9,838	7,335	N.D
1986	2,519	1,167	40,186	9,384	6,996	3,460
1987	3,071	1,476	46,219	8,555	6,378	24,002
1988	3,322	1,829	38,785	8,101	6,040	22,722
1989	3,389	1,953	61,972	8,990	6,703	24,296
1990	4,000	2,097	47,403	8,010	5,972	25,803

Sources: Carlos Salinas de Gortari, *Tercer informe de gobierno: Anexo estadístico* (México, 1991), anexo, p. 303. Deflated using the wholesale price index in the International Monetary Fund, *International Financial Statistics* (1990 and January 1992). **Note:** T = thousands.

At the same time that the State Food Agency was shifting to meet the consumer demands of the rural population, it was trimming many of its services to producers. In particular, the 1980s saw some of the most prolonged declines in the real guaranteed prices offered by the Agency. Real guaranteed prices of basic grains generally reached their peak in 1981, but with the onset of double- and triple-digit inflation in the 1980s, they fell substantially for beans, corn, and wheat. For corn, the price dropped steadily under de la Madrid to 70 percent of the 1981 level. The guaranteed price for beans plummeted 61 percent from that of 1981. Wheat prices fell 72 percent by 1987. It was likely that if campesino organizations had not placed pressure on the state, real guaranteed prices might have plummeted further. Such sharp dips in guaranteed prices had a profound effect on rural incomes, compounded by a general decapitalization of government investment in the countryside. These shifts in government policy helped lead to a drop in production of basic grains in Mexico.

Beginning in 1982, the federal government's investment in agriculture, including credit and investment in irrigation, did not keep pace with inflation and instead plummeted to new lows. In fact, between 1982 and 1990, the amount of investment in the countryside fell to 517.4 billion real pesos, a 62 percent decline. Individual agencies fared worse than the aggregate data reveal. For example, the Banco Nacional de Crédito Rural (BANRURAL) showed a 76 percent real decline in funds allocated to it by the federal government (Table 9-5).[21]

The drastic declines in real guaranteed prices coupled with the general decapitalization of the countryside contributed to a further reduction in grain production and the resultant large imports of grain to supplement the production deficiencies. For corn, the mainstay of the popular diet, imports averaged nearly 3 million tons of corn per year, nearly triple the amount of the 1970s.[22] These large amounts of imports at a time of substantial decline in government revenues placed greater financial stress on the government. Consequently, there were renewed calls for a strategy to increase agricultural productivity to eliminate imports.[23]

Mounting pressure from peasants led to constant readjustments of the guaranteed price. Between 1983 and 1987, independent peasant organizations initiated a wave of protests against the pricing policy of the State Food Agency, including the occupation of various Agency warehouses and marches that blocked major highways. These protests led in many cases to increased producer bargaining powers and price concessions by the Agency.[24] Such pressure led to frequent adjustments of the guaranteed price of basic grains in an attempt to keep pace with inflation.

Table 9-5. Real Federal Government Investment in the Countryside, 1980–1990 (billions of pesos)

Year	A^a Total Government Investment in Countryside	B^a Amount Allotted to BANRURAL	C^b WPI^e 1985 = 100	D^c Real Total Government Investment in Countryside	E^d Real Amount Allotted to BANRURAL
1980	139.6	22.4	9.5	1,469.5	235.8
1981	191.8	39.4	11.8	1,625.4	333.9
1982	249.8	45.9	18.4	1,357.6	249.5
1983	408.1	104.9	38.2	1,068.3	274.6
1984	604.7	124.9	65.1	928.9	191.9
1985	856.8	181.3	100.0	856.8	181.3
1986	1,411.0	339.0	188.4	748.9	179.9
1987	2,500.8	524.4	443.9	563.4	118.1
1988	4,003.2	951.1	922.5	434.0	103.1
1989	4,868.1	1,030.4	1,070.8	454.6	96.2
1990	6,833.9	797.3	1,320.8	517.4	60.4

[a]Carlos Salinas de Gortari, *Tercer informe de gobierno, 1991* (México, 1991).
[b]International Monetary Fund, *International Financial Statistics* (1990 and January 1992).
[c]D = A/C.
[d]E = B/C.
[e]WPI = wholesale price index.

During the presidency of Miguel de la Madrid the State Food Agency served to maintain social peace in the city and the countryside. Because of its unique role as a catch-all social welfare agency, it did not undergo massive restructuring during the early years of the crisis. Instead, it gradually decentralized its operation and slowly shifted away from providing general subsidies to targeting specific sectors of the population. Indeed, many government officials publicly proclaimed that the Agency would be spared privatization due to its overwhelming social importance. The continued use of the Agency as a relief agency placed pressure on government expenditures, accounting for a growing portion of the government's public debt.

Although Agency expansion during this period maintained social peace, the nutrition of many poor Mexicans worsened. The stores concentrated in the countryside were no panacea to a growing portion of the *campesinado* that were restructured out of their livelihoods: inexpensive foodstuffs cannot replace declining credit and plummeting guaranteed prices. Official data demonstrate that between 1980 and 1988 there was a rise in infant and preschool mortality caused by nutritional deficiencies: from 1 percent to 5.2 percent for infants and from 1.5 percent to 9.1 percent for preschool-age children.[25] While rural poverty expanded, however, social peace was maintained—at least temporarily.

Salinas and the Dismantling of the State Food Agency

Following one of the most contested elections in Mexican history, Carlos Salinas de Gortari was inaugurated president of Mexico on December 1, 1988. Salinas claimed to have received 50.1 percent of the vote to 31.1 percent for the left-of-center candidate, Cuauhtémoc Cárdenas, other estimates showed that Cárdenas had actually won. Since not all of the ballots were released for counting, many doubts as to the validity of the election were raised.[26] With a weak political base, Salinas was forced to move quickly to consolidate his power. He carried forward his plan to modernize the economy by stepping up the privatization and liquidation of state agencies at a much more aggressive pace than did his predecessor. Salinas's moves to restructure the public sector led him to sell, liquidate, or merge most government operations, including the State Food Agency.

Many of the intellectual justifications for Salinas's economic programs and his view of the role of the state were similar to those of de la Madrid. In fact, as planning secretary during the de la Madrid administration, Salinas had been the architect of the first wave of privatizations. Intellectually, he relied on a number of studies that argued that the old justification for social programs—to gain political support—was not very effective. His 1978 Harvard doctoral dissertation, "Political Participation, Public Investment and System Support: A Study of 3 Rural Communities in Central Mexico," argued that the most politically effective form of government intervention is "to provide service slowly and moderately, thus obtaining relatively higher public support."[27]

Salinas's plan for the State Food Agency was shaped by his overall strategy for reforming the countryside. He called for reactivation of agricultural production by encouraging private and foreign investment in agriculture; government would withdraw from active participation in the market to assume the role of regulator. A number of cost-benefit studies carried out at the Instituto Tecnológico Autónoma de México demonstrated that the Agency was using resources inefficiently, benefiting neither consumers nor producers as much as it intended to do.[28] These studies provided an intellectual and "empirical" justification for the reduction of the role of the Agency.

Within a year of assuming the presidency, Salinas launched his plans to reform the State Food Agency. In October 1989, Salinas's head of the Agency, Ignacio Ovalle Fernández, announced that the downsizing was aimed at making the government responsive to the poorest sectors of the population. By eliminating operations that were deemed too costly and did not directly benefit the very poor, the Agency's nonpriority activities were reduced: nine of its industrial plants were put up for sale; a number of its urban stores were put up for sale or transferred to unions and consumer cooperatives; its warehouses were transferred to ANDSA; and the grains that it purchased were limited to corn and beans. In addition to the closures, the Agency announced plans to open up to seventy large stores in the countryside, called solidarity warehouses, to make basic goods available to isolated populations.[29] During the weeks prior to the reorganization, rumors had been circulating in Mexico that the Agency's entire operation would be privatized, but government officials repeatedly explained that reorganization would allow the Agency to carry out its tasks more effectively. According to Ovalle, it was only "slimming for the wealthy but expanding for the poor."[30]

On the surface, both public and private sector leaders embraced the reduction of the State Food Agency's operations. Two major private sector organizations—CONCANACO and Confederación Nacional de Cámaras Industriales (CONCAMIN)—lauded the government's initiatives and called on the government to move further and completely privatize the remaining stores.[31] The official peasant and worker organizations joined in expressing their support for restructuring the Agency. Immediately following the announcement, CTM and CNC made official statements praising the change. However, over the next few days, daily press accounts began to show that there was much more opposition to government policy than was initially expressed.

Although the official spokespersons of the CNC and the CTM publicly supported the restructuring, the rank and file were divided. The government newspaper *El Nacional* proclaimed that the CT backed the restructuring, but the left-of-center *La Jornada* stated that the CT wanted the Agency expanded and that its leaders were upset that they had not been consulted about the proposed changes.[32] Likewise, many members of the executive committee of the CNC, with the exception of its leader, began to question the move and argued that it was contrary to what they had been struggling for.[33]

One of the few government officials to openly criticize the downsizing of the State Food Agency was Demetrio Sodi de la Tijera, a PRI congressman known for his independence. Sodi de la Tijera, an expert on agrarian affairs and on the provisioning of Mexico City, had been publicly challenging any proposed Agency reorganization that would weaken it. In a series of articles, Sodi argued that the poorer classes would be victims of the downsizing process.[34] Nineteen other PRI congressmen joined Sodi in a meeting with Ovalle in which they expressed their opposition to the sale of the Agency's industrial plants, the reduction in state purchases, and the elimination of urban stores. Ovalle acknowledged their concerns, but he explained that the decision to reduce operations was a presidential one that did not emanate from the Agency and that therefore there was little that he could do.[35]

Aside from factions within the official party, a number of other groups condemned the restructuring of the State Food Agency. Left-of-center opposition parties charged that less state intervention would subject both the producer and the consumer to exploitation by the middleman.[36] Popular protests condemning the restructuring were numerous in the days following the announcement of the restructuring, and women's groups even stormed the offices of the Agency to condemn the withdrawal of subsidies.

Protests soon waned, however, and the Agency stopped producing industrial products and began to close its stores in urban areas. When the industrial plants of the Agency were put up for sale, there were not many potential buyers seeking to purchase them. The best prospect for sale was the corn flour mill (MICONSA), which it was speculated would be purchased by MICONSA's only major competitor since 1949, Molinos Aztecas (MASECA), which had grown to be a major producer of tortilla-related products with multinational dealings.[37] In the end, MICONSA was purchased by another consortium and renamed MINSA, returning to its original name.

The initial restructuring in October 1989 led to a qualitatively distinct State Food Agency entity. Operations were so reduced that the government projected that the Agency's income would fall from 2,618,700 billion pesos in 1989 to 447 billion in 1990.[38]

As the State Food Agency reduced its operations by closing down stores, it began to place greater emphasis on subsidizing milk and tortillas. A month after announcing the restructuring of the

Agency's operations, Ovalle announced a 48 percent increase in the subsidies for bread, milk, and tortillas for those living in rural areas and on the margins of the larger cities.[39] In targeting specific sectors of the population, many of the activities of the Agency were run in cooperation with President Salinas's national solidarity program (PRONASOL). Announced in his inaugural address on December 1, 1988, PRONASOL was an umbrella social welfare agency that sought to develop health, education, housing, nutrition, employment, basic infrastructure for the poorest sectors of the Mexican population. PRONASOL consolidated programs located in different government agencies in order to coordinate their operation in a more cost-effective manner. According to government figures, in over a two-year period the government program had disbursed 3.4 billion dollars and had undertaken some 204,000 social welfare projects. PRONASOL's supporters argued that by concentrating resources in one agency, the government could more efficiently use its scarce resources to target the poor. Critics claimed that PRONASOL was merely a sophisticated way for the poor to receive social welfare benefits from the president, thus winning political support for the official party.[40]

Throughout the country, the State Food Agency closed stores and then began to reopen them in cooperation with PRONASOL. The Agency planned to establish seventy solidarity stores, offering wholesale goods at a discount to small businesses and allowing organized labor and consumer cooperatives a chance to purchase basic products at an average discount of 25 percent. In inaugurating the first of the solidarity stores in May 1990, Agency manager Ignacio Ovalle reaffirmed that the purpose of the new Agency was to serve only those who needed it most. To support this venture, state governments invested 1,627 million pesos, and the Agency invested 2,371 million pesos. The participation of state governments eased the Agency's financial burden.[41]

Another major area of concentration of government resources by the Salinas administration was in LICONSA, the State Food Agency's milk subsidiary. Subsidizing milk consumption had been one of the primary symbols of the state's concern for popular welfare during Mexico's intense economic crisis. Consequently, the importation of powdered milk rose at a phenomenal rate during the 1980s. By 1990 Mexico was the world's largest powdered milk importer.[42] The government stepped up its distribution of milk to the rural and urban poor by expanding LICONSA outlets. The number of beneficiaries more than quadrupled between 1980 and 1988 and increased by over 10 percent between 1988 and 1990 (Table 9-4). Despite the investment, Salinas plunged forward with his plan for completely dismantling the State Food Agency, ridding it of its last industrial operations—milk recombination. In 1991 he announced the sale of the milk agency's three production plants, including operations in Aguascalientes, Veracruz, and Chihuahua.[43] Nevertheless, LICONSA would continue to exist in streamlined form.

Under PRONASOL, the State Food Agency shifted its policy from granting tortilla coupons to the poor to giving tortillas directly to the poor and gradually liberalizing the price of tortillas to the general public. In a last-ditch effort to eliminate the indiscriminate tortilla subsidy and help the truly needy, the government, through its *tortivales* program, began to give away a kilogram of tortillas daily to 3.2 million families earning less than two minimum wages. According to government officials, this new policy has saved 700 billion pesos in yearly subsidies, despite the fact that the government continued to subsidize the tortilla for 500 pesos a kilogram in order to maintain its price to consumers at 600 pesos.[44] Critics charged that *tortivales* were granted to those who voted for the official party and not necessarily to those who truly needed it. Mexico's independent political weekly, *Proceso*, charged that PRONASOL interviewers sent to determine if families qualified for the tortivales program also asked questions about official party affiliation and voting preferences. *Proceso* found that people were being offered *tortivales* even though they were economically ineligible. Detractors of the policy opined that a more apt name for the *tortivales* program would be *tortivotos* because, according to them, it was used to buy votes for the official party.[45]

Although targeting subsidies to those who "truly need it" will eventually reduce public expenditure in this area, a number of problems of definitions arise. Who qualifies as "truly needy" is a subject that has plagued government policymakers. Although the definition of the equivalent of two minimum wages has been used, purchasing power varies with family size and the area in which the family lives. Problems in defining precisely the number of truly needy has led to a fairly large disparity in government estimates. The nutritional impact that the government's withdrawal from the marketplace has had on the poorer populations has yet to be fully investigated, but it is clear that in the short term poor workers have even less access to basic foods.[46]

As part of the government strategy to modernize the economy and reduce public expenditure, governments during the past two *sexenios* reoriented the countryside by targeting producers of certain crops. The slogan for the agricultural sector has been "modernization and increased productivity." In line with these goals, the government gradually retreated from its traditional role of active intervention in the countryside by limiting its role in the marketing of grain and by liberalizing land reform laws. The latter enabled *ejidos* to sell their parcels of land, paving the way for increased private and foreign investment in the countryside.

The massive decapitalization of the countryside that began with the economic crisis of 1982 continued into the 1990s. Despite the fact that inflation was brought under control within the first two years of the Salinas administration, agricultural investment grew very slowly, and government extension of agricultural credit declined by 40 percent (Table 9-5). Coupled with the general decline in investment in the countryside was the liquidation during the 1980s of a number of agencies that operated in the countryside. Following the general streamlining trend, many of these agencies have been shut down or privatized.[47]

During the 1980s, the State Food Agency contributed to the decapitalization of the countryside by reducing real guaranteed prices for agricultural products. Between 1982 and 1987 the guaranteed price of the four basic grains (beans, corn, rice, and wheat) fell by 30 percent in the case of corn. With the reorganization of the Agency in 1989, the number of crops that it purchased at a guaranteed price was reduced from twelve to two—beans and corn. The real guaranteed prices of these two staples continued to decline, even though corn prices still remained slightly above the world price.

Corn in Mexico faced a bleak future under NAFTA. Many analysts have predicted that when Mexico's corn prices were liberalized there would be a massive shifting of the population away from corn production to the cultivation of other crops, either sparking a mass migration to the cities and to the United States or causing them to shift to more competitive crops. One study suggests that as many as 850,000 heads of household, some 12 percent of the rural labor force, would leave the Mexican countryside.[48] Although the State Food Agency did not end guaranteed prices on corn and beans prior to the implementation of NAFTA, it planned to do so soon after 1994.

Decline in agricultural output during the 1980s enabled the Salinas administration to argue that the Mexican countryside needed massive private investment. To encourage investment, Salinas oversaw the December 1991 revision of Article 27 of the Mexican Constitution, which ended the requirement for state distribution of land and provided for the rental and sale of *ejido* lands if *ejido* members voted to do so.[49] Although President Salinas publicly stated that the government will provide credit to those *ejidatarios* who wished to maintain their land, it does seem that such credit is channeled mainly through PRONASOL. It is still unclear how this new privatization and reduced public sector participation in the countryside can lead to renewed agricultural prosperity or to a general increase in the standard of living of rural dwellers.

In October 4, 1993, President Salinas announced his effort to "modernize agricultural policy and promote rural welfare" with his Programa de Apoyo al Campo (PROCAMPO).[50] The purpose of PROCAMPO was to grant direct payments to more than 3 million producers (two-thirds of whom have not had access to government support) to encourage modernization of production and increased output. The payment structure gave smaller producers more aid than larger producers. Over time, however, PROCAMPO payments were to be gradually reduced and phased out, well before the fifteen-year phase-out period allotted by NAFTA. The stated goal, then, was to aid the smallest producers, making them more competitive and easing their transition.[51] Critics of PROCAMPO charged that the program was a ploy to slow down some of the more obvious rural inequities created by over a decade of rural neglect and decapitalization. Some went so far as to suggest that the timing of PROCAMPO's announcement was aimed at helping the PRI in the countryside.[52] PROCAMPO was the government's way of attempting to cushion the effects of liberalizations in the countryside and to support those rural producers that had been particularly hard hit by a decade of economic crisis and dwindling government resources. It exemplified the fact that the functions of the State Food Agency, by the end of the Salinas administration, had been substantially supplanted by market forces.

Neoliberalism and the Reemergence of Social Conflict in the Countryside

Could the major reforms in the countryside be accomplished without social upheaval? Until the beginning of 1994, the Salinas ad-

ministration seemed to be successful at implementing its rural reforms, relatively free of widespread opposition and indeed, at times
with seemingly strong support. The uprising in Chiapas beginning
on January 1, 1994, and the support given to the rebels by both
urban and rural groups, however, called into question many of the
Salinas reforms. According to Subcomandante Marcos, spokesper-
son for the Ejército Zapatista de Liberación Nacional (EZLN), "it
seems to me that what most radicalized the comrades was the reform of Article 27." The EZLN has called for a renewed agrarian
reform, the first step of which would include the reversal of Salinas's
changes to Article 27.[53] Many campesino and indigenous groups
throughout the country pledged their support for the EZLN and
its proposals. Within a few weeks of the outbreak of hostilities, there
were indications that many of these organizations had radicalized,
and some threatened to join the armed rebellion.[54]

Scholars analyzing the rise of the EZLN have also linked the
group's emergence and popularity to the economic and agrarian
change that occurred in the region since the 1970s. Stanford University anthropologist George Collier has convincingly argued that
part of the roots of rebellion lie in the neglect of small-scale agriculture. In Tabasco and Chiapas, for example, an energy boom lured
many corn farmers and farm laborers to work in higher paying jobs
on these public works projects or on the numerous construction
projects that developed with the boom. At the same time, agriculture in the region changed as many workers left the countryside
and landowners increasingly converted acreage to pasture lands
or introduced labor-saving devices that required fewer workers.
When these public works were reduced in the 1980s, large numbers of workers had little to fall back on, creating significant unemployment that exacerbated existing conflicts in the region and
contributed to the rebellion of January 1994.[55]

With the ascension of President Ernesto Zedillo at the end of
1994, most analysts predicted a continuation of the economic policies of neoliberalism that were associated with the administration
of Salinas. Indeed, Zedillo vowed to continue transforming Mexico
to a market economy and pledged full support to NAFTA and the
concept of free trade. President Zedillo's first major crisis came a
month after taking office. On December 20, 1994, he sought to deal
with Mexico's overvalued currency by allowing the peso to float
against the dollar. The result was the plummeting of the currency
during several weeks of economic uncertainty. The peso eventually settled at approximately seven to the U.S. dollar (up from three),

but the process led to greater economic crisis, with GDP plummeting and businesses closing and laying off people in large numbers.
President Zedillo's response included accelerating the liberalization of prices and further reducing government spending. Privatization was introduced in areas that for political reasons had been
spared previously, namely, the railroad, Pétroleos Mexicanos
(PEMEX), and electricity. The United States stepped in to help bail
Mexico out of the crisis by extending a line of credit to prevent the
depletion of Mexico's reserves.[56]

As with the crisis of the 1980s, there was substantial economic
and social fallout from the peso crisis. Economically, the crisis meant
a 7.5 percent decline in the official GDP, when the predicted growth
rate was about 3–4 percent. Domestic sales declined by between
30 and 80 percent, and a large percent of small- and medium-sized
businesses were forced to close or streamline their operations. Res-
taurant business was halved; car sales plummeted 75 percent. New
investment was suspended: Nissan cut 1,000 jobs, and Walmart
suspended plans to build twenty-five additional stores throughout the country.

Despite President Zedillo's campaign slogan, "For the Welfare
of Your Family," the burden of the crisis fell disproportionately on
Mexican workers. The year 1995 witnessed a devastating impact
on Mexican workers: there were an estimated 750,000 to 1 million
layoffs (in addition to 1 million new job entrants); official unemployment rose from 3.2 percent in December 1994 to 7.6 percent in
August 1995.[57] Historically, this rate was extremely high, and un-
official estimates placed unemployment as high as 19 million, or
nearly 50 percent of the economically active population (EAP). Official statistics demonstrated that two-thirds of the EAP, approximately 23 million out of 35 million people, were underemployed,
either working at jobs below their training or in part-time positions, often piecing several jobs together to try to recuperate their
income.[58] Indeed, children have been entering the workforce in
larger numbers, selling chewing gum or performing on street corners before and after school as a way to supplement family income.

Unlike past crises, President Zedillo confronted the peso crisis
and the resulting economic malaise with austerity measures that
have added extra burdens for the majority of Mexicans. In December 1995, the price to ride the Metro, electric train, and trolley buses
increased from 40 centavos to 1 peso—a bargain by U.S. standards
but a great burden to hundreds of thousands of riders a day who
depend on daily travel from outlying *colonias* to work. Rates for

public utilities increased and in April 1995, the federal sales tax increased. The inflation rate in 1995 was at least 54 percent. Although government moved to place controls on some prices, it liberalized others. The secretary of commerce announced that prices of basic foods—bread, rice, cookies, cleaning products, and soaps—would increase approximately 40 percent.[59]

It is apparent that the economic fallout accelerated Mexico's crime rate. After one year of economic crisis, the *Los Angeles Times* reported that "Mexico's economic crisis has brought not 'red flags' and revolt, as many feared, but a brutal wave of robberies and murders." In 1995 car thefts increased 161 percent in Mexico City, armed robberies and home burglaries by 30 percent, and homicide by 10 percent.[60] In 1996, Mexico witnessed an additional 10 percent increase in the already record levels of crime, despite a high profile effort to fight crime.[61] This is a clear indication that Mexico's social fabric is tattered.

From 1994 through 1996, the countryside has grown increasingly unstable. Foreign capital apparently has not flowed as continuously as was expected. Meanwhile, poorer peasants have become increasingly marginalized, and many have been forced to become involved in the illicit drug trade. In the middle of 1996, a second guerrilla army began operating in the Mexican countryside, Ejército Popular Revolucionario (EPR), which gained support in the poorer regions of the country such as Guerrero and Oaxaca. The importance of this group remains to be seen, but their actions and government counteractions do not bode well for stability in the countryside.[62]

As part of the political fallout of the economic crisis, former President Salinas and his brother Raúl came under intense scrutiny. While Raúl Salinas was jailed in 1995 in connection with the assassination of PRI presidential candidate Luis Donaldo Colosio, many of his past business dealings came under scrutiny. An expert on rural questions, Raúl Salinas had a longtime association with the State Food Agency. Many began to speculate that Salinas had amassed a fortune during his tenure at the agency. Such accusations led a number of members of Congress to call for a special investigation into CONASUPO's operations. After a ten-month investigation, Congress voted along party lines (219 to 129) to send the president a report that found no widespread corruption in the agency and only reported isolated incidents of wrongdoing. Opposition politicians argued that the investigation was unable to probe deep enough and that the PRI was engaged in a coverup.[63]

Such scandal has clearly discredited much of the reputation that the State Food Agency once had.

In the early 1990s other abuses in the activities of the State Food Agency came to light. For example, because the demand for powdered milk was so great during the 1980s and the secrecy with which policymaking was carried out was so entrenched it was alleged that a number of abuses were committed. The most high-profile allegation was the case of radioactive milk shipments. During late 1987, between 17,000 and 43,000 tons of milk infected by the Chernobyl nuclear accident were imported to Mexico from Ireland. Later, it is alleged, thousands of tons more might have been imported despite knowledge of the possibilities of contamination. Although it was very difficult to determine how much of the contaminated milk was ingested by consumers, investigative reporters and popular outcry led to a congressional investigation. However, such investigations have met numerous bureaucratic and political obstacles due to the historical secrecy of such policymaking.[64]

During the late 1980s and 1990s, then, widespread corruption in the State Food Agency was hinted at for the first time. It is likely that such abuses represented the tip of the iceberg. Nevertheless, the growing recognition of corruption in the Agency was used by government officials to justify downsizing the Agency and privatizing its functions. Even Fidel Velásquez, head of the CTM, in calling for increased government programs to maintain social peace, said that the eventual disappearance of CONASUPO would be healthy since "it only functions to favor dishonest officials."[65]

The Zedillo administration has continued the food policy of the Salinas administration: it liberalized prices and greatly reduced the role of government to allow the free market to allocate food resources. The State Food Agency would be gradually eliminated. In November of 1998, the government took a step toward dismantling the Agency by firing over 1,000 employees and closing over half of its national offices. As the government cut its budget to account for income lost from economic crisis and declining petroleum prices, the Agency, as the last symbol of the social welfare state, was severely weakened. Although government officials stated that the Agency would continue to exist for a couple of years until the private sector could fully take over its functions, by mid-1999 it had been dismantled.[66]

In a further blow to the welfare state, the government announced the elimination of the tortilla subsidy and the end of price controls, starting in January 1999. Although no one is quite sure what this will mean for tortilla prices, any increase would be harmful to the large number of Mexicans who subsist on incomes of double the minimum wage or less. The large corn flour producers, MASECA and MINSA, applauded the plan as a further step to allow the free market to determine prices.[67] Because most small family-owned *tortillerias* will not be able to survive, this change will increase their market share.

Many argued that eliminating the tortilla subsidy would have a devastating effect on children and families who are already reeling from nearly two decades of neoliberal policy.[68] A recent study on purchasing power conducted by researchers from the Universidad Nacional Autónoma de México (UNAM) demonstrated that in 1988 eight hours of work were sufficient to purchase the basic basket of food items, but in 1998 it requires thirty-four hours of work.[69] This study further documented the devastating impact of the dismantling of the welfare state.

Conclusion

The economic crisis of the 1980s forced the Mexican government to drastically rethink the role of the government in the economy. Instead of active state intervention, President Miguel de la Madrid initiated a wave of privatization and liquidation of state companies in an effort to cut public expenditures. Because the economic crisis had disastrous effects on wages, the federal government opted not to dismantle the State Food Agency immediately and instead used it to cushion the impact of the economic crisis. It continued to expand the number of its retail outlets during the early 1980s to provide inexpensive foodstuffs to a wider sector of the population. After the most intense period of crisis was felt during 1983, the government scaled back the operations of the Agency by decentralizing its bureaucracy and allowing federal government transfers to the Agency to fall below the rate of inflation. In the countryside, guaranteed prices did not keep pace with inflation, and producers shifted production to other crops.

With the presidency of Carlos Salinas de Gortari, the State Food Agency experienced a radical transformation of its operations. In one swift blow, in October 1989, the Agency was directed to liquidate its industrial plants and its urban retail stores, to transfer all of its warehouses to ANDSA, and to reduce the number of grains that it purchased at a guaranteed price from twelve to two. The Agency that emerged from the 1989 restructuring was one that was designed to use its resources to target poorer sectors of the population by indirect means. Subsequently, it saw most of its remaining functions, primarily social welfare operations, merged with PRONASOL, so that the way had been paved for the Agency's complete liquidation.

By the end of the 1990s the Agency that emerged under Cárdenas and saw its apogee in the early 1980s was effectively dead. The political and economic crisis beginning in 1994, characterized by the Chiapas uprising and the peso devaluation of 1994, can be linked to the unraveling of the social welfare programs represented by the State Food Agency. Additionally, the lack of a social safety net in the midst of economic crisis has cut deeply into the purchasing power of both producers and consumers.

Notes

1. For a general overview of the economy during this period, see James W. Wilkie, "The Six Ideological Phases of Mexico's 'Permanent Revolution' since 1910," in James W. Wilkie, ed., *Society and Economy in Mexico* (Los Angeles: UCLA Latin American Center Publications, 1990); James M. Cypher, *State and Capital in Mexico: Development Policy since 1940* (Boulder, Colo.: Westview Press, 1990), esp. chap. 6. For the impact of the crisis on minimum wages, see Kevin J. Middlebrook, "The Sounds of Silence: Organised Labour's Response to Economic Crisis in Mexico," *Journal of Latin American Studies* 21:2 (May 1989), p. 195.

2. Judith A. Teichman, *Privatization and Political Change in Mexico* (Pittsburgh, Pa.: University of Pittsburgh Press, 1995), pp. 131, 4.

3. Middlebrook, "The Sounds of Silence," pp. 204–205.

4. Teichman, *Privatization and Political Change in Mexico*, p. 74.

5. For discussion of de la Madrid's austerity program, see Wayne A. Cornelius, "The Political Economy of Mexico under de la Madrid: Austerity, Routinized Crisis, and Nascent Recovery," *Mexican Studies/Estudios Mexicanos* 1:1 (winter 1985), pp. 83–124.

6. Teichman, *Privatization and Political Change in Mexico*, p. 79.

7. Compañía Nacional de Subsistencias Populares, *Cinco años de realizaciones, 1983–87* (México: CONASUPO, 1988), p. 4.

8. Presidencia de la República, *Las razones y la obras: Gobierno de Miguel de la Madrid, crónica del sexenio, 1982–88, primer año* (México: Presidencia de la República, 1984), p. 137.

9. Calculated from the statistical appendix of CONASUPO, *El mercado de las subsistencias populares*, vol. 2 (México: CONASUPO, 1988).

10. Ibid.

11. Carlos Salinas de Gortari, *Tercer informe de gobierno, 1991* (México, 1991), statistical annex, p. 178.

12. José Iturriaga de la Fuente, "1983–88: CONASUPO y el cambio estructural," p. 165.

13. CONASUPO, *Cinco años de realizaciones, 1983–87*, p. 5.

14. CONASUPO, *Cambio estructural del sistema de distribuidoras CONASUPO: Informe de labores, 1982–1988* (México: Sistema de Distribuidoras, 1988), vol. 2.

15. Presidencia de la República, *Las razones y la obras*, primer año, p. 183.

16. "El cambio estructural en el comercio interior de México, 1983–1986," *El Mercado de Valores* 77:30 (July 27, 1987), p. 803.

17. Presidencia de la República, *Las razones y las obras*, fourth year, p. 80.

18. *Proceso*, no. 563 (August 17, 1987), p. 11.

19. Manrrubio Muñoz Rodríguez, "Limites y potencialidades del sistema de la leche en México," *Comercio Exterior* 40:3 (September 1990), p. 887.

20. Presidencia de la República, *Las razones y las obras*, first year, p. 139. For data on imports, see Aida Mostkoff and Enrique C. Ochoa, "Complexities of Measuring the Food Situation in Mexico: Supply versus Self-Sufficiency of Basic Grains, 1925–86," in James W. Wilkie, ed., *Society and Economy in Mexico* (Los Angeles: UCLA Latin American Center Press, 1990).

21. *El Financiero*, May 16, 1989, claims a 56 percent decline. The discrepancy here can be largely accounted for by updated data in Table 9-5. Neil Harvey, in *Rebellion in Chiapas: Rural Reforms, Campesino Radicalism, and the Limits to Salinismo*, revised and updated edition (La Jolla: Center for U.S.-Mexican Studies, University of California at San Diego), discusses discrepancies in the amount of credit received by producers in Chiapas during this period. For further discussion of decapitalization of the countryside during the first half of the 1980s, see José Luis Calva, *Crisis agrícola y alimentaria en México, 1982–1988* (México: Distribución Fontamara, 1988), pp. 38–44.

22. Mostkoff and Ochoa, *Complexities of Measuring the Food Situation in Mexico*.

23. *El Financiero*, May 11, 1990.

24. Presidencia de la República, *Las razones y las obras*, cuarto año, pp. 224–229; Jonathan Fox and Gustavo Gordillo, "Between State and Market: The Campesino's Quest for Autonomy," in Wayne A. Cornelius, Judith Gentleman, and Peter H. Smith, eds., *Mexico's Alternative Political Futures* (La Jolla: Center for U.S.-Mexican Studies, University of California at San Diego, 1989), pp. 153–155.

25. Santiago Friedmann, Nora Lustig, and Arianna Legovini, "Mexico: Social Spending and Food Subsidies during Adjustment in the 1980s," in Nora Lustig, ed., *Coping with Austerity: Poverty and Inequality in Latin America* (Washington, D.C.: Brookings Institution, 1995), p. 369.

26. The various estimates of the election outcome can be found in Wilkie, "The Six Ideological Phases," pp. 49–53.

27. Carlos Salinas de Gortari, "Political Participation, Public Investment and System Support: Study of 3 Rural Communities in Central Mexico," Ph.D. diss., Harvard University, 1978, p. 143.

28. Oscar H. Vera Ferrer, *El caso CONASUPO: Una evaluación* (México: Centro de Estudios en Economia y Educación, A.C., 1987).

29. *La Jornada*, October 23, 1989; *A quién sirve la nueva CONASUPO* (México: CONASUPO, 1989).

30. Quoted in *La Jornada*, October 23, 1989; *El Nacional*, October 26, 1989.

31. *La Jornada*, October 30, 1989.

32. *El Nacional*, October 26, 1989; *La Jornada*, October 26, 1989.

33. *La Jornada*, November 7, 1989. For the CNC's continued support of the restructuring of the State Food Agency, see the comments of its leader, Maximiliano Silerio Esparza, "La CNC apoya la modernización de CONASUPO," *La Jornada*, November 9, 1989.

34. Prior to becoming a congressman, Demetrio Sodi was the general coordinator of provision and distributions in the Federal District. As a result of his work in this area, he coauthored, with Fernando Rello, *Abasto y distribución de alimientos en las grandes metropolis: El caso de la ciudad de México* (México: Nueva Imagen, 1988). Among the articles Sodi wrote for *La Jornada* was "Un paso atrás en la rectoria del estado," *La Jornada*, October 24, 1989; see also *Mexico City News*, October 23, 1989.

35. *La Jornada*, November 15, 1989.

36. *La Jornada*, October 26, 1989.

37. P. Dugan, "Tortilla Technology," *Forbes*, April 29, 1991, pp. 147–148.

38. Billion refers to mil millones (1,000 million). *El Financiero*, November 15, 1989.

39. *El Financiero*, November 23, 1989.

40. For discussion of PRONOSAL's operations and its political ramifications, see Denise Dresser, *Neopopulist Solutions to Neoliberal Problems: Mexico's National Solidarity Program* (La Jolla: Center for U.S.-Mexican Studies, University of California at San Diego, 1992); Sergio Sarmiento, "Solidarity Offers Hope for Votes," *El Financiero Internacional*, September 30, 1991, p. 12; Julio Moguel, "Salinas' Failed War on Poverty," *NACLA Report on the Americas* 18:1 (July–August 1994), pp. 38–41.

41. *El Financiero*, May 11, 1990.

42. *El Sol de México*, June 17, 1991.

43. Mike Zellner, "Mexico's Milk Industry: Half Full or Half Empty?" in *El Financiero Internacional*, August 26, 1991, pp. 10–11.

44. *Excelsior*, July 7, 1990; *La Jornada*, July 19, 1990.

45. *Proceso*, no. 732, November 12, 1990, pp. 6–8; Dresser, *Neopopulist Solutions to Neoliberal Problems*, pp. 28–29.

46. For initial attempts to assess the social impact of the crisis and economic restructuring, see Nora Lustig, *Mexico: The Remaking of an Economy* (Washington, D.C.: Brookings Institution, 1992).

47. For a list of the various public sector acts taken in the countryside, by *sexenio*, see Raúl Salinas de Gortari, "Agrarismo y agricultura en el México independiente y posrevolucionario," in *México: Setenta y cinco años de revolución, tomo 1, Desarrollo social* (México: Fondo de Cultura Económica, 1988), pp. 368–384. In 1991, Gustavo Gordillo, undersecretary of Agriculture, announced the discorporation of twenty-four parastate entities coordinated by the Secretary of Agriculture; see *Uno Más Uno*, February 2, 1991.

48. See Sherman Robinson, Mary Burfisher, Raúl Hinojosa, and Karen Thierfelder, "Agricultural Policies and Migration in a U.S.-Mexican Free Trade Area: A Computable General Equilibrium Analysis," California Agricultural Experiment Station, Giannini Foundation, University of California at Berkeley, Working Paper No. 617, December 1991. For a clear discussion of the various issues related to agriculture and the North American Free Trade Agreement, see Jonathan Fox, "Agriculture and the Poli-

tics of the North American Trade Debate: A Report from the Trinational Exchange on Agriculture, the Environment, and the Free Trade Agreement," *LASA Forum* 23:1 (spring 1992), pp. 3–9.

49. "New Horizons for Agriculture," BANAMEX, *Review of the Mexican Economic Situation*, no. 794 (January 1992), pp. 9–13. The November 25, 1991, edition of *Proceso* was dedicated to the reform of Article 27.

50. Carlos Hank González, "El Procampo: Estrategia de apoyos al productor del agro," *Comercio Exterior* (October 1993), pp. 982.

51. David M. Baer, "PROCAMPO: Analyzing State Agricultural Policy in Mexico in the Context of Economic Liberalization, NAFTA, and GATT," M.A. thesis, University of Florida, 1995.

52. For critiques of PROCAMPO, see Armando Bartra, "¿Subsidios para qué? Los quiebres finisexenales de la política rural," and Julio Moguel, "Procampo y la vía campesina de desarrollo," in *La Jornada del Campo* 2:20 (October 26, 1993); Armando Bartra, "A Persistant Rural Leviathan," in Laura Randall, ed., *Reforming Mexico's Agrarian Reform* (Armonk, N.Y.: M. E. Sharp, 1996), pp. 173–184.

53. Blanche Petrich, "Parte de las armas del EZLN se las compramos al Ejército: Marcos," *La Opinión* (Los Angeles), February 9, 1994.

54. "Campesinos e indígenas con el EZLN," *La Opinión* (Los Angeles), February 9, 1994.

55. George A. Collier, *Basta! Land and the Zapatista Rebellion in Chiapas* (Oakland, Calif.: Institute for Food and Development Policy, 1994); and George A. Collier, "The Rebellion in Chiapas and the Legacy of Energy Development," in *Mexican Studies/Estudios Mexicanos* 10:2 (summer 1994), pp. 371–382. See also Harvey, *Rebellion in Chiapas.*

56. See Jorge G. Castañeda, *The Mexican Shock: Its Meaning for the U.S.* (New York: New Press, 1995).

57. David E. Lorey, "The Status of Social Development under Zedillo," in M. Delal Baer and Roderic Ai Camp, eds., *Presiding over Change? Zedillo's First Year* (Washington, D.C.: Center for Strategic and International Studies, 1997). See also Enrique Valencia Lomelí, ed., *A dos años: La política social de Ernesto Zedillo* (México: Red Observatorio Social, 1997).

58. *El Financiero*, January 18, 1996.

59. Víctor Manuel Juárez, "Las alzas rebasaron al aument salarial," *Epoca*, April 8, 1996, pp. 36–37.

60. *Los Angeles Times*, December 30, 1995.

61. *Los Angeles Times*, December 15, 1996.

62. For a discussion of the EPR, see *Proceso*, no. 1034 (August 25, 1996).

63. Mark Fineman, "Opposition Cries Foul as PRI Ends Investigation of State Firm," *Los Angeles Times* (September 27, 1996); and Francisco Robles, "Proponen juicios políticos contra los directores de CONASUPO," *La Opinion* (September 27, 1996).

64. The story of the radioactive milk is told by Guillermo Zamora in *Caso CONASUPO: La leche radiactiva, el crimen más atroz contra el pueblo mexicano* (México: Editorial Planeta, 1997). Zamora is an investigative reporter who helped uncover this story.

65. Arturo Gómez Salgado, "Mantendrá la paz social la generación de empleo, advierte Fidel Velásquez," *El Financiero*, August 23, 1996.

66. G. Burke and V. González, "Cutbacks Hit Corn Distributor," *El Financiero Internacional*, November 9–15, 1998.

67. "SHCP: Liberado, el precio de la tortilla," *La Jornada* (November 16, 1998); and Adolfo Garza, "Poor Fear Free Tortilla Market," *Orange County Register*, November 17, 1998.

68. *La Jornada* (November 25, 1998)

69. Francisco Robles, "Disminuye poder adquisitivo del salario en México," *La Opinion* (November 28, 1998).

10

The State Food Agency and the Persistence of Poverty

A lthough many have concluded that the Mexican government irrationally created a number of runaway state enterprises, this study has argued that, at least in the case of foodstuffs, government policy grew in response to short-term political crises. Government intervention in the basic food market in Mexico has deep historical roots, and it can only be explained by understanding the political and socioeconomic context from which it arises. When examined on these terms, we can better understand the motivations for the creation of such policy programs and therefore see why despite massive state expenditures, poverty and malnutrition continue to be a reality in Mexico. This concluding chapter will examine four broad themes that have recurred throughout this work: the reasons for the form that government intervention took, the link between State Food Agency policy and presidential policy, the Agency and the city, and the Agency and the countryside. These themes highlight the interrelations between setting food policy and maintaining political support in Mexico and can be seen as an example of why the Mexican government since the 1930s has been a relatively stable regime that has hitherto been able to thwart any major challenges to its legitimacy.

Political forces have been the primary shapers of government intervention in the marketing of basic foods. The State Food Agency saw its greatest expansion during periods of crisis. In 1938, it began to purchase and sell beans, corns, and wheat and established a chain of retail stores largely in response to the political pressure exerted by unions in the wake of the inflationary wave of late 1937 and 1938. During the 1940s, with Mexico's participation in World War II, the Agency became pivotal as the federal government expanded its financial resources to deal with food shortages and inflation. Such problems arose due both to a poor corn harvest and to the difficulties of importing grain during a war. Shortfall and inflation were met with protests that spread to cities throughout the country and even became violent on some occasions. Responding to such conditions, the federal government increased its real financial allotment to the State Food Agency more than sixfold. In the process of this expansion, however, the state had to maintain its balancing act between the demands of consumers and organized labor and those of the vocal merchant organizations. Instead of heeding the demands of the CTM and abolishing all private food stores, a solution that merchants obviously disliked, the Agency began to operate as an alternative merchant. Although this solution seemed to appease both organized labor and merchants, both continued to be vigilant and critical of the Agency's activities in order to assure that their interests were not ill-served.

Similarly, the State Food Agency expanded its operations during three other periods of economic and political crisis. In the early 1950s, as inflation began to reach double-digit figures after two years of relatively low rates, President Alemán responded to pressure from consumers who demanded further price controls and an expanded role for the State Food Agency by cautiously abandoning many of his plans to streamline government subsidies. Indeed, the rise in prices and the government's slow response became an issue in the hotly contested 1952 election.

Facing a crisis in legitimacy in 1968, the official party had to deal with the rise of urban and rural guerrilla movements and with low voter turnout. President Echeverría used the State Food Agency to reach out to all the disaffected groups by establishing retail stores in middle-class as well as in working-class areas to bolster his support. He also used the Agency to try and incorporate the peasant sector into the folds of the state. President López Portillo expanded the Agency's operation to meet more of the needs of rural consumers and the urban poor. By the early 1980s the Agency was one of the largest corporations in Mexico and the second-largest public enterprise.

In the wake of the plummeting of oil prices and the onset of Mexico's economic crisis, President de la Madrid strengthened the Agency in the early 1980s, providing short-term relief for consumers who suffered from both inflation and rising employment problems. Only after the initial impact of the crisis began to subside in the mid-1980s did he begin to decentralize the operations of the Agency, as he had been doing with other public sector enterprises.

Thus, the mere expansion of State Food Agency activities can be seen as a response to essentially political considerations, at first in urban areas and then in the countryside. However, the way in which it grew or contracted can be partially explained by the close relationship between the activities of the Agency and presidential policy. Agency goals and actions have largely been shaped by the goals and policies set forth by the president. The analysis of specific policy actions by each president yields insight into how goals actually were implemented and help explain how such goals and policy plans were modified to meet the changing political and economic environment.

Although public entities were granted a certain amount of legal and fiscal autonomy, the president appointed public agency heads and held them accountable. Aside from appointing the manager of the Agency, members of the board of directors were all members of the presidential cabinet. Recent research into the composition of presidential appointments and cabinets has demonstrated the importance of presidential "teams" composed of like-minded individuals whose political careers are usually tied to the president or to one of his close advisers. Therefore, it has been in the interest of appointees not to deviate too far from the presidential program if they want to keep their jobs.

In the case of the State Food Agency, the choice of manager has generally reflected the direction that the administration wished the Agency to take. During periods of crisis, politicians skilled in buildings coalitions and public relations have generally led the agency, as in 1943, and more recently during the presidency of Salinas. During a period of relative calm and low rates of inflation in 1946, President Alemán chose low-profile individuals to downsize its operations and increase its efficiency. Alemán tried to use the Agency to enhance and modernize Mexico's storage and handling of grains and to lay plans for a commodities exchange. Such programs were part of his larger strategy for the agricultural sector, which entailed the expansion of output so as to drive food prices downward. Under renewed pressure for government intervention after 1949, he did so only reluctantly and stressed the temporary nature of the intervention, in a manner that was most consistent with his overall economic strategy.

The ability of the president to tighten the reins on the State Food Agency is probably best illustrated by the lack of major opposition within the Agency to the various presidential initiatives to reorganize the Agency, such as President Salinas's efforts to essentially dismantle it in the 1990s. Salinas's gradual substitution of statists with his own key personnel, who in turn brought in their teams, rooted out entrenched elements whose careers and lives were linked inextricably with the State Food Agency. After those changes, the agency was rendered virtually powerless.

That the general goals and direction of the State Food Agency have been tied to presidential policy does not deny the fact that the Agency has taken on a life of its own with its own agendas and motivations. Throughout its history, the Agency has been involved in heated bureaucratic struggles over scarce resources, causing the president to intercede to negotiate a resolution. This was the case with the struggle between the Agency and the national railway company during World War II over the battle for the apportionment of railcars to transport grains from the various regions to Mexico City. At other times the size and operations of the Agency have been such that it was unable to keep track of its goods, often leading to corruption and mismanagement.

As Mexico transformed itself from a rural agricultural society into an urban industrial one, increased pressure was placed on the urban infrastructure, which at times strained to accommodate the swelling numbers of rural migrants. Mounting urban pressure throughout the century led to greater potential for the outbreak of political instability in the city. In the face of urban volatility during periods of sharp inflation, food scarcity, or during times of political disaffection, the State Food Agency grew to favor the urban sector over the countryside.

Although President Cárdenas initially established the first State Food Agency to meet producer and consumer demands, he and his followers soon found that they had to expand urban operations at the expense of the countryside. Because urban labor was one of the primary sectors within the official party, it won greater government intervention to cushion the impact of cost-of-living increases, especially during the late 1930s, World War II, and the early 1950s. Beyond labor, industrialists shaped the form that government intervention was to take. Mexico's struggle to industrialize required that its presidents, especially Cárdenas, be very careful to listen to industrialists. Thus, rather than meet organized labor's demands for wage increases, the government used the Agency to respond to many of labor's demands.

The State Food Agency's most visible attack on inflation was through its chain of retail stores. It first opened a retail store in Mexico City during 1938, after first trying to lower the general trend of basic grain prices by subsidizing the sales to selected merchants. Great increases in the number of state stores in urban areas followed sharp price increases in 1943 and 1944. The number of retail stores, which had hovered near 100 under Cárdenas, expanded to some 2,000 by the end of World War II. As prices declined in the postwar slump, a number of stores were closed. But by the early 1950s, the number of stores again shot up as the Agency began to build them on the outskirts of Mexico City, where thousands of new migrants had flocked hoping to participate in Mexico's industrial boom. By the late 1950s, aside from fixed stores, the Agency purchased a fleet of trucks and began to operate mobile stores, traveling to the more remote neighborhoods surrounding Mexico City. Throughout the 1960s and 1970s the number of stores targeted for urban consumers skyrocketed. As Echeverría tried to rebuild the coalition that had supported the official party by appealing to both working and middle classes, he had the State Food Agency build numerous stores in working class neighborhoods as well as large-scale shopping centers in middle-class neighborhoods. By 1985, there were over 20,000 such stores.

The State Food Agency's response to the urban sector can be seen in its other types of undertakings, which also display a crisis-driven pattern. Responding first to the difficulties of enforcing sanitary regulation of milk in Mexico City and then to shortages of milk caused by the outbreak of hoof and mouth disease in 1946, the government gradually began to intervene in the milk market. It first encouraged the importation of milk, and then it provided incentives for a private company to build a plant to recombine imported powdered milk. However, when the less expensive recombined milk failed to reach all corners of the city, the government began to build its own recombination plants. By the late 1950s, then, the State Food Agency was supplying Mexico City with some 15 percent of its milk supply. Throughout the 1960s and 1970s, the Agency continued to invest in milk recombination plants in order to maintain a constant and inexpensive supply for the poorer sectors of the population. This was one of the few areas of government food policy that continued to expand throughout the 1980s. Even after the downsizing of the Agency in 1989, the recombination and sale of milk continued to be a mainstay, albeit one that directly targeted the poor.

A linchpin in the official party's fifty-year pact with labor, the Agency cushioned the impact of cost-of-living rises on the working classes, thus helping to diffuse many of their demands for wage increases. As we have seen, the expansion of the State Food Agency often coincided with labor unrest. During inflationary times, the CTM often called for wage increases but settled for greater job control as well as for price controls and greater accessibility to subsidized foodstuffs.

For much of its history, the State Food Agency had an urban bent. For nearly three decades following the massive land distribution programs of the Cárdenas administration, there was relative social peace in the rural areas. That peasant communities received land or had hopes of benefiting from land reform programs served to pacify much of the countryside that only a few years earlier, between 1910 and the 1930s, had been in the midst of constant turmoil.* This relative rural tranquillity allowed the government to use the State Food Agency, between the late 1930s and the 1960s, as a means for coordinating production to meet the needs of the city.

Although Cárdenas originally planned that the State Food Agency would provide market support for the new recipients of land, this goal proved difficult to meet and was abandoned as food scarcity and inflation demanded that grains be instantly brought to the city. The primary reasons for shifting away from market support for the new recipients of land were the Agency's lack of purchasing agents in the countryside, poor transportation, and inadequate storage infrastructure in the countryside. These factors combined to make purchasing from small producers economically and physically unfeasible. Although rhetorical overtures continued to be made toward the peasantry, the escalation of World War II and the persistence of food shortages caused the government to abandon the small producer, purchase mainly from large producers closer to the railroad lines, and buy imports to make up for the deficit.

Following World War II, the State Food Agency was used to coordinate the expansion and modernization of the storage infrastructure as a means of stimulating agricultural production. Under the presidency of Alemán the Agency helped ANDSA construct and operate large storage depots outside Mexico City and at the ports to facilitate the maintenance of sufficient grain reserves. The introduction in 1953 of a uniform guaranteed price announced prior to planting further served to stimulate the production of certain crops.

---

*John Tutino, *From Insurrection to Revolution in Mexico: Social Bases of Agrarian Violence, 1750–1940* (Princeton, NJ: Princeton University Press, 1986).

Although initially the pricing policy enabled producers to profit from the harvest, by the mid-1950s, the real guaranteed prices for beans, corn, and wheat were on a downhill spiral. With the exception of a few years, this downward trend continued.

Yet as real prices fell throughout the 1950s and 1960s they were maintained above the import price, and the State Food Agency was caught in a dilemma: lowering the guaranteed price for grains even as the guaranteed prices of other crops such as sorghum rose discouraged farmers from planting basic grains. It was also more attractive for the Agency to purchase grains abroad during periods of crisis because imports were inexpensive and could be transported quickly. During periods of crisis, the Agency often opted to import goods, thus choosing expediency over self-sufficiency.

Beginning in the late 1960s, and continuing throughout the 1980s, the Agency paid greater attention to the countryside and particularly to smaller producers and *ejidatarios*. This attention grew out of renewed unrest in the countryside with the rise of both dissident peasant organizations and guerrilla movements as land distribution slowed and credit declined. The State Food Agency was used to actively attempt to incorporate smaller producers and *ejidatarios* into the country's politico-economic system. This was done first through the construction of small-scale silos, thus enabling the peasants to store their own grain and to sell it flexibly for the best price. The Agency used these small silos as an organizing point in which the members of *ejidal* communities were given instructions on the technical aspects of grading grains and on other methods of grain reception. Thus, nearly forty years after Cárdenas established the Agency, it was finally complying with one of its original aims.

By the middle of the 1970s, the State Food Agency began to expand its retail store operations into the countryside at an unprecedented rate. In 1979, the number of country stores surpassed that of urban stores, and the gap continued to widen during the de la Madrid presidency. These Agency stores often broke the monopoly that small neighborhood stores had on remote towns and villages. These stores became visible signs of the government's reach into the countryside. During the administration of President Salinas, with the virtual dismantling of the Agency, rural stores persisted because of their collaboration with Salinas's poverty and regional development organization, PRONASOL.

The rise and growth of the State Food Agency and the investment of billions of pesos did not, obviously, solve Mexico's food problems. In the late 1990s, Mexico continued to be a country where some 40 million people still suffered from some form of malnutrition. This study has shown, however, that it was not the purpose of the Agency to solve Mexico's hunger and nutrition problems. Instead, by participating in the marketplace it served to increase access to foodstuffs at slightly below the going rate and in the process attempted to win political support for the PRI. Throughout this study, we have seen how the political concerns that shaped policy have often been motivated by efforts to maintain political support without restructuring power relations. Government subsidies served to cushion both consumers as well as employers who were often alleviated of pressures to increase wages. It is little wonder, then, that poverty persists in Mexico. The Agency was not created to eradicate poverty; only real structural reform could address this issue. And as the state began to withdraw from providing even short-term relief during the 1980s and 1990s and continued to chip away at the remaining social programs, Mexico's political, social, and economic stability was threatened.

Bibliography

Archival Collections

Mexico

Archivo General de la Nación (AGN)
    Fondo Departamento de Trabajo (DT)
    Fondo de Presidentes
        Sección-Lázaro Cárdenas (LC), Manuel Avila Camacho
           (MAC), Miguel Alemán (MA), Adolfo Ruiz Cortines (ARC),
           Adolfo López Mateos (ALM)
    Fondo Eduardo Chavez (EC)
    Fondo de Secretaría de Trabajo y Previsión Social (STPS)
    Fondo Dirección General de Industrias (DGI)
    Fondo Gonzalo Robles (GR)
Archivo General de la Secretaría de Relaciones Exteriores (AG-SRE)
Archivo Ramón Fernández y Fernández, Colegio de Michoacán
    (Zamora, Michoacán) (ARFF)
Biblioteca del Banco de México (BBM)
Biblioteca Miguel Lerdo de Tejada, Secretaría de Hacienda y
    Crédito Público
        Colección de recortes periodísticas sobre CEIMSA y
           CONASUPO, 1949–1962
Compañía Nacional de Subsistencia Populares-Biblioteca y
    Archivo Técnico (CONASUPO-BAT)
Hermeoteca Nacional

United States

United States National Archives (USNA)
    Record Group 59 (RG 59)
    Record Group 166. Office of Foreign Agricultural Affairs
        (RG 166)

Periodicals

Agricultura, 1937–1939
Almacenes, 1954–1956

Boletín de Estudios Especiales (Banco Nacional de Crédito Ejidal), 1953–1960

Boletín del Archivo General de la Nación, 1983

Carta Semanal, 1939–1945

Diario Oficial, 1938–1945

El Economista, 1933–1940

EPOCA (Mexico City), 1996

Examen de la situación económica de México (Banco Nacional de México), 1946–1990

Excelsior (Mexico City), 1936–1998

El Financiero (Mexico City), 1989–1998

El Financiero Internacional, 1991–1999

Foreign Agriculture (U.S. Department of Agriculture), 1940–1950

Futuro, 1937

Gaceta Oficial del Departamento del Distrito Federal, 1936–1938, 1941–1966

Ideario Ruíz-Cortinista, 1952

La Jornada (Mexico City), 1989–1999

Mexico City News, 1989–1998

El Nacional (Mexico City), 1934–1998

New York Times, 1937–1965

Novedades, 1936–1960

La Opinion (Los Angeles), 1988–1999

Política (Mexico City), 1961–1964

¿Por Que?, 1968

La Prensa, 1936–1960

Problemas Agrícolas y Economicos de México, 1946–1955

Proceso (Mexico City), 1987–1998

Publicación del Departamento Comercial (Banco Nacional de Crédito Agrícola), 1931

Revista de Economia, 1938–1951

Revista de Estadística, 1933–1970

Revista de Hacienda, 1937–1939

Revista de Trabajo, 1937–1941, 1947–1951

Servicio de Información Agricola y Comercial (Banco Nacional Comercio Exterior), 1956–1958

Siembra, 1943–1946

Sistema: Organismo de Difusión del Sistema CONASUPO, 1983–1987

Ultimas Noticias, 1936–1960

El Universal (Mexico City), 1937–1990

Primary Documents

Alemán, Miguel. *Programa de Gobierno*. México, 1945.

Almacenes Nacional de Depósito, S.A. *Informe del consejo de administración a la asamblea general ordinaria de accionistas*, 1949; 1952, 1954, 1956, 1964–65; 1966–67; 1967–68; 1968–69; 1969–70.

Archivo General de la Nación. *Boletín del Archivo General de la Nación,* tercera serie, tomo VII, vol. I (22) (January–March 1983).

Banco Nacional de Comercio Exterior. *Informe del consejo de administración a la asamblea general ordinaria de accionistas,* 1938–1962.

Banco Nacional de Crédito Agrícola. *Boletín de Departamento comercial,* 1931–1933.

———. *Informe anual,* 1925–1961.

———. *El trigo en México,* 6 vols. México: Banco Nacional de Crédito Agrícola, 1937–1939.

Banco Nacional de Crédito Ejidal. *Informe anual,* 1936–1961.

———. *El sistema de producción colectiva en los ejidos del valle del Yaqui, Son.* México, 1945.

Banco Nacional de México. *Examen de la situación económica de México, 1925–1976.* México, 1978.

Cámara de Diputados. *La cámara de diputados y el problema de las subsistencias.* México: Ediciones de la "Editorial de Izquierda" Cámara de Diputados, 1945.

El Comité de Afóros y Subsidios al Comercio Exterior. "El subsidio a la importación del trigo." México: Oficina de Subsidios y Estudios Especiales, mimeo, 1944.

Comité Regulador del Mercado de las subsistencias. *Informes anuales, 1938–1939.* Mimeo, 1940.

Compañía Nacional de Subsistencias Populares. *A quién sirve la nueve CONASUPO.* México: CONASUPO, 1989.

———. "Almacenamiento y conservación de alimentos agrícolas básicos." México: Coordinación de Comunicación Social de CONASUPO, 1986.

———. *Cambio estructural del sistema de distribuidores CONASUPO: Informe de labores, 1982–1988,* vol. 2. México: Sistema de Distribuidora, 1988.

———. *Cinco años de realizaciones.* México, 1988.

———. *La CTM en la Lucha por la Alimentación.* México: Sistema de Distribuidors CONASUPO, 1987.

———. *CONASUPO en cífras, 1965–1981.* México, 1981.

———. *CONASUPO, 1977–1982.* México, n.d.

———. *50 años de lucha por la alimentación: Raices constitucionales.* México, 1987.

———. *Informe anuales y memorias de labores,* 1961; 1962; 1963; 1964; 1968–1969; 1970–1973.

———. *El mercado de las subsistencias populares: Cincuenta años de regulación,* 2 vols. México, 1988.

———. "Los precios de garantia." México: Coordinación de Comunicación Social, 1986.

———. "Los subsidios." México: Coordinación de Comunicación Social, 1986.

Compañía Rehidratadora de Leche CONASUPO. *Informe de labores, 1970.* México: CONASUPO, 1971.

Confederación Nacional Campesina. *Historia documental del CNC,* vol. 1: 1938–1942. México, 1981.

Confederación de Trabajadores Mexicanos. *CTM 1936–1941.* México, 1942.

Departamento del Distrito Federal. *Boletín Mensual de Estadísticas del Departamento del Distrito Federal,* 1937–1945.

———. *Memoria del Departamento del Distrito Federal,* 1935–1947.

Departamento del Trabajo. *Memoria del Departamento del Trabajo, septiembre de 1937–agosto de 1938.* México: DAAP, 1938.

Díaz Ordaz, Gustavo. *Cuarto informe que rinde al H. Congreso de la union el C. presidente de la república Gustavo Díaz Ordaz del 1° septiembre 1968.* México: Secretaría de Gobernación, 1968.

———. *Primer informe que rinde al H. Congreso de la union el C. presidente de la república Gustavo Díaz Ordaz del 1° septiembre 1965.* México: Secretaría de Gobernación, 1965.

Estados Unidos Mexicanos. *Directorio del gobierno federal 1948.* México: Dirección Técnica de Organización, Secretaría de Bienes Nacionales e Inspeccion Administracion, 1998.

López Mateos, Adolfo. *Informe que rinde al H. Congreso de la union el C. presidente de la república Adolfo López Mateos del 1° diciembre 1958 al 31 de agosto de 1959.* México: Secretaría de Gobernación, 1959.

———. *Informe que rinde al H. Congreso de la union el C. presidente de la república Adolfo López Mateos del 1° septiembre 1960 al 31 de agosto de 1961.* México: Secretaría de Gobernación, 1961.

———. "El Licenciado Adolfo López Mateos, al abrir el congreso sus sesiones ordinarias, el 1° de septiembre de 1962," in Luis González y González, ed., *Los Presidentes de México ante la nación: Informes, manifiestos, y documento de 1821 a 1966.* México: Cámara de Diputados, 1966.

López Portillo, José. *Quinto informe de Gobierno: Anexo programático II-A, 1980.* México, 1981.

———. *Sexto informe de Gobierno: Anexo programático II-A, 1981.* México, 1982.

———. *Tercer informe de Gobierno: Anexo programático II-A, 1978.* México, 1979.

México: Desarrollo regional y decentralización de la vida nacional, 1982–88. México: SPP, 1988.

Nacional Financiera, S.A. *50 años de revolución mexicana en cífras.* México, 1963.

———. *La industria de la harina de maíz.* México: NAFINSA, 1982.

Nuevo Sistema para la compra, recepción y almacenamiento de maíz, frijol y trigo. México: CEIMSA, ANDSA, BANJIDAL, BANGRICOLA, 1959.

Partido Nacional de la Revolución. *Plan sexenal del PNR.* México, 1934.

Partido Revolucionario Nacional, Secretaria de Acción Agraria. *Los problemas agrícolas de México,* vol. 2. México, 1934.

Presidencia de la República. *Crónica del gobierno de Carlos Salinas de Gortari*, 7 vols. México: Presidencia de la República, Unidad de la Crónica Presidencial and Fondo de Cultura Económica, 1994.

———. *Las razones y la obras: Gobierno de Miguel de la Madrid, Crónica del sexenio, 1982–88.* México, 1984–1988.

Salinas de Gortari, Carlos. *Tercer informe de gobierno: Anexo estadístico.* México: SPP, 1991.

Secretaría de Agricultura y Fomento. Comisión Consultativa de Costos de Producción Agrícola. *Memoria de trabajos ejecutados y métodos adaptados para la determinación de los costos de produción agrícola.* México, 1939.

———. Dirreción de Economia Rural, Instituto de Economia Rural. *Estudio agro-económico del maíz.* México, 1940.

———. *Memoria de la primera convención triguera nacional.* México, 1934.

———. *Memoria de los trabajos ejecutados por las direcciones de agricultura y ganaderia e Instituto Biotecnico del año de 1935 a mayo de 1940 y dentro del periodo presidencial del C. Gral. de División Lázaro Cárdenas.* México, 1940.

———. *Monografias comerciales.* México, 1920s–1930s.

———. *Plan de modernización agricola de la república mexicana.* México, 1945.

Secretaría de Agricultura y Ganadería. *Boletín mensual de la Dirección General de Economía Rural.* 1934–1955.

———. *Resumen del informe de labores de la Secretaría de Agrícultura y Ganadero del 1° de septiembre de 1953 al 31 de agosto de 1954.* México: Talleres Gráficos de la Nación, 1954.

Secretaría de Agricultura y Recursos Hidraulicos, Subsecretaria de Agricultura y Operación- Dirección General de Economía Agrícola. *Consumos aparentes de productos agrícolas, 1925–1982*, vol. 7, no. 9. México, 1983.

Secretaría de Bienes Nacionales e Inspección Administrativa. *Directorio del gobierno federal 1947.* México, 1947.

———. *Directorio del gobierno federal 1948.* México, 1948.

Secretaría de la Economía Nacional. *Informe de la actividades desarrolladas por la Secretaría de la Economía Nacional durante el periodo del 1° de agosto de 1934 al 31 de julio de 1935.* (México, 1935).

———. *La industria harinera: Materia prima, molienda y transportes.* México: Talleres Gráficos de la Nación, 1934.

———. *Memoria* (1934–1957).

Secretaría de la Economía Nacional, Dirección General de Estadísticas. *Anuarío estadístico*, 1930–1975.

———. *Compendio estadístico*, 1948–1963.

Secretaría de Economía, Dirección de Estudios Económicos. *Desarrollo de la economía nacional, 1939–1947.* México, 1947.

———. *El desarrollo de la economía nacional bajo la inflación de la guerra, 1939–45.* México: Oficina de Barometros Economicos, 1945.

Secretaría de Gobernación. *Seis años de actividad nacional.* México, 1946.

Secretaría de Hacienda y Crédito Público. "Estadisticas de finanzas públicas: Cifras anuales, 1971–86." México, 1986.

———. *La hacienda pública atráves de los informes presidenciales,* 2 vols. México, 1963.

———. *Memoria de la Secretaría de Hacienda y Crédito Público* (December 1, 1940–November 30, 1946), vol. 1. México, 1955.

Secretaría de Industria y Comercio. *Censo industrial 1955, resumen general,* vol. 1. México, 1955.

———. *Estadisticas básicas de la actividad pesquera nacional, 1959–1965.* México, 1966.

———. *Memoria de labores,* 1959–1964, 1973, 1975, 1977.

United Nations Food and Agriculture Organization. *Production Yearbook.* Various years.

———. *Yearbook of Food and Agricultural Statistics,* 1951, 1956.

U.S. Department of Agriculture. *Hearing before the Committee on Agriculture, House of Representatives, Eighty-Fourth Congress,* May 27, 1955.

U.S. Senate, Committee on Agriculture and Forestry. *Report of the Subcommittee on Foot-and-Mouth Disease,* March 24, 1950.

Secondary Sources

Acosta L., Agustín. "La política de subsistencias," in Jorge Echaniz et al., *Cuestiones nacionales,* vol. 1, pp. 69–141. México: Ediciones del Instituto Nacional de la Juventud Mexicana, 1964.

Adler, Ruth. "La administración obrera en los FFNN," *Revista Mexicana de Sociología* 50:3 (July–September 1988), pp. 97–124.

Alanís Patiño, E., and E. Vargas Torres. "Observaciones sobre algunas estadísticas agrícolas," *Trimestre Económico* (1946), pp. 589–625.

Alarcón Mendizabal, Adolfo. "La política mexicana en el mercado de productos agrícolas," *Problemas Agrícolas y Economicos de México* 1:2 (October–December 1946), pp. 85–100.

Alderete-Haas, José A. "The Decline of the Mexican State?: The Case of State Housing Intervention (1917–1988)." Ph.D. diss., MIT, 1989.

Alisky, Marvin. "CONASUPO: A Mexican Agency Which Makes Low-Income Workers Feel Their Government Cares," *Inter-American Economic Affairs* 27:3 (winter 1973–74), pp. 47–61.

Alonso, Antonio. *El movimiento ferrocarriles en México, 1958/1959: De la conciliación a la lucha and claser.* México: Ediciones ERA, 1972.

Altman, Ida, and James Lockhart, eds. *Provinces of Early Mexico: Variants of Spanish American Regional Evolution.* Los Angeles: UCLA Latin American Center Publications, 1976.

Amorós, Roberto. "La política de distribución y la intervención marginal de sector público," in *Nuevos aspectos de la política económica*

y de la administración pública en México, conferencias de invierno 1960.
México: Escuela Nacional de Economia, 1960.

Anderson, Bo, and James D. Cockcroft. "Control and Cooptation in Mexican Politics," in Irving Louis Horowitz, Josué de Castro, and John Gerassi, eds., *Latin American Radicalism: A Documentary Report on Left and Nationalist Movements*, pp. 366–389. New York: Random House, 1969.

Anderson, Charles W. "Bankers as Revolutionaries: Politics and Development Banking in Mexico," in William P. Glade Jr. and Charles W. Anderson, eds., *The Political Economy of Mexico*. Madison: University of Wisconsin Press, 1968.

Anderson, Rodney. *Outcasts in Their Own Land: Mexican Industrial Workers, 1906–1911*. De Kalb: Northern Illinois University Press, 1978 .

Andrade , Manuel, ed. *Constitución política mexicana: Con reformas y adiciones*. México: Editorial Información Aduanera de México, 1936.

Anguiano, Arturo. *El estado y la política obrera del cardenismo*. México: ERA, 1975.

Ardito-Barletta, Nicolás. "Costs and Social Benefits of Agricultural Research in Mexico." Ph.D. diss., University of Chicago, 1971.

Armstrong, George M. *Law and Market Society in Mexico*. New York: Praeger, 1989.

Ashby, Joe C. *Organized Labor and the Mexican Revolution under Cárdenas*. Chapel Hill: University of North Carolina Press, 1963.

Austin, James E., and Gustavo Esteva, eds., *Food Policy in Mexico: The Search for Self-Sufficiency*. Ithaca, N.Y.: Cornell University Press, 1987.

Austin, James E., and Jonathan Fox. "State-Owned Enterprises: Food Policy Implementers," in James E. Austin and Gustavo Esteva, eds., *Food Policy in Mexico: The Search for Self-Sufficiency*, pp. Ithaca, N.Y.: Cornell University Press, 1987.

Austin, James E., and Kenneth L. Hoadley. "State Trading and the Future Market: The Experience of CONASUPO in Mexico," in Bruce F. Johnston, Cassio Luiselli, Celso Cartas Contreras, and Roger Norton, eds., *U.S. Mexican Relations: Agriculture and Rural Development*, pp. 159–175. Stanford, Calif.: Stanford University Press, 1987.

Azpeitia Gómez, Hugo. *Compañía Exportadora e Importadora Mexicana, S.A. (1949–1958): Conflicto y abasto alimentario*. México: Centro de Investigaciones y Estudios Superiores en Antropología Social, 1994.

Bach, Federico. "La nacionalización de los ferrocarriles," *Revista de Hacienda* 4:19 (September, 1939), pp. 137–148.

Baer, David M. "PROCAMPO: Analyzing State Agricultural Policy in Mexico in the Context of Economic Liberalization, NAFTA, and GATT," M.A. thesis, University of Florida, 1995.

Banco Nacional de México. *Examen de la situación económica de México, 1925–1976*. México: Fondo Cultural BANAMEX, 1978.

Bantjes, Adrian A. *As If Jesus Walked on Earth: Cardenismo, Sonora, and the Mexican Revolution*. Wilmington, Del.: Scholarly Resources, 1998.

Baranda, Marta y Lia García Verástegui. *Adolfo López Mateos, estadísta mexicano*. Toluca: Gobierno del Estado de México, 1987.

Barkin, David. "Mexico's Albatross: The U.S. Economy," in Nora Hamilton and Timothy F. Harding, eds., *Modern Mexico: State, Economy, and Social Conflict*. Beverly Hills, Calif.: Sage Publications, 1986, pp. 106–127.

Barkin, David, and Blanca Suárez. *El fin de la autosuficiencia alimentaria mexicana*. México: Ediciones Océano, 1985.

Bartra, Armando. *Los herederos de Zapata: Movimientos posrevolucionarios en México*. México: Ediciones ERA, 1985.

———. "A Persistant Rural Leviathan," in Laura Randall, ed., *Reforming Mexico's Agrarian Reform*, pp. 173–184. Armonk, N.Y.: M. E. Sharp, 1996.

Basurto, Jorge. *Cárdenas y el poder sindical*. México: Ediciones ERA, 1983.

———. *La clase obrera en la historia de México: Del avilacamachismo al alemanismo (1940–1952)*. México: Siglo Veintiuno Editores, 1984.

———. *La clase obrera en la historia de México: En el regimen de Echeverría: Rebelión e independencia*. México: Siglo Veintiuno Editores, 1983.

Bauer, Arnold J. "Millers and Grinders: Technology and Household Economy in Meso-America," *Agricultural History* 64:1 (Winter 1990): pp. 1–17.

Bazdresch, Carlos, and Santiago Levy. "Populism and Economic Policy in Mexico, 1970–1982," in Rudiger Dornbusch and Sebastian Edwards, eds., *The Macroeconomics of Populism in Latin America*, pp. 223–262. Chicago, Ill.: University of Chicago Press, 1990.

Becker, Marjorie. *Setting the Virgin on Fire: Lázaro Cárdenas, Michoacán Peasants, and the Redemption of the Mexican Revolution*. Berkeley: University of California Press, 1995.

Beezley, William H., Cheryl English Martin, and William E. French, eds. *Rituals of Rule, Rituals of Resistance: Public Celebrations and Popular Culture in Mexico*. Wilmington, Del.: Scholarly Resources, 1994.

Benjamin, Thomas, and Mark Wasserman, eds. *Provinces of the Revolution: Essays on Regional Mexican History, 1910–1929*. Albuquerque: University of New Mexico Press, 1990.

Bennett, Douglas, and Kenneth Sharpe, "The State as Banker and Entrepreneur: The Last Resort Character of the Mexican State's Economic Intervention, 1917–1970," in Sylvia Ann Hewlett and Richard S. Weinert, eds., *Brazil and Mexico: Patterns in Late Devel-*

opment, pp. 169–211. Philadelphia, Pa.: Institute for the Study of Human Issues, 1982.

Bernstein, Marvin D. *The Mexican Mining Industry, 1890–1950: A Study of the Interaction of Politics, Economics, and Technology*. Albany: State University of New York Press, 1965.

Bethell, Leslie, ed. *Mexico since Independence*. Cambridge: Cambridge University Press, 1991.

Bortz, Jeffrey Lawrence. *Los salarios industriales en la ciudad de México, 1939–1975*. México: Fondo de Cultura Económica, 1988.

Brachet-Márquez, Viviane. *The Dynamics of Domination: State, Class, and Social Reform in Mexico, 1910–1990*. Pittsburgh, Pa.: University of Pittsburgh Press, 1994.

Brandenberg, Frank. *The Making of Modern Mexico*. Englewood Cliffs, N.J.: Prentice-Hall, 1964.

Brannon, Jeffrey, and Eric Baklanoff. *Agrarian Reform and Public Enterprise: The Political Economy of Yucatan's Henequen Industry*. Tuscaloosa: University of Alabama Press, 1987.

Brothers, Dwight S., and Leopoldo Solís M. *Mexican Financial Development*. Austin: University of Texas Press, 1966.

Brown, Lyle C. "Cárdenas: Creating a Campesino Power Base for Presidential Policy," in George Wolfskill and Douglas Richmond, eds., *Essays on the Mexican Revolution: Revisionist Views of the Leaders*. Austin: University of Texas Press, 1979.

Calva, José Luis. *Crisis agrícola y alimentaria en México, 1982–1988*. México: Distribución Fontmara, 1988.

Camp, Roderic A. *Entrepreneurs and Politics in Twentieth-Century Mexico*. New York: Oxford University Press, 1989.

———. *Mexican Political Biographies, 1935–1981*. Tucson: University of Arizona Press, 1982.

———. *Mexico's Leaders: Their Education and Recruitment*. Tucson: University of Arizona Press, 1980.

Cárdenas, Enrique. *La hacienda pública y la política económica, 1929–1958*. México: El Colegio de México, 1994.

———. *La industrialización mexicana durante la Gran Depresión*. México: El Colegio de México, 1987.

Cárdenas, Lázaro. *Palabras y documentos públicos de Lázaro Cárdenas*, vol. 2: *Informes de Gobierno y Mensajes Presidenciales de Año Nuevo, 1928–40*. México: Siglo Veintiuno Editores, 1978.

Carmagnani, Marcello. *Estado y mercado: La economía pública del liberalismo mexicano, 1850–1911*. México: Fondo de Cultura Económica, 1994.

Carr, Barry. *Marxism and Communism in Twentieth-Century Mexico*. Lincoln: University of Nebraska Press, 1992.

Carrillo Castro, Alejandro. *La reforma administrativa en México*. México: Instituto Nacional de Administración Pública, 1975.

Cartas Contreras, Celso, and Luz María Bassoco. "The Mexican Food System (SAM): An Agricultural Production Strategy," in Bruce F.

Johnson, Casio Luiselli, Celso Cartas Contreras, and Roger D. Norton, eds., *U.S.-Mexico Relations: Agriculture and Rural Development*, pp. 319–332. Stanford, Calif.: Stanford University Press, 1987.

Casar, María Amparo, and Wilson Peres. *El estado empresario en México: ¿Agotamiento o renovación?* México: Siglo Veintiuno Editores, 1988.

Castañeda, Jorge A. *The Mexican Shock: Its Meaning for the U.S.* (New York: New Press, 1995).

Caulfield, Norman. "Mexican Labor and the State in the Twentieth Century: Conflict and Accommodation." Ph.D. diss., University of Houston, 1990.

Cline, Howard F. *Mexico: Revolution to Evolution, 1940–1960.* New York: Oxford University Press, 1963.

———. *The United States and Mexico.* Cambridge, Mass.: Harvard University Press, 1953; revised and enlarged edition published in 1963 by Atheneum Press, New York.

Coatsworth, John H. "Anotaciones sobre la producción de alimentos durante el porfiriato," *Historia Mexicana* 26:2 (October–December 1976).

———. "Obstacles to Economic Growth in Nineteenth-Century Mexico," *American Historical Review* 83:1 (1978), pp. 80–100.

Cockcroft, James D. "Mexico," in Ronald H. Chilcote and Joel C. Edelstein, eds., *Latin America: The Struggle with Dependency and Beyond.* Cambridge, Mass.: Schenkman Publishing, 1974, pp. 221–303.

Coerver, Don M. "The Perils of Progress: The Mexican Department of Fomento during the Boom Years 1880–1884," *Inter-American Economic Affairs* 31:2 (autumn 1977).

Collier, George A. *Basta! Land and the Zapatista Rebellion in Chiapas.* Oakland, Calif.: Institute for Food and Development Policy, 1994.

———. "The Rebellion in Chiapas and the Legacy of Energy Development," *Mexican Studies/Estudios Mexicanos* 10:2 (summer 1994), pp. 371–382.

Combined Mexican Working Party of the International Bank for Reconstruction and Development. *The Economic Development of Mexico.* Baltimore, Md.: Johns Hopkins University Press, 1953.

Cornelius, Wayne A. "The Political Economy of Mexico under de la Madrid: Austerity, Routinized Crisis, and Nascent Recovery," *Mexican Studies/Estudios Mexicanos* 1:1 (winter 1985), pp. 83–124.

Cosío Villegas, Daniel. *La cuestión arancelaria en México.* México, 1932.

Cotter, Joseph Eugene. "Before the Green Revolution: Agricultural Science Policy in Mexico, 1920–1950." Ph.D. diss., University of California at Santa Barbara, 1994.

———. "The Origins of the Green Revolution in Mexico: Continuity or Change?" in David Rock, ed., *Latin America in the 1940s:*

War and Postwar Transitions. Berkeley: University of California Press, 1994.

Cotter, Joseph, and Michael A. Osborne. "Agronomía Afranceada: The French Contribution to Mexican Agronomy, 1880–1940," *Science, Technology and Society* 1:1 (1996), pp. 25–49.

"La CTM Frente el Alza de los Precios," *Futuro* (April 1937), pp. 20–25.

Cypher, James M. *State and Capital in Mexico: Development Policy since 1940.* Boulder, Colo.: Westview Press, 1990.

Danzós, Ramón. *Ramón Danzós: Desde la cárcel de Atlixco.* México: Ediciones de Cultura Popular, 1974.

Davis, Diane E. *Urban Leviathan: Mexico City in the Twentieth Century.* Philadelphia, Pa.: Temple University Press, 1994.

de Appendini, Kirsten A. "Políticas macroeconómicas y abasto de maíz," *Economía Informa* (UNAM) no. 247 (May 1996).

de Appendini, Kirsten A., and Vania Almeida Salles. "Algunas consideraciones sobre los precios de garantía y la crisis de produción de los alimentos básicos." *Foro Internacional* 19:3 (January–March 1979), pp. 402–428.

de Grammont, Hubert C. "Los empresarios también se organizan: La unión nacional de cosecheros," in Julio Moguel, ed., *Historia de la cuestión agraria mexicana: Política estatal y conflictos agrarios 1950–1970.* México: Siglo Veintiuno Editores, 1989.

———. "Jaramillo y las luchas campesinos en Morelos," in Julio Moguel, ed., *Historia de la cuéstion agraria mexicana: Política estatal y conflictos agrarios 1950–1970.* México: Siglo Veintiuno Editores, 1989.

de la Garza Toledo, Enrique. "Independent Trade Unionism in Mexico: Past Developments and Future Perspectives," in Kevin Middlebrook, ed., *Unions, Workers, and the State in Mexico.* La Jolla: University of California at San Diego, Center for U.S.-Mexican Studies, 1991.

de la Peña, Joaquín, José Crowley, Santos Amaro, and Héctor Calles. *El maíz en México: Datos y apreciaciones.* México: EDIAPSA, 1955.

de la Peña, Moisés T. "El Comité Regulador," *Revista de Economía* 2:4 (February, 1942), pp. 91–102.

———. "Crítica de las tarifas ferrocarrileras," *El Trimestre Económico*, no. 4 (1937), pp. 3–24.

———. "La industrialización de México y la política arancelaria," *El Trimestre Económico* 12:2 (July–September 1945), pp. 187–218.

———. "El maíz, su influencia nacional," *El Trimestie Económico* 3:10 (April–June 1936), pp. 186–220.

———. *Zacatecas económico.* México, 1948.

de la Peña, Sergio, and Marcel Morales. *Historia de la cuestión agraria mexicana: El agrarismo y la industrialización de México, 1940–1950.* México: Siglo Veintiuno Editores, 1989.

DeBeers, John S. "El peso mexicano, 1941–1949," *Problemas Agrícolas e Industriales de México* 5:1 (January–March 1953), pp. 7–134.

De Walt, Billie R. "Mexico's Second Green Revolution: Food for Feed," *Mexican Studies/Estudios Mexicanos* 1:1 (winter 1985), pp. 29–60.

Dresser, Denise. *Neopopulist Solutions to Neoliberal Problems: Mexico's National Solidarity Program*. San Diego: Center for U.S.-Mexican Studies, University of California at San Diego, 1992.

Echeverría, Leonardo Martín. *La ganadería en México*. México: Banco de México, 1960.

Eckstein, Salomon. *El ejido colectivo en México*. México: Fondo de Cultura Económica, 1966.

"El cambio estructural en el comercio interior de México, 1983–1986." *Mercado de Valores* 47:30 (July 27, 1987), pp. 797–811.

Esteva, Gustavo. "La experiencia de la intervención estatal en la comercialización agropecuario de 1970 a 1976," in Ursula Oswald, ed., *Mercado y dependencia*. México: Editorial Nueva Imagen, 1979.

Esteva, Gustavo, and David Barkin. *El papel del sector público en la comercialización y la fijación de precios de los productos agrícolas basicos en México*. México: CEPAL, 1981.

Feijoo, Rosa. "El tumulto de 1624," *Historia Mexicana* 14:1 (July–September, 1964), pp. 656–679.

Fernández y Fernández, Ramón. *El comercio del trigo en México*, 2 vols. México: BNCA, 1939.

———. "El comercio del trigo en México," unpublished draft of a report for the Comisión de Estudios Especiales of the Banco Nacional de Crédito Agrícola, BBM, 1937.

———. "La guerra y las finanzas agrícolas en Estados Unidos," *Investigación Económica* 4:4 (1944), pp. 333–361.

———. *Historia de la estadístca agrícola en México*. México: Talleres Gráficos de la Nación, 1933.

———. "La regulación de precios de los productos agrícolas," *El Trimestre Económica* 22:3 (July–September 1955), pp. 297–328.

Fernández y Fernández, Ramón, and Ricardo Acosta. *Política agrícola: Ensayo sobre normas para México*. México: Fondo de Cultura Económica, 1961.

Flores, Rodolfo T. "Interpretaciones económicas del salario minimo," *Revista de Trabajo* 2:2 (March 1938), pp. 111–121.

Flores Caballero, Romeo. "Comercio interior," in Luís González et al., *La economía mexicana en la época de Juárez*. México: Secretaría de Industria y Comercio, 1972.

Flores Caballero, Romeo R. *Administración y política en la historia de México*. México: Instituto Nacional de Administración Pública, 1988.

Florescano, Enrique. "El abasto y la legislación de granos en el siglo XVI," *Historia Mexicana 56* 14:4 (April–June 1965), pp. 567–630.

Fox, Jonathan. "Agriculture and the Politics of the North American Trade Debate: A Report from the Trinational Exchange on Agriculture, the Environment, and the Free Trade Agreement," *LASA Forum* 23:1 (spring 1992), pp. 3–9.

————. *The Politics of Food in Mexico: State Power and Social Mobilization*. Ithaca, N.Y.: Cornell University Press, 1992.

Fox, Jonathan, and Gustavo Gordillo. "Between State and Market: The Campesino's Quest for Autonomy," in Wayne A. Cornelius, Judith Gentleman, and Peter H. Smith, eds., *Mexico's Alternative Political Futures*. La Jolla: Center for U.S.-Mexican Studies, University of California at San Diego, 1989.

Friedmann, Santiago, Nora Lustig, and Arianna Legovini. "Mexico: Social Spending and Food Subsidies during Adjustment in the 1980s," in Nora Lustig, ed., *Coping with Austerity: Poverty and Inequality in Latin America*. Washington, D.C.: Brookings Institution, 1995.

Frischmann, Donald H. "Misiones Culturales, Teatro CONASUPO, and Teatro Comunidad: The Evolution of Rural Theater," in William H. Beezley, Cheryl English Martin, and William E. French, eds., *Rituals of Rule, Rituals of Resistance: Public Celebrations and Popular Culture in Mexico*. Wilmington, Del.: Scholarly Resources, 1994.

Gamble, Stephen Holland. *The Despensa System of Food Distribution: A Case Study of Monterrey, Mexico*. New York: Praeger Publishers, 1970.

Gavaldón Enciso, Enrique, and Eduardo Pérez Haro. "CONASUPO: Un esfuerzo sistemático," *EL Cotidiano* (November–December 1987), pp. 409–413.

————. "A proposito de la 'Debildad y forteleza de CONASUPO'" in *El Cotidiano* (May–June 1987), pp. 182–186.

Gaxiola, Francisco J. *Memorias*. México: Porrúa, 1975.

Gilly, Adolfo. *El cardensimo, una utopía mexicana*. México: Cal y arena, 1994.

Glade, William P. "Las empresas gubermentales descentralizadas," *Problemas Agrícolas e Industriales de México* 11:1 (January–March 1959), pp. 1–210.

————. "Entrepreneurship in the State Sector: CONASUPO of Mexico," in Sidney M. Greenfield, Arnold Strickon, and Robery T. Aubry, eds., *Entrepreneurs in Cultural Context*. Albuquerque: University of New Mexico Press, 1979.

————. *The Latin American Economies: A Study of their State and Society*. Princeton, N.J.: Princeton University Press, 1978.

Gledhill, John. *Casi Nada: A Study of Agrarian Reform in the Homeland of Cardenismo*. Albany: Institute for Mesoamerican Studies, State University of New York, 1991.

Gómez, Marte R. *Vida política contemporánea: Cartas de Marte R. Gómez*, 2 vols. México: Fondo de Cultura Económica, 1978.

González Gallardo, Alfonso. "La orientación de la agricultura mexicana," *El Trimestre Económico* 11:4 (1943), pp. 506–535.

González y González, Luís. *San José de Gracia: Mexican Village in Transition*, trans. by John Upton. Austin: University of Texas Press, 1972.

González y González, Luis, ed. *Los presidentes de México ante la nación: Informes, manifiestos, y documento de 1821 a 1966.* México: Cámara de Diputados, 1966.

González Ibarra, Juan de Dios. *Interpretaciones del cardenismo.* México: Universidad Autónoma Metropolitana, 1988.

González Navarro, Moisés. *La colonización en México, 1877–1910.* México: Talleres de Impresión de Estampillas y Valores, 1960.

———. *La Confederación Nacional Campesina en la reforma agraria mexicana.* México: El Día en Libros, 1985.

———. *La pobreza en México.* México: Fondo de Cultura Económica, 1985.

Greenberg, Martin Harry. *Bureaucracy and Development: A Mexican Case Study.* Lexington, Mass.: D. C. Heath, 1970.

Gregory, Peter. " 'The Effect of Mexico's Postwar Industrialization on the U.S.-Mexico Price and Wage Comparison' by Jeffrey Bortz: A Comment," in Jorge A. Bustmante, Clark W. Reynolds, and Raúl A. Hinojosa Ojeda, eds., *U.S.-Mexico Relations: Labor Market Interdependence.* Stanford, Calif.: Stanford University Press, 1992.

———. *The Myth of Market Failure: Employment and the Labor Market in Mexico.* Baltimore, Md.: Johns Hopkins University Press, 1986.

Grindle, Merrilee Serrill. *Bureaucrats, Politicians, and Peasants in Mexico: A Case Study in Public Policy.* Berkeley: University of California Press, 1977.

———. "Official Interpretations of Rural Underdevelopment: Mexico in the 1970s," Working Paper in U.S.-Mexican Studies. La Jolla: Center for U.S.-Mexican Studies, University of California at San Diego, 1981.

———. *Searching for Rural Development: Labor, Migration, and Employment in Mexico.* Ithaca, N.Y.: Cornell University Press, 1988.

Grunstein, Arturo. "Railroads, Revolution, and the State: The Emergence of the National Railways of Mexico," in Samuel Schmidt, James W. Wilkie, and Manuel Esparza, eds., *Estudios cuantitativos sobre la historia de México.* México: Universidad National Autonoma de México, 1988.

Guthrie, Chester Lyle. "Riots in Seventeenth Century Mexico City: A Study of Social and Economic Conditions," in Adele Ogden and Engel Sluiter, eds., *Greater America: Essays in Honor of Herbert Eugene Bolton.* Berkeley: University of California Press, 1945.

Haag, Herman M., and José Soto Angli. *El mercado de los productos agropecuarios.* México: Editorial Limusa, Wiley, S.A., 1969.

Haber, Stephen H. "Assessing the Obstacles to Industrialisation: The Mexican Economy, 1830–1940," *Journal of Latin American Studies* 24, pp. 1–32.

———. *Industry and Underdevelopment: The Industrialization of Mexico, 1890–1940.* Stanford, Calif.: Stanford University Press, 1989.

Hamilton, Nora. *The Limits of State Autonomy: Post-Revolutionary Mexico.* Princeton, N.J.: Princeton University Press, 1982.

Hank González, Carlos. "El Procampo: Estrategia de apoyos al productor del agro," *Comercio Exterior* (October 1993), pp. 982–989.

Hansen, Roger D. *The Politics of Mexican Development*. Baltimore, Md.: Johns Hopkins University Press, 1971.

Hart, John Mason. *Revolutionary Mexico: The Coming and Process of the Mexican Revolution*. Berkeley: University of California Press, 1987.

Harvey, Neil. *Rebellion in Chiapas: Rural Reforms, Campesino Radicalism, and the Limits to Salinismo*, revised and updated. La Jolla: Center for U.S.-Mexican Studies, University of California at San Diego, 1994.

Heath, John R. "El abasto alimentario en la economía de guerra," in Rafael Loyola, ed., *Entre la guerra y la estabilidad política: El México de los 40*. México: Grjalbo, 1990.

———. "Further Analysis of the Food Crisis in Mexico," *Latin American Research Review* 27:3 (1992), pp. 123–145.

———. "Por qué los campesinos no venden su grano al estado? Algunos limitantes respecto a la captación de maíz por la CONASUPO," *Revista Mexicana de Sociologia* (January–March 1988), pp. 169–187.

Hernán Ortiz, Sergio. *Los ferrocarriles de México: Una visión social y económica*, 2 vols. México: FFNN, 1988.

Hernández Chávez, Alicia. *La mecánica cardenista*. México: El Colegio de México, 1979.

Hernández Enriquez, Gustavo Abel, and Armando Rojas Trujillo. *Manuel Avila Camacho: Biografía de un revolucionario con historia*, vol. 2. México: Ediciones del Gobierno de Puebla, 1986.

Hernández Fujigaki, Gloria. *La CTM en la lucha por la alimentación*. México: Sistema de Distribuidores CONASUPO, 1987.

———. "1915–1938 Antecedentes: El Comité Regulador del Mercado del Trigo," in Compañía Nacional de Subsistencias Populares, *El mercado de las subsistencias populares: Cincuenta años de regulación*, vol. 1. México: CONASUPO, 1988.

Hewitt de Alcántara, Cynthia. "Feeding Mexico City," in James E. Austin and Gustavo Esteva, eds., *Food Policy in Mexico: The Search for Self-Sufficiency*. Ithaca, N.Y.: Cornell University Press, 1987.

———. "The 'Green Revolution' As History: The Mexican Experience," *Development and Change* 5:2 (1973–1974).

———. *La modernización de la agricultura mexicana, 1940–1970*. México: Siglo Veintiuno editores, 1978.

Hilger, Mary Tharp. "Consumer Perceptions of a Public Marketer: The Case of CONASUPO in Monterrey, Mexico," Ph.D. diss., University of Texas at Austin, August 1976.

Hodges, Donald C. *Mexican Anarchism after the Revolution*. Austin: University of Texas Press, 1995.

Holden, Robert H. *Mexico and the Survey of Public Lands: The Management of Modernization, 1876–1911*. De Kalb: Northern Illinois University Press, 1994.

————. "Priorities of the State in the Survey of Public Land in Mexico, 1876–1911," *Hispanic American Historical Review* 70:4 (November 1990), pp. 579–608.

Hunzicker, Otto Frederick. *Condensed Milk and Powdered Milk Prepared for Factory, School, and Laboratory,* 7th ed. La Grange, Ill., 1949.

Instituto Nacional de Estadística, Geografia, e Informática. *Estadisticas históricas de México.* 2 vols. México, 1985.

Iturriaga de la Fuente, José. "1983–88: CONASUPO del cambio estructural," in *El mercado de las subsistencias populares: Cincuenta años de regulación,* vol. 2. México: CONASUPO, 1988.

Jacobsen, Nils, and Joseph Love, eds. *Guiding the Invisible Hand: Economic Liberalism and the State in Latin America.* New York: Praeger, 1988.

Johnson, Kenneth F. *Mexican Democracy: A Critical View.* Boston: Allyn and Bacon, 1971.

Joseph, Gilbert. *Revolution from Without: Yucatán, Mexico, and the United States, 1880–1924.* New York: Cambridge University Press, 1983.

Joseph, Gilbert M., and Daniel Nugent, eds. *Everyday Forms of State Formation: Revolution and the Negotiation of Rule in Modern Mexico.* Durham, N.C.: Duke University Press, 1994.

Katz, Friedrich. "The Liberal Republic and the Porfiriato, 1867–1910," in Leslie Bethell, ed., *Mexico since Independence.* New York: Cambridge University Press, 1991.

————. *The Secret War in Mexico: Europe, the United States, and the Mexican Revolution.* Chicago: University of Chicago Press, 1983.

Kemmerer, Edwin Walter. *Inflation and Revolution: Mexico's Experience of 1912–1917.* Princeton, N.J.: Princeton University Press, 1940.

Keremitsis, Dawn. "Del metate al molino: La mujer mexicana de 1910 a 1940," *Historia Mexicana* 33:2 (October–December 1983), pp. 285–302.

Knight, Alan. "Cardenismo: Juggernaut or Jalopy," *Journal of Latin American Studies* 26 (1994), pp. 73–107.

————. *The Mexican Revolution,* 2 vols. New York: Cambridge University Press, 1986.

Kroeber, Clifton B. *Man, Land, and Water: Mexico's Farmland Irrigation Policies, 1885–1911.* Berkeley: University of California Press, 1983.

Langley, Lester D. *Mexico and the United States: The Fragile Relationship.* Boston: Twayne Publishers, 1991.

Lee, Raymond L. "Grain Legislation in Colonial Mexico, 1575–1585," *Hispanic American Historical Review* (November 1947), pp. 647–660.

Lerman Alperstein, Aída. *Comercio exterior e industria de transformación en México, 1910–1920.* México: Plaza y Valdés Editores, 1989.

Lewis, Oscar. *Five Families: Mexican Case Studies in the Culture of Poverty*. New York: John Wiley and Sons, fourth printing, 1964.

López Malo, Ernesto. *Ensayo sobre localización de la industria en México*. México: Universidad Nacional Autónoma de México, 1960.

López Rosado, Diego G. *El abasto de productos alimenticios en la ciudad de México*. México: Fondo de Cultura Económica, 1988.

Lorey, David E. "The Status of Social Development under Zedillo," in M. Delal Baer and Roderic Ai Camp, eds., *Presiding over Change? Zedillo's First Year*. Washington, D.C.: Center for Strategic and International Studies, 1997.

Lugo V., Adolfo. "La acción de DICONSA en el abastecimiento de subsistencias populares," in Ifigenia Martinez de Navarrete, Iván Restrepo Fernández, and Clementina Zamora M. de Equihua, eds., *Alimentación básica y desarrollo agroindustrial*. México: Fondo de Cultura Económica, 1977.

Luiselli, Cassio. *The Mexican Food System: Elements of a Program of Accelerated Production of Basic Foodstuffs in Mexico*, Research Report Series 22. San Diego: Center for U.S.-Mexican Studies, University of California at San Diego, 1982.

Lustig, Nora. *Mexico: The Remaking of an Economy*. Washington, D.C.: Brookings Institution, 1992.

Lustig, Nora, ed. *Coping with Austerity: Poverty and Inequality in Latin America*. Washington, D.C.: Brookings Institution, 1995.

Lustig, Nora, and Antonio Martín del Campo. "Descripción del funcionamiento del sistema CONASUPO," *Investigación Económico* 173 (July–September 1985), pp. 215–243.

Macín, Francisco J. *Los salarios en México*. México, 1947.

Markiewicz, Dana. *Ejido Organization in Mexico, 1934–1976*. Los Angeles: UCLA Latin American Center Publications, 1980.

———. *The Mexican Revolution and the Limits of Agrarian Reform, 1915–1946*. Boulder, Colo.: Lynne Rienner, 1993.

Marti, Judith Ettinger. "Subsistence and the State: Municipal Government Policies and Urban Markets in Developing Nations: The Case of Mexico City and Guadalajara, 1877–1910," Ph.D. diss., University of California at Los Angeles, 1990.

Martínez Assad, Carlos. *El henriquismo, una piedra en el camino*. México: Martin Casillas editores, 1982.

Martínez de Alva, Ernesto. "El crédito agrícola como fundamento de la reorganización de la economía agricola," in Secretaria de Acción Agraria del Partido Revolucionario Nacional, *Los problemas agrícolas de México*, vol. 2. México: PNR, 1934.

Martínez de Navarrete, Ifigenia. *La distribución del ingreso y el desarrollo económico de México*. México: Instituto de Investigaciones Económicos, Esceula Nacional de Economía, 1960.

Martínez de Navarrete, Ifigenia, Iván Restrepo Fernández, and Clementina Zamora M. de Equihua, ed., *Alimentación básica y desarrollo agroindustrial*. México: Fondo de Cultura Económica, 1977.

Martínez Dominguez, Guillermo. *Intentos de control de precios en México*. México: Secretaria de Educación Pública, 1950.

———. *Quince años de periodismo al servicio de México*. México: Ediciones Asociación Mexicana de Periodistas, 1958.

Medin, Tzvi. *El sexenio alemanista*. México: Ediciones ERA, 1990.

Merla, Pedro. *El costo de la vida obrera en México*. México: Secretaría de Trabajo y Previsión Social, 1942.

———. *Estadísticas de salarios*. México: Secretaría de Trabajo y Previsión Social, 1942.

Mesa-Lago, Carmelo. "The Case of Mexico," in Mesa-Lago, *Social Security in Latin America: Pressure Groups, Stratification, and Inequality*. Pittsburgh, Pa.: University of Pittsburgh Press, 1978.

Meyer, Lorenzo. *El conflicto social y los gobiernos del maximato*. México: El Colegio de México, 1978.

Michaels, Albert L. "The Crisis of Cardenismo," *Journal of Latin American Studies* 2:1 (May 1970), pp. 51–79.

Middlebrook, Kevin J. *The Paradox of Revolution: Labor, the State, and Authoritarianism in Mexico*. Baltimore, Md.: Johns Hopkins University Press, 1995.

———. "The Sounds of Silence: Organised Labour's Response to Economic Crisis in Mexico," *Journal of Latin American Studies* 21:2 (May 1989), pp. 195–220.

———. *Unions, Workers, and the State in Mexico*. La Jolla: University of California at San Diego, Center for U.S.-Mexican Studies, 1991.

Miller, Richard Ulric. "The Role of Labor Organizations in a Developing Country: The Case of Mexico," Ph.D. diss., Cornell University, 1966.

Miller, Robert Ryal. "Mexico under Avila Camacho: Major Aspects of the 1940–46 Administration," M.A. thesis, University of California at Berkeley, 1951.

Mogab, John W. "Public Credit Institutions as Development Agencies: The Case of Mexico's Ejido Credit System," Ph.D. diss., University of Tennessee at Knoxville, 1981.

Moguel, Julio, ed. *Historia de la cuestión agraria mexicana: Política estatal y conflictos agrarios, 1950–1970* . México: Siglo Veintiuno Editores S.A., 1989.

———. "Salinas' Failed War on Poverty," *NACLA Report on the Americas* 18:1 (July–August 1994), pp. 38–41.

Moguel, Julio, and Hugo Azpeitia. "Precios y política agrícola en dos décadas de desarrollo agropecuario," in Julio Moguel, ed., *Historia de la cuestión agraria mexicana: Política estatal y conflictos agrarios, 1950–1970*. México: Siglo Veintiuno Editores S.A., 1989.

Moguel, Julio, Rosario Robles, and Blanca Rubio. *Historia de la cuestión agraria mexicana: La época de oro y el principio de la crisis de la agricultura mexicana, 1950–1970*. México: Siglo Veintiuno Editores S.A., 1988.

Montanari, Mario. "The Conception of SAM," in James E. Austin and Gustavo Esteva, eds., *Food Policy in Mexico: The Search for Self-Sufficiency.* Ithaca, N.Y.: Cornell University Press, 1987.

Mora Ortiz, Gonzalo. *El Banco Nacional de Comercio Exterior.* México: Editorial Ruta, 1950.

Moreno Pérez, Juan. "La economía mexicana desde 1900: Nuevos series largas sobre la producción interna bruta y la inflación," unpublished manuscript, Los Angeles, 1992.

Morris, Stephen D. *Corruption and Politics in Contemporary Mexico.* Tuscaloosa: University of Alabama Press, 1991.

Mostkoff, Aída, and Enrique C. Ochoa. "Complexities of Measuring the Food Situation in Mexico: Supply versus Self-Sufficiency of Basic Grains, 1925–86," in James W. Wilkie, ed., *Society and Economy in Mexico.* Los Angeles: UCLA Latin American Center Press, 1990.

Muldoon, Juan, and Daniel Servitje. *El comercio de alimentos en México: Presente y futuro.* México: Editorial Trillas, 1984.

Mummert, Gail, ed. *Almacenamiento de productos agropecuarios en México.* Zamora: El Colegio de Michoacán, 1987.

Muñoz Rodríguez, Manrrubio. "Limites y potencialidades del sistema de la leche en México," *Comercio Exterior* 40:3 (September, 1990), pp. 886–893.

Newell, Roberto G. and Luis F. Rubio. *Mexico's Dilemma: The Political Origins of Economic Crisis.* Boulder, Colo.: Westview Press, 1984.

Newman, Lucile F., ed. *Hunger in History: Food Shortage, Poverty, and Deprivation.* Cambridge, Mass.: Basil Blackwell, 1990.

Niblo, Stephen R. "Decoding Mexican Politics: The Resignation of Francisco Javier Gaxiola," *Anales* (University of New South Wales) 2:1 (1993), pp. 23–39.

———. "The Impact of War: Mexico and World War II," La Trobe University Institute of Latin American Studies, Occasional Paper No. 10, 1988.

———. *War, Diplomacy, and Development: The United States and Mexico, 1938–1954.* Wilmington, Del.: Scholarly Resources, 1995.

Niemeyer Jr., E. V. *Revolution at Querétaro: The Mexican Constitutional Convention of 1916–1917.* Austin: University of Texas Press, 1974.

Nugent, Daniel. *Spent Cartridges of Revolution: An Anthropological History of Namiquipa, Chihuahua.* Chicago: University of Chicago Press, 1993.

Ochoa, Enrique C. "Instituto mexicana de seguro social," in Michael S. Werner, ed., *Encyclopedia of Mexico: History, Society, and Culture.* Chicago: Fitzroy Dearborn, 1997, vol. 1, pp. 708–711.

———. "Reappraising State Intervention and Social Policy in Mexico: The Case of Milk in the Distrito Federal during the Twentieth Century," *Mexican Studies/Estudios Mexicanos* 15:1 (winter 1999), pp. 73–99.

———. "The Politics of Feeding Mexico: The State and the Market-place since 1934." Ph.D. diss., University of California at Los Angeles, 1993.

———. "The Urban Roots of Mexican Food Policy: The State and Basic Grains since 1934," in Enrique C. Ochoa and David E. Lorey, eds., *Estado y agricultura en México: Antecedentes e implicaciones de las reformas salinistas.* México: UAM, Azcapotzalco, 1994.

Ochoa, Enrique C., and David E. Lorey. *Estado y agricultura en México: Antecedentes e implicaciones de las reformas salinistas.* México: UAM, Azcapotzalco, 1994.

Olizar, Marynka. *Guía a los mercados de México.* México, 1968.

Orive Alba, Adolfo. *La política de irrigación en México.* México: Fondo de Cultura Económica, 1960.

Ortega Cruz, Leopoldo. "El control de precios y su importancia en la economía del país," licenciatura thesis, México, Escuela Nacional de Economía, UNAM, 1965.

Palavicini, Félix F. *Historia de la Constitución de 1917.* México, 1938.

Paredes Arévalo, Oscar. *Los almacenes generales de depósito en México.* México: Almacenes Nacionales de Depósito, S.A., 1955.

Patiño, E. Alanís, and E. Vargas Torres. "Observaciones sobre algunas estadísticas agrícolas, *Trimestre Económico* (1946), pp. 589–625.

Patiño Alvarez, Miguel. "DICONSA como reguladora de artículos de primera necesidad," Licenciatura thesis, México, UNAM, 1974.

Paz, Octavio. *The Other Mexico: Critique of the Pyramid.* New York: Grove Press, 1972.

Pellicer de Brody, Olga. "La oposición en México: El caso del henriquismo," in *La Crisis en el sistema politico Mexicano, 1928–1977.* México: El Colegio de México, 1977.

Pellicer de Brody, Olga, and Esteban L. Mancilla. *El entendimiento con los Estados Unidos y la gestión de desarrollo estabilizador, 1952–1960.* México: El Colegio de México, 1978.

Pellicer de Brody, Olga, and José Luis Reyna. *Historia de la revolución mexicana: El afianzamiento de la estabilidad política, 1952–1960.* México: El Colegio de México, 1978.

Peschard, Jacqueline. "Las elecciones en el Distrito Federal (1946–1970)," *Revista Mexicana de Sociología* 50:3 (July–September 1988), pp. 229–245.

Pilcher, Jeffrey M. *¡Que Viván los Tamales! Food and the Making of Mexican Identity.* Albuquerque: University of New Mexico Press, 1998.

Poniatowska, Elena. *Massacre in Mexico.* New York: Viking Penguin, 1975.

Purcell, Susan Kaufman. *The Mexican Profit-Sharing Decision: Politics in an Authoritarian Regime.* Berkeley: University of California Press, 1975.

Pyle, Jane. "The Public Markets of Mexico City," Ph.D. diss., University of Oregon, 1968.

Randall, Laura, ed. *Reforming Mexico's Agrarian Reform*. Armonk, N.Y.: M. E. Sharp, 1996.

Reyes Osorio, Sergio Rodolfo Stavenhagen, Salomón Eckstein, and Juan Ballestros. *Estructura agraria y desarrollo agrícola en México*. México: Fondo de Cultura Económica, 1974.

Reynolds, Clark W. *The Mexican Economy: Twentieth-Century Structure and Growth*. New Haven, Conn.: Yale University Press, 1970.

Richmond, Douglas W. *Venustiano Carranza's Nationalist Struggle, 1893–1920*. Lincoln: University of Nebraska Press, 1983.

Richmond, Patricia McIntire. "Mexico: A Case in One-Party Politics," Ph.D. diss., University of California at Berkeley, 1965.

Rickman, Geoffery. *The Grain Supply of Ancient Rome*. Oxford: Oxford University Press, 1980.

Rius, Eduardo. *Rius (1955–1958): Primeras porquerías*. México: Editorial Heterodoxa, 1973.

Robinson, Sherman, Mary Burfisher, Raúl Hinojosa, and Karen Thierfelder. "Agricultural Policies and Migration in a U.S.-Mexican Free Trade Area: A Computable General Equilibrium Analysis," California Agricultural Experiment Station, Giannini Foundation, University of California at Berkeley, Working Paper No. 617, December 1991.

Rochlin, James F. *Redefining Mexican "Security": State, Society, and Region under NAFTA*. Boulder, Colo.: Lynne Rienner, 1997.

Rodríguez Adame, Julián. *La CEIMSA: Su función económica y social*. México: Editorial La Justicia, 1958.

Rodríguez Batista, María. " El problema del reparto agrario en el régimen alemanista," *Estudios Sociales* 6:2:4, pp. 77–91.

Roseberry, William, et al. *Coffee, Society, and Power in Latin America*. Baltimore, Md.: Johns Hopkins University Press, 1995.

Ruiz, Ramón E. *The Great Rebellion: Mexico, 1905–1924*. New York: W. W. Norton, 1980.

Salinas de Gortari, Carlos. "Political Participation, Public Investment and System Support: A Study of 3 Rural Communities in Central Mexico," Ph.D. diss., Harvard University, 1978.

Salinas de Gortari, Raúl. "Agrarismo y agricultura en el México independiente y posrevolucionario," in *México: Setenta y cinco años de revolución, tomo 1, Desarrollo social*. México: Fondo de Cultura Económica, 1988.

Salinas Lózano, Raúl. *La intervención del estado y la cuestión de los precios*. México: Editorial America, 1944.

Sánchez, Gerardo. "Crisis agrícola y abastecimiento de granos en Michoacán, 1880–1910," in Gail Mummert, ed., *Almacenamiento de productos agropecuarios en México*. Zamora: El Colegio de Michoacán, 1987.

Sanchez Daza, Alfredo, and Sergio Vargas Velázquez. "Debildad y fortaleza de CONASUPO," *El Cotidiano* (September–October 1986), pp. 40–46.

Sanderson, Steven E. *Agrarian Populism and the Mexican State: The Struggle for Land in Sonora*. Berkeley: University of California Press, 1981.

————. *The Transformation of Mexican Agriculture: International Structure and the Politics of Rural Change*. Princeton, N.J.: Princeton University Press, 1986.

Santillán López, Roberto, and Ancieto Rosas Figueroa. *Teoria general de las finanzas públicas y el caso de Méxcio*. México: UNAM, 1962.

Schmidt, Samuel. *The Deterioration of the Mexican Presidency: The Years of Luis Echeverría*. Tucson: University of Arizona Press, 1991.

Schuler, Friedrich E. *Mexico between Hitler and Roosevelt: Mexican Foreign Relations in the Age of Lázaro Cárdenas, 1934–1940*. Albuquerque: University of New Mexico Press, 1998.

Scott, James C. *Seeing Like a State: How Certain Schemes to Improve the Human Condition Have Failed*. New Haven, Conn.: Yale University Press, 1998.

Shafer, Robert Jones. *Mexican Business Organization: History and Analysis*. Syracuse, N.Y.: Syracuse University Press, 1973.

————. *Mexico: Mutual Adjustment Planning*. Syracuse, N.Y.: Syracuse University Press, 1966.

Sherman, John W. "Reassessing Cárdenismo: The Mexican Right and the Failure of a Revolutionary Regime, 1934–1940," *The Americas* 54:3 (January 1998), pp. 357–378.

Simpson, Eyler N. *The Ejido: Mexico's Way Out*. Chapel Hill: University of North Carolina Press, 1937.

Simpson, Lesley Byrd. *Many Mexicos*. Berkeley: University of California Press, 1966.

Sodi, Demetrio, and Fernando Rello. *Abasto y distribución de alimientos en las grandes metropolis: El caso de la ciudad de México*. México: Nueva Imagen, 1988.

Solís Rosales, Ricardo. "Precios de garantía y política agraria: Un análisis de largo plazo," *Comercio Exterior* 40:10 (October 1990), pp. 923–937.

Stakman, E. C., Richard Bradfield, and Paul C. Mangelsdorf. *Campaigns against Hunger*. Cambridge, Mass.: Belknap Press of Harvard University Press, 1967.

Stavenhagen, Rodolfo, Fernándo Paz Sánchez, Cuahtémoc Cárdenas, and Arturo Bonilla. *Neolatifundismo y explotación: De Emiliano Zapata a Anderson Clayton*. México: Editorial Nuestro Tiempo, 1968.

Strobel, D. R and C. J. Babcock. *Recombined Milk: A Dependable Supply of Fluid Milk Far from the Cow*. Washington, D.C.: U.S. Department of Agriculture, Foreign Agriculture Report No. 84, 1955.

Suárez, Eduardo. *Comentarios y recuerdos (1926–46)*. México: Editorial Porrúa, 1977.

Super, John C. "Bread and the Provisioning of Mexico City in the Late Eighteenth Century," in *Jahrbuch Für Geschichte: Von Staat,*

Wirrschaft und Gesellschaft Lateinamerikas no. 19 (1982), pp. 159–182.

———. *Food, Conquest, and Colonization in Sixteenth-Century Spanish America.* Albuquerque: University of New Mexico Press, 1988.

Taracena, Alfonso. *La vida en México bajo Avila Camacho.* México: Editorial Jus, 1976.

Teichman, Judith A. *Policymaking in Mexico: From Boom to Crisis.* Boston: Allen and Unwin, 1988.

———. *Privatization and Political Change in Mexico.* Pittsburgh, Pa.: University of Pittsburgh Press, 1995.

Tello, Carlos. *La política económica en México, 1970–1976.* México: Siglo Veintiuno Editores, 1979.

Tenenbaum, Barbara. *The Politics of Penury: Debt and Taxes in Mexico 1821–1856.* Albuquerque: University of New Mexico Press, 1986.

Thomson, Guy P.C. *Puebla de los Angeles: Industry and Society in a Mexican City, 1700–1850.* Boulder, Colo.: Westview Press, 1989.

Torres, Blanca. "1938–1949: El Comité Regulador del Mercado de Subsistencias y la Nacional Reguladora y Distribuidora, S.A.," in Compañía Nacional de Subsistencias Populares, *El Mercado de la Subsistencias Populares,* tomo 1. México: CONASUPO, 1988.

———. *Hacia la utopía industrial, 1940–1952.* México: El Colegio de México, 1984.

———. *México en la segunda guerra mundial.* México: El Colegio de México, 1979.

Trejo, Delarbe. *Crónica del sindicalismo en México, 1976–1988.* México: Siglo Veintimo Editores, 1990.

Tutino, John. *From Insurrection to Revolution in Mexico: Social Bases of Agrarian Violence, 1750–1940.* Princeton, N.J.: Princeton University Press, 1988.

Unikel, Luis, Crescencio Ruíz Chiapetto, and Gustavo Garza Villarreal. *El desarrollo urban en México: Diagnostico e implicaciones futuras.* México: El Colegio de México, 1976.

Valencia Lomelí, Enrique, ed. *A dos años: La política social de Ernesto Zedillo.* México: Red Observatorio Social, 1997.

Van Young, Eric. *Hacienda and Market in Eighteenth-Century Mexico; The Rural Economy of the Guadalajara Region, 1675–1820.* Berkeley: University of California Press, 1981.

Vásquez de Warman, Irene. "El pósito y la alhóndiga en la Nueva España," *Historia Mexicana 67* 17:3 (January–March 1968), pp. 395–426.

Vásquez Tercero, Héctor, and José Luis Robles Glenn. *Control de precios.* México: Editorial Tecnos, S.A., 1976.

Vaughan, Mary Kay, *Cultural Politics in Revolution: Teachers, Peasants, and Schools in Mexico, 1930–1940.* Tucson: University of Arizona Press, 1997.

Vera Ferrer, Oscar H. *El caso CONASUPO: Una evaluación.* México: Centro de Estudios en Economia y Educación, 1987.

Vernon, Raymond. *The Dilemma of Mexico's Development: The Role of the Public and Private Sectors.* Cambridge, Mass.: Harvard University Press, 1963.

Vernon, Raymond, ed. *Public Policy and Private Enterprise in Mexico.* Cambridge, Mass.: Harvard University Press, 1964.

Villafuerte, Carlos. *Ferrocarriles.* México: Fondo de Cultura Económica, 1959.

Vitela, Manuel. *El cultivo del trigo.* México: Oficina Tip. de la Secretaría de Fomento, 1900.

Ward, Peter M. *Mexico City: The Production and Reproduction of an Urban Enviornment.* Boston: G. K. Hall, 1990.

———. *Politicas de bienestar social en México, 1970–1989.* México: Nueva Imagen, 1989.

Warman, Arturo. *Los campesinos: Hijos predilectos del régimen.* México: Editorial Nuestro Tiempo, 1972.

Weyl, Nathaniel, and Sylvia Weyl. *The Reconquest of Mexico: The Years of Lázaro Cárdenas.* New York: Oxford University Press, 1939.

Whetten, Nathaniel. *Rural Mexico.* Chicago: University of Chicago Press, 1948.

Wilkie, James W. "From Economic Growth to Economic Stagnation in Mexico: Statistical Series for Understanding Pre- and Post-1982 Change," in James W. Wilkie, David E. Lorey, and Enrique Ochoa, eds., *Statistical Abstract of Latin America*, vol. 26. Los Angeles: UCLA Latin American Center Publications, 1988.

———. *The Mexican Revolution: Federal Expenditure and Social Change since 1910.* Berkeley: University of California Press, 1970.

———. "Mexico City as a Magnet for Mexico's Economically Active Population, 1935–65," in James W. Wilkie, ed., *Statistics and National Policy.* Los Angeles: UCLA Latin American Center Publications, 1974.

———. "New Hypotheses for Statistical Research," in James W. Wilkie, ed., *Statistics and National Policy.* Los Angeles: UCLA Latin American Center Publications, 1974.

———. "The Six Ideological Phases of Mexico's 'Permanent Revolution' since 1910," in James W. Wilkie, ed., *Society and Economy in Mexico.* Los Angeles: UCLA Latin American Center Publications, 1990.

Wilkie, James W., ed. *Society and Economy in Mexico.* Los Angeles: UCLA Latin American Center Publications, 1990.

Wilkie, James W., David E. Lorey, and Enrique Ochoa, eds. *Statistical Abstract of Latin America*, 26. Los Angeles: UCLA Latin American Center Publications, 1988.

———. *Statistical Abstract of Latin America*, vol. 28. Los Angeles: UCLA Latin American Center Publications, 1990.

Wilkie, James W., and Edna Monzon de Wilkie. *México visto en el siglo XX: Entrevistas de historia oral.* México: Instituto de Investigaciones Económicos, 1969.

Wilkie, James W., and Enrique Ochoa, eds. *Statistical Abstract of Latin America* 27. Los Angeles: UCLA Latin American Center Publications, 1989.

Wilkie, Raymond. *San Miguel: A Mexican Collective Ejido*. Stanford, Calif.: Stanford University Press, 1971.

Wise, George S. *El México de Alemán*, trans. by Octavio Novaro. México: Editorial Atlanta, S.A., 1952.

Womak, John. "The Mexican Revolution, 1910–1920," in Leslie Bethell, ed., *Mexico since Independence*. New York: Cambridge University Press, 1991.

Wright, Thomas C. "The Politics of Urban Provisioning in Latin American History," in John C. Super and Wright, eds., *Food, Politics, and Society in Latin America*. Lincoln: University of Nebraska Press, 1985.

Wylie, Kathryn H. "Production and Marketing Policies in Mexico," *Foreign Agriculture* 11:11–12 (1947).

Yates, Paul Lamartine. *Mexico's Agricultural Dilemmna*. Tucson: University of Arizona Press, 1981.

Young, Dolly J. "Mexican Literary Reactions to Tlatelolco 1968," *Latin American Research Review* 20:2 (1985), pp. 71–85.

Zamora, Guillermo. *Caso CONASUPO: La leche radiactiva, el crimen más atroz contra el pueblo mexicano*. México: Editorial Planeta, 1997.

Zellner, Mike. "Mexico's Milk Industry: Half Full or Half Empty?" in *El Financiero Internacional*, August 26, 1991.

Zermeño, Sergio. *La sociedad derrotada: El desorden mexicano del fin de siglo*. México: Siglo Veintiuno Editores, 1996.

Zevada, Ricardo J. "México," in Erik T. H. Kjellström et al., *El control de precios*, trans. by Javier Márquez. México: Fondo de Cultura Económica, 1943, pp. 209–254.

———. "Política de precios," *Investigación Económica* 5:4 (1945), pp. 471–506.

Index

Latin American Silhouettes
Studies in History and Culture

William H. Beezley and
Judith Ewell
Editors

Volumes Published

Silvia Marina Arrom and Servando Ortoll, eds., *Riots in the Cities: Popular Politics and the Urban Poor in Latin America, 1765–1910* (1996). Cloth ISBN 0-8420-2580-4   Paper ISBN 0-8420-2581-2

Roderic Ai Camp, ed., *Polling for Democracy: Public Opinion and Political Liberalization in Mexico* (1996). ISBN 0-8420-2583-9

Brian Loveman and Thomas M. Davies, Jr., eds., *The Politics of Antipolitics: The Military in Latin America*, 3d ed., revised and updated (1996). Cloth ISBN 0-8420-2609-6   Paper ISBN 0-8420-2611-8

Joseph S. Tulchin, Andrés Serbín, and Rafael Hernández, eds., *Cuba and the Caribbean: Regional Issues and Trends in the Post-Cold War Era* (1997). ISBN 0-8420-2652-5

Thomas W. Walker, ed., *Nicaragua without Illusions: Regime Transition and Structural Adjustment in the 1990s* (1997). Cloth ISBN 0-8420-2578-2   Paper ISBN 0-8420-2579-0

Dianne Walta Hart, *Undocumented in L.A.: An Immigrant's Story* (1997). Cloth ISBN 0-8420-2648-7   Paper ISBN 0-8420-2649-5

Jaime E. Rodríguez O. and Kathryn Vincent, eds., *Myths, Misdeeds, and Misunderstandings: The Roots of Conflict in U.S.-Mexican Relations* (1997). ISBN 0-8420-2662-2

Jaime E. Rodríguez O. and Kathryn Vincent, eds., *Common Border, Uncommon Paths: Race, Culture, and National Identity in U.S.-Mexican Relations* (1997). ISBN 0-8420-2673-8

William H. Beezley and Judith Ewell, eds., *The Human Tradition in Modern Latin America* (1997). Cloth ISBN 0-8420-2612-6   Paper ISBN 0-8420-2613-4

Donald F. Stevens, ed., *Based on a True Story: Latin American History at the Movies* (1997). Cloth ISBN 0-8420-2582-0   Paper ISBN 0-8420-2781-5

Jaime E. Rodríguez O., ed., *The Origins of Mexican National Politics, 1808–1847* (1997). Paper ISBN 0-8420-2723-8

Che Guevara, *Guerrilla Warfare*, with revised and updated introduction and case studies by Brian Loveman and Thomas M. Davies, Jr., 3d ed. (1997). Cloth ISBN 0-8420-2677-0   Paper ISBN 0-8420-2678-9

Adrian A. Bantjes, *As If Jesus Walked on Earth: Cardenismo, Sonora, and the Mexican Revolution* (1998; rev. ed., 2000). Cloth ISBN 0-8420-2653-3   Paper ISBN 0-8420-2751-3

Henry A. Dietz and Gil Shidlo, eds., *Urban Elections in Democratic Latin America* (1998). Cloth ISBN 0-8420-2627-4   Paper ISBN 0-8420-2628-2

A. Kim Clark, *The Redemptive Work: Railway and Nation in Ecuador, 1895–1930* (1998). ISBN 0-8420-2674-6

Joseph S. Tulchin, ed., with Allison M. Garland, *Argentina: The Challenges of Modernization* (1998). ISBN 0-8420-2721-1

Louis A. Pérez, Jr., ed., *Impressions of Cuba in the Nineteenth Century: The Travel Diary of Joseph J. Dimock* (1998). Cloth ISBN 0-8420-2657-6   Paper ISBN 0-8420-2658-4

June E. Hahner, ed., *Women through Women's Eyes: Latin American Women in Nineteenth-Century Travel Accounts* (1998). Cloth ISBN 0-8420-2633-9   Paper ISBN 0-8420-2634-7

James P. Brennan, ed., *Peronism and Argentina* (1998). ISBN 0-8420-2706-8

John Mason Hart, ed., *Border Crossings: Mexican and Mexican-American Workers*

(1998). Cloth ISBN 0-8420-2716-5 Paper ISBN 0-8420-2717-3

Brian Loveman, *For* la Patria: *Politics and the Armed Forces in Latin America* (1999). Cloth ISBN 0-8420-2772-6 Paper ISBN 0-8420-2773-4

Guy P. C. Thomson, with David G. LaFrance, *Patriotism, Politics, and Popular Liberalism in Nineteenth-Century Mexico: Juan Francisco Lucas and the Puebla Sierra* (1999). ISBN 0-8420-2683-5

Robert Woodmansee Herr, in collaboration with Richard Herr, *An American Family in the Mexican Revolution* (1999). ISBN 0-8420-2724-6

Juan Pedro Viqueira Albán, trans. Sonya Lipsett-Rivera and Sergio Rivera Ayala, *Propriety and Permissiveness in Bourbon Mexico* (1999). Cloth ISBN 0-8420-2466-2 Paper ISBN 0-8420-2467-0

Stephen R. Niblo, *Mexico in the 1940s: Modernity, Politics, and Corruption* (1999). ISBN 0-8420-2794-7

David E. Lorey, *The U.S.-Mexican Border in the Twentieth Century* (1999). Cloth ISBN 0-8420-2755-6 Paper ISBN 0-8420-2756-4

Joanne Hershfield and David R. Maciel, eds., *Mexico's Cinema: A Century of Films and Filmmakers* (2000). Cloth ISBN 0-8420-2681-9 Paper ISBN 0-8420-2682-7

Peter V. N. Henderson, *In the Absence of Don Porfirio: Francisco León de la Barra and the Mexican Revolution* (2000). ISBN 0-8420-2774-2

Mark T. Gilderhus, *The Second Century: U.S.-Latin American Relations since 1889* (2000). Cloth ISBN 0-8420-2413-1 Paper ISBN 0-8420-2414-X

Catherine Moses, *Real Life in Castro's Cuba* (2000). Cloth ISBN 0-8420-2836-6 Paper ISBN 0-8420-2837-4

K. Lynn Stoner, ed./comp., with Luis Hipólito Serrano Pérez, *Cuban and Cuban-American Women: An Annotated Bibliography* (2000). ISBN 0-8420-2643-6

Thomas D. Schoonover, *The French in Central America: Culture and Commerce, 1820–1930* (2000). ISBN 0-8420-2792-0

Enrique C. Ochoa, *Feeding Mexico: The Political Uses of Food since 1910* (2000). ISBN 0-8420-2812-9

Thomas W. Walker and Ariel C. Armory, eds., *Repression, Resistance, and Democratic Transition in Central America* (2000). Cloth ISBN 0-8420-2766-1 Paper ISBN 0-8420-2768-8

William H. Beezley and David E. Lorey, eds., *Viva Mexico! Viva Independencia! Celebrations of September 16* (2001). Cloth ISBN 0-8420-2914-1 Paper ISBN 0-8420-2915-X

Jeffrey M. Pilcher, *Cantinflas and the Chaos of Mexican Modernity* (2001). Cloth ISBN 0-8420-2769-6 Paper ISBN 0-8420-2771-8